ש . אײזבאן

„אומלעגאלע" ייִדן טרעפאלטן יפּפּן

(די געשיכטע פון אן אומלעגאלער רייזע קיין ארץ ישראל)

D1364555

First published as: אומלעגאַלע ייִדן שפּאַלטן ימען

Umlegale yidn shpaltn yamen

By צענטראַל-פֿאַרבאַנד פֿון פּוילישע ייִדן אין אַרגענטינע

Tsentral-farband fun poylishe yidn in argentine, Buenos Aires, 1948.

Cover photo: "Immigration to Israel" from the Palmach Archive.

Typesetting and book design by Daniel Kennedy.

www.danielkennedy.fr

Samuel Isban
"Illegal" Jews Part the Seas

Translated from the Yiddish by Daniel Kennedy

CONTENTS

HISTORICAL INTRODUCTION

The events that gave birth to the state of Israel are complicated. After WWI, in 1917, as a result of war reparations, the Ottomans were extricated from Palestine by the Allied Powers. Consequently, the League of Nations mandated Britain to administrate the land area known as Palestine, which was occupied by both Arabs and Jews at the time. Lord Arthur Balfour, a British statesman and former Prime Minister of the United Kingdom, issued what would become known as the Balfour Declaration, calling for a homeland for the Jewish people in Palestine. This legitimized the Zionist claim for a Jewish state in their ancestral homeland. In response to an unsuccessful three-year revolt by the Arabs in Palestine for sovereignty of the region, the British issued a White Paper in 1939 reaffirming the establishment of a Jewish National home in an independent Palestine within ten years.

These British policies and promises made to the world and to the Jewish people, became a betrayal when the British began to blockade refugee ships from entering Palestine, calling them "illegal." It was outrageous that in 1947, when the Jewish survivors were leaving behind a battered and destroyed Europe to go to their homeland that they should be blockaded from getting in by the very people who were supposed to deliver them. The British, instead, sent thousands to detention camps in Cyprus.

Samuel Isban, was a Yiddish journalist who was assigned to go undercover by his NYC newspaper, *Der Morgn Zhurnal*, the Jewish Morning Journal, and write an exposé about one of the ships making this journey. He sailed with 1,500 refugees on The Hatikva ("The Hope" in Hebrew) and wrote a firsthand account of his experience.

Isban's intention in writing the book was to inform the world of the plight of the destitute Jews trying to enter their rightful homeland. Although the British couldn't have foreseen it, things changed dramatically after WWII, when six million Jews were annihilated in the holocaust. Isban's argument is that there was no excuse for anyone to prevent or curtail their return to the Jewish homeland, especially given these dire circumstances.

This exposé written in 1947 perhaps set the stage that led to an independent Israel. What he wrote in installments as a newspaper assignment evolved into a much bigger story which became a book in 1948 before the United Nations recognized Israel as a Jewish state.

First published in Yiddish in 1948, now, in 2020, it has finally been translated and published in English, seventy-three years after it was written, documenting these important historical events.

R. C. Stone

FOREWORD

THE SAGA of the legally sanctioned wave of immigration of Jews to their own land began in 1935 on a tiny sail-boat named Velos. Sixty *halutzim*,[1] most of them from Poland, made *aliyah*[2] on that boat.

The emissaries from the Haganah who oversaw this pioneering achievement did not have the support and blessing of everyone, but what they did have was drive and vision. They were not professional seamen. They knew nothing of how to run a ship, aside from what they had observed as fourth-class passengers when they themselves had made the journey to the Land of Israel.

Until 1939 these ships would sporadically make their way to the shores of the Jewish homeland. [. . .]

*

Between Velos and the Exodus many ships lie in the depths of foreign seas; the Salvador, the Struma the Patria; the wreckage of the salvaged Mevkura appears before our eyes. Scattered and murdered, lie the millions turned to ash, while tens of thousands of living witnesses

....

1 Halutz: Jewish Immigrants to Palestine, especially those who came to work the land.

2 Aliyah (lit. Ascent) term describing Jewish immigration from the diaspora to the Land of Israel.

to this annihilation and rebirth stand waiting on every coast of Europe.

The living corpses from the extermination camps Bergen-Belsen, Dachau, Buchenwald, Ravensbrück; the weary heads of the Jewish survivors from the occupied areas of Italy, France, Belgium, the Netherlands, Romania, Czechoslovakia and Hungary; those few escaped vestiges of the partisans and ghetto-fighters of Poland and Lithuania—the breath returned to their bodies and the light to their eyes when they first came face to face with their allies from the Land of Israel and beheld the uniforms of the Jewish Brigade, or those of the *halutzim*, or of the parachutists.

They shook hands with these emissaries who swore not to rest until each of them arrived safely in their own land.

And the hands of Israel united with the hands of the survivors, working together with widows and American rabbis, ordinary Jewish boys and with a few Righteous among the Nations—from simple fishermen, to high-ranking personalities—doing everything possible to gather everyone together, via broken trains on broken rails, and over perilous border crossings.

Ships, which had their best days long behind them, shaking with every movement, found renewed energy.

No harbor welcomed these ships to nourish them, no oil or coal depots were open to them. Even drinking water had to be sourced clandestinely.

The strong hands of the Haganah led these ships and brought them to their destination, those Jewish sons and daughters, who answered the call of their nation, understanding the privilege and responsibility of their mission.

*

For many years a select few have tended the secrets of this great rescue. The history of the grandiose saga will be written by the generations to come, by those who will be the grandchildren of the rescuers and rescued.

Then, on the green fields and valleys, from the hills of Galilee and Judea to Mount Scopus, the eternal Jewish state will stand.

The tiny flashes of illumination from this book, just like Stone's and Mary Sirkin's books provide fragments of valiant heroism and pioneering achievement.

And perhaps this history will be written by the children who were born on these ships . . .

Can you imagine what a mother feels as she brings a Jewish life into the world on such a ship? Can you begin to comprehend what it feels like to be one of those fortunate passengers? And can you imagine how the Jews of Palestine felt, trembling in anticipation of the ship's arrival? And what do the young men and women of the coastal settlements feel when providence choses them to be the first to greet these children, men, and women disembarking from a ship that has broken through the British blockade?

Can you place yourself in Haifa as our armed enemies forced our brothers and sisters—after they had already laid eyes on Mount Carmel and breathed in the air of their homeland—to board ships bound for Cyprus for months of captivity?

Do you know how they fought with their bare hands against outrageous persecution?. . .

*

I recall, on a warm summer Sabbath when 300 pious Jews—men, women, and children—arrived at the train station in Marseille and did not want to travel on the buses that were waiting to take them the seven kilometer distance to the shore where a ship was waiting to take them home.

When I tried to explain that the distance was too great, and the sun was blazing, a pale boy, barely Bar-Mitzvah age, newly freed from the camps, answered me proudly:

"If we could march under the Nazi whips for hundreds of kilometers toward death, then we can march seven kilometers toward life . . ."

The present book by Samuel Isban shows us an outline of the path traced by the Haganah to bring the Jewish people into a new eternal life.

Ruth Kluger
Buenos Aires, January 1948.

"Illegal" Jews
Part the Seas

1
THE BEGINNINGS OF THE EXODUS FROM EUROPE

The history of the ironically named "illegal immigration" currently streaming toward Palestine has not yet been written. Meanwhile, this history is being recorded in the memories of the immigrants themselves. Caravans of refugee ships are crossing the seven seas, while British vessels of every sort lie in wait, intercepting them and sending the passengers to concentration camps on the island of Cyprus.

Little has been said concerning the background of this movement to bring masses of displaced persons to the Jewish Homeland.

But the world must learn about the struggle the Jewish survivors are currently engaged in for their existence. It is a chapter in human history of extraordinary valor, endurance, strength, and self-sacrifice.

From Moses to Joshua, from Nebuchadnezzar to Cyrus the Great, from Titus to the Biluim,[1] Jews in various states of exile have launched illegal expeditions to Palestine. No force on earth could halt the return of the Eternal People to their ancestral land. But no migration in the history of the Jewish Exile can compare in scope, or elemental drive with the current one.

....

1 See glossary p. 364 for selected historical and religious terms.

Their path is one of pain and suffering, a path strewn with obstacles and dangers. But it is the only concrete path to redemption for those of our nation who have already lost the earth under their feet.

The worst has already come to pass. Millions of Jews have been annihilated. The displaced persons yearn to reach Palestine, but Britain—just as Amalek in the desert on the flight from Egypt—is blocking their path to deliverance, hunting down their leaders, and demanding official documentation. In 1939, just after Britain published the illegitimate White Paper of 1939, the idea was born to allow large numbers of Jews—the rightful owners of the Land of Israel—to enter the country. The six horrible years of war that followed ensured the idea never came to maturity and was never put into practice. The plan was fostered by its initiators, grew ripe, and found supporters in Jewish communities throughout the world. And when the final shot rang out on the battlefield, and when it became known that the blood of six million Jews had been spilled, the plan of a return to Israel began to take on concrete form.

The initiators of this grandiose enterprise were to be found in New York and Jerusalem, in London and Rome, in Stockholm and in Oslo. These were no dreamers or fantasists, but men of deeds and vision who foresaw that the life-and-death battle to come would demand considerable effort, and that a combination of forces—spiritual, intellectual, and political—would be needed to save the Jewish refugees. Every move would have to be weighed and measured. Haste could lead to failure. Instinct must not be allowed to overpower reason. Every step, whether in broad strokes or in fine detail, must be disciplined and unified. The test we have to face is great; obstacles and pitfalls lie in wait at every turn. Safely extricating ourselves from these perils will require unity of strength and considerable responsibility from each of us. The Yishuv[2] in Palestine and the Jewish communities around the world are engaged in a common struggle—The Jewish community cannot afford to indulge anyone who would break ranks.

Those leading the flight from Europe understand this, as do the captains of the refugee ships and those leading the transports; therefore the work is being carried out discreetly, without clamor or publicity, without fanfare. If this vital work can be called "conspiracy"— the term Bevin, the British Foreign Secretary, uses— then it is conspiracy in the noblest and most idealistic sense of the word. It is plotting against a regime that signs agreements only to later break them, that makes ardent promises it does not intend to keep, a regime that took on international responsibilities and then trampled them underfoot. It is a conspiracy against a malicious state that—in the time of our gravest national catastrophe—besieges the Jewish land and cuts

----

2 The community of Jewish residents in Ottoman Syria and later Palestine prior to the establishment of the state of Israel.

the lifebelts from the drowning vestiges of our people as they struggle to make it ashore.

These conspirators are our vigilant heroes. They are sounding the alarm; they are modern day Paul Reveres galloping through the Jewish world to awaken the people to its total liberation. And their call has been answered by the very best that American Jewry has to offer.

The fires of Majdanek burned six million children of Israel, but as a by-product they have also sparked the zeal and determination of a large portion of America's Jewish youth. The flames of martyrdom have also illuminated a fervor. Hearts have caught fire, an iron will has been forged. Israel's sentinels began to seek volunteers, and a select few American boys answered the call, willing to do anything, to crawl through underground tunnels if needs be, in order to save those few of their people who have survived.

Who are these Jewish-American boys who have decided to become mariners, to perform this service for their nation in its hour of need?

An astute observer will notice that there is something these young people have in common that differentiates them from the average American, something intangible and hard to define. They stand out from the gray monotony. At first glance they appear to be the typical all-American boys that you'd see on the subway, in the universities, or in places of entertainment. You meet such faces at sporting events, and swimming competitions. These are the perennial readers of the funny pages in the daily newspapers, they are the moviegoers without a care in the world.

But a careful observer should not be too hasty. One must wait before passing judgement. A patient glance into the eyes of one such boy will convince you that the boy standing before you is one of a select few, the chosen of the Jewish youth. Notice the spirited earnestness on his face, the stamina, the audacity, the Jewish spirit of "*nevertheless*," and you will be forced to recognize that such select young men are the *crème de la crème* of the Jewish youth in America, with a purpose and mission in life. Their existence is a refutation of the notion that their generation is synonymous with fun and frivolity. Among those volunteering to join the movement to lead the refugee ships are boys who might, to careless observers, appear to be curious specimens, outlandish oddballs, the colorful characters you'd encounter on the bustling streets of New York. But these are no oddballs, no characters. These are healthy Jewish boys, with healthy bodies and minds, in whom the national instinct to serve their people has awakened.

And they perform this sacred service with all the fire and enthusiasm their souls have to offer. They know what their predecessors achieved aboard the first ships. The high adventures of the first sea-pioneers bore fruit: the results were considerable. Our boys also know a thing or two about statistics. Last year thirty ships succeeded in reaching Palestine's shores: not all of them were captured by the British. The world knows nothing about the fates of those ships, which succeeded in landing on the shores of the Jewish Homeland, but we know they increased the population of Jewish citizens by forty thousand. Furthermore, one must not forget that the deported Jews in Cyprus are also potential citizens of Jewish-Palestine.

Characteristically the British are stepping up their anti-Jewish propaganda in proportion to Jewish victories. The more Jews succeed in entering the country, the more refugee ships there are in Mediterranean waters, the more fear and terror the Bevin regime wishes to unleash upon the Jewish world. The British telegraph agency bombards all five continents with reports of international shipping agencies profiteering off Jewish suffering, forcing tens of thousands onto ramshackle dinghies, putting at risk those very lives most deserving of protection. Note the hypocrisy, which has but one aim—to scare off the displaced Jews, discouraging them from embarking on the journey.

But the British propaganda campaign is doomed from the outset. If it is intended as a battle of nerves, it is pathetic. If the aim is to instill terror among the humiliated, abased Jews of the camps it serves only to strengthen their resolve. These false reports will not fool the uprooted Jews setting off for Palestine. Nor will they dupe the organizers of the sea crossings into giving up information about their ships, their condition, their capacity or providence. One thing we can say to reassure the British, who are so worried about Jewish lives, is that each and every ship that sets off toward

Palestine is in perfect working order, with the best installations and the finest equipment. The Haganah, the mighty defence wing of the Jews in British Palestine, has seen to that.

The holy texts tell us that the Messiah was born in the days of the destruction of the Temple, in a similar fashion it is an undeniable fact that in the hours when the smoke ceased to rise from the chimneys and ovens, the first migrant ships set out toward Palestine.

My newspaper, the *Morgn Zhurnal*,[3] has assigned me to follow the clandestine refugee ships' organizers—over seven seas if necessary—entrusted me with a mission that is awe inspiring, nerve wracking and that requires the utmost responsibility.

With a sense of reverence, I open the door to the headquarters of the movement, at a secret location in New York, where a group of brave lads who have taken it upon themselves to be the guardians over the floating tents of Israel are gathering on the eve of their departure.

----

3 Der Morgn zhurnal, a.k.a. The Jewish Morning Journal, was a New York-based Yiddish language newspaper that published six days a week between 1901 and 1971. The paper was pro-Zionist and catered predominantly to an orthodox/traditional readership.

2

THE "SEA-WOLVES"

The quiet building in New York, where the boys from the volunteer crew—the future "Sea-Wolves" of the refugee ships—gather a few hours before their departure, looks for all the world like an art gallery. Paintings adorn the walls, the rooms are filled with priceless antiques. Even the solid furniture is reminiscent of a curated rare collection. There is a young man watching over his crew with utmost earnestness. He speaks leisurely; he is friendly, but cautious. His secretary, seated at a nearby desk, is a radiant, well-dressed girl. She has a bright, well-kept face and a head of unruly hair. Judging by the deft, skillful drum-roll of her fingers on the typewriter, and the nonchalance with which she does her routine work, she must be one of the thousands of everyday stenographers who daily fill the bustling offices in the skyscrapers of New York. But she's a Jewish girl who knows the discreet responsibilities of her work. She is naturally no enthusiast of the Jitterbug. In different circumstances, under a different sky, she could have been a nurse in Hadera, a kibbutznik in Beit Alfa.

The young man dictating a letter to her is growing impatient. He glances at his watch every couple of minutes—a sign that his people should have been here by now. His anxiety is accompanied by the hasty finger clapping of his secretary on her typewriter. Suddenly several doors open at once, the movement and open entrances shattering the illusion that we are in a museum, or an art gallery. In a matter of minutes the comfortable rooms are transformed into a noisy train-station.

One after another the strong, well-built young crew members stream into the room. They throw down heavy rucksacks from their shoulders, and place straining suitcases on the floor. They huddle together in smaller groups engaged in secretive discussion. These are the peaceful Jewish "conspirators" conspiring against the British power which is deaf to the cries of the uprooted Jews of the camps, of the humbled and humiliated Jews, the Jews of fire and flame.

The ice is swiftly broken. A sense of mutual trust is established much faster than I'd anticipated. Trusting eyes look at me. They don't have much time before their departure and there's a lot to talk about. I must feed my curiosity as to how such an occurrence is possible, how so many Jewish boys from sweatshops, schools, and offices are prepared to leave their positions, leave the spreads of their parent's dining tables and throw themselves with such feverish enthusiasm into the plight of the migrants. Is it the call of adventure? Is it disappointment in the post-war world order?

Sealed lips open up. Opened tongues become loose. Let us hear what the ordinary people have to say. There before me stands Chaim, brown-eyed, with a burning Jewish stubbornness etched on his young face. Determination in the corners of his mouth, fire in his gaze. His entire expression tells of stamina and an unbroken drive to help the displaced, uprooted Jews to reach the land where they belong.

One look at Chaim and you forgive the fact he cannot read a page of Talmud, that he failed to study a chapter of the Mishnah as our scholars of old did. His service to the people, his willingness to cross the seas and oceans in order to save Jewish refugees from annihilation, makes up for everything.

Chaim has a score to settle with the Gentile world. He has a score to settle with the English. He knows the whole backstory of diplomacy that Britain is pursuing with the United States in relation to Jewish aspirations in Palestine. Every political manoeuvre is a link in the chain of duplicity and chicanery the likes of which only "perfidious Albion" is capable of. Even the most recent plan that Britain has proposed for the Jewish people is no plan at all, but a wily trick—a trick, for there can be no more just solution to the Israel-Problem in light of our tragedy.

Chaim speaks brusquely; he doesn't pull any punches. His words, which exude proud, Jewish consciousness, surprise me. How does a young American Jew, from that generation the Jewish establishment likes to paint as dull and shallow, lacking in ideals, like everyday playboys, become so well-versed in Jewish matters?

Chaim is not the only example of this new breed of American Jews. Behind him, impetuous and uneasy, stands Isaac. Isaac is short, with a typical Jewish appearance, a stubby, idiosyncratic nose, a shock of curly blond hair. Why Isaac? Why doesn't he call himself Izzy, as his sweetheart, his mother, and his greenhorn uncle call him? Isaac is original. Isaac was the second of our patriarchs. The name is weightier, prouder, it calls to mind the tribe, an ancestry that stretches back to before the exile in Egypt.

Isaac is twenty-six years old. But his young shoulders are already those of an experienced seafarer. His journey has been no picnic, no walk in the park. He has been through the Seven Circles of Hell. It was a year ago: the first refugee ship made its way across the Adriatic Sea. The enthusiastic young Isaac fell ill; he caught a cold which he ignored until it developed into full-blown pneumonia. The negligence almost cost him his life. Isaac the "illegal" sailor was left behind in Italy. It took three months in the hospital before he was back on his feet. Do you think Isaac gave up his ambition of becoming a Sea-Wolf? The path back to New York lay open to him. There was a legal American ship waiting for him. But Isaac chose the illegal path. He found his way aboard a second refugee ship. For twenty-one days the waves rocked that ship. The captain was a Greek who used to run a steam-ship through the Corinth Canal. Keeping control over a teeming passenger ship as it crossed the breadth of the Mediterranean was a difficult mission beyond his capabilities. He strayed off course, the crew was inexperienced; this was the very early days of the sea-crossings. There was a shortage of drinking water, the food portions were meagre. Finally they came in view of Haifa's golden shores, but the port was blockaded by British warships.

The refugees did not leave the ship without a fight. They were all deported to Cyprus. Isaac was among them. He eventually made his way to Palestine, and from there back to America. Now here he is again, preparing to join another crew which will guard a refugee ship.

From within the huddled group emerges a strong, broad-shouldered youth with ruddy cheeks. There is joy in his blue eyes, a smile around his white teeth. He wants to tell his story. Joseph is his name. He comes from Chicago. He speaks like a windmill: impossible to get a word in. He tells me about his father's house, about his assimilated background. I just about succeed in asking him a question.

"What brought you to make such a decision, Joseph?"

During the war he had been a mariner, serving in the merchant marines. In his travels through Europe he had encountered all kinds of Jews the likes of which he'd never met before—Australian Jews, exotic Jews—all of them sad, all of them orphaned. Each the sole remaining scion of many-branched families that had been decimated through countless violent deaths. Hearing stories about the gruesome extermination of millions of Jews stirred something inside Joseph.

Thoughts he'd never before entertained now burned within him, plaguing him. He became anxious, and the anxiety did not leave him even when he had returned to civilian life. When he heard about the Jewish sea-crossings he reached out and joined the movement with ardor.

Joseph is sincere and unassuming as he explains that he has been waiting for just such an opportunity. The generations before him did not have the privilege of being able to do something so tangible to help save their people. He is happy to have the good fortune of living in our generation.

As he finishes speaking, Joseph's blue eyes become sad. The smile around his white teeth vanishes. A grimace passes over his face. He looks pensive for a moment, before asking me if I want to meet a good friend of his, a Gentile who has also decided to cross the seas and lend a hand in the struggle against the British and their unjust edicts.

I shake hands with Joseph's friend, an angular, brown-skinned young man in an immaculate suit. His white shirt-collar is starched rigid; his wide-brimmed hat, without a wrinkle; his black shoes, polished to a shine. At first glance I take him to be mixed-race, a half-black man from the more up-market end of Harlem. But as it turns out he's Puerto Rican. Nothing about his manner indicates that he's nervous about being an hour away from embarking on an ocean-crossing. He looks more like someone out for a leisurely stroll on Coney Island. The aim of his voyage? It would be an exaggeration to say he was enthralled in the Jewish cause. Only loyalty to his friend, the impossibility of parting from the courageous Joseph, has brought him to bind his destiny with that of the Jewish migrants.

The Puerto Rican is not the only idealistic Gentile willing to take on the burden of Jewish suffering.

I'm introduced to an energetic young Irishman with bulging shoulders. His face is reddish-brown like a fried cutlet. Genuine Scotch-Irish, a Catholic, twenty-five years old. He wants to help Jews in some way. He's about to graduate from Harvard University. But he's happy to put off his plan of becoming a professor by a year or two.

The Irishman has come with the mystical conviction that his world, the non-Jewish world, owes a debt to the Jewish people. With that conviction he will board an illegal ship bound for Cypriot exile. He tells me about his personal life, shedding light on his entire background. He is a Catholic, while his wife, a Southern protestant, is relentlessly anti-Catholic. His prejudiced in-laws are constantly trying to turn their daughter against him. At the same time, our typical Irishman has seen no shortage of antisemitism among his own Irish Catholic community. The constant quarrels with his wife's Protestant parents has made him understand the mindset of the wronged and persecuted. The inferiority complex of an offended party plays—psychologically speaking—no small part in his decision to become an ally in the Jewish struggle.

Another curious specimen among the Gentile passengers is a young priest. A colorful character. Silent as a sphinx. His provisions: the Gospels and a small suitcase. He's a member of the Christian Committee for Israel, and at their initiative he is to travel on a refugee ship. When he returns he will report to the wider world on what he has seen and on who is the legitimate side in the struggle over the Land of Israel.

The Puerto Rican, the Irishman, the priest—these non-Jewish passengers are the aptly named Righteous Among the Nations in a world of malice, a world teeming with oppressors and antisemitism. They are a small minority, but they are here and it's good to have them on the crew of the Jewish Sea-Wolves.

And what a motley crew it is, containing so many contradictory elements. A boxer from California and a farmer from Pennsylvania. A Mexican bullfighter and a Yeshiva boy from Brownsville. Gentiles, both hired-hands and idealists.

These disparate elements make up the first group of adventurers ready to leave America's shores.

These are the seamen of the Jewish fleet. These are the heroes who will outsmart the British naval powers, who with their packed refugee ships will break the mighty blockade of the shores of Palestine.

3

THE PLANE JOURNEY TO EUROPE

It's Sunday evening. I'm in New York on my way to the airport where a plane is waiting to take me to one of Europe's capitals. There I will get an opportunity to see how the uprooted Jews from the camps are grouped and sorted, before being placed on the so-called "illegal" ships, which, from now on, will form an unbroken chain, streaming like sea-caravans, toward Palestine.

Time is short. There is feverish activity afoot over there on the other side of the Atlantic. The "Jewish invasion" is being prepared. As a journalist I always look for the fastest way from A to B and this steel bird will get to Europe in time to witness the "recruitment" process of tens of thousands of sea-passengers. I use the word "recruitment" not as a wry turn of phrase: the passengers waiting in European ports are no mere undocumented migrants. They are being carefully screened and selected because in reality they are being trained as soldiers, as seamen who must be prepared for the unexpected eventualities and nasty surprises that lay in wait for everyone who takes up the burden of risk and adventure. Only the brave and strong may go—the fainthearted will have to stay behind.

It's already eight p.m., New York time, and I'm being driven to the airport at great speed. Half an hour later and I'm already at LaGuardia airport. Once I've checked in my luggage and shown my passport, I'm approached by a thin young man. He stands in front of me, looks at me, and smiles. I recognize him immediately. It's Sidney, one of the future Sea-Wolves who I didn't get a chance to speak with before my departure. He knew I was flying out today, and he didn't want to miss his last chance to tell me his story. Over the past few weeks, while waiting for my travel papers to be in order, I've paid several visits, here in New York, to the gathering places of the young men volunteering for the ships. I interviewed as many of them as I could, but I had overlooked Sidney. Sidney, however, wanted to correct my omission and so has come to the airport to find me.

As it happens Sidney has not come alone; his companion is booked to fly to Paris on the same flight as me. It turns out the passenger is no less interesting than Sidney himself. He is a Norwegian captain and a pillar of New York society who wishes to join the movement; he wants to watch over and guide the Jewish refugee ships. Their friendship intrigues me. I'd like to extract as much information as I can out of him. But Sidney stands in the way: this time he has no intention of being overlooked. Besides: on the plane I'll have the Gentile captain all to myself. Sidney's staying in New York, so he takes precedence.

Even though there's still another hour or two before the flight leaves, Sidney wastes no time. The habitual caution—standard during such conspiratorial encounters—which usually hinders longer conversations, has vanished. Sidney lets his guard down and is an engaging speaker. Every now and then he glances around, on the lookout for eavesdroppers. The general lack of interest in our conversation reassures him.

His story is the typical story of an American Jew whose sense of national consciousness awoke soon after the war. And this consciousness pushed him toward action: not just arousing words and desires, but urging him to transform those desires into deeds. The time had come to do something for his own tormented people which was living through a decisive moment in its history. A great many young American Jews were undergoing the same transformation. I've met hundreds of similar young men, active in the liberation movement, here in New York. His own words best illustrate the crisis that has occurred in the hearts of these young Jews.

Sidney is in fact cosmopolitan by nature. Until now he had no truck with the idea of a Jewish national life. He ignored Jewish national aspirations. His father in the Bronx was a radical in his youth. In the old country he had been a member of various Socialist parties. In America too he had flirted with different political groups, both Jewish and Gentile. Zionism was alien to him. In his older years he had become more and more of a "fellow traveler." When the Holocaust came in all its horror Sidney's father was deeply affected. For the first time he began telling Sidney stories about Jewish life in the old country. He painted a vivid picture of the vibrant, teeming, communal Jewish life on the European continent spanning generations. That world had now vanished. Sidney did not just hear his father's depiction; he also served in the American army. He was too late to see the living, seething Jewish life in Europe, but he did witness its downfall and destruction. The experience changed him, so much so that the quiet, pragmatic lad no longer had any peace. His blood simmered. The urge for revenge for spilled Jewish blood began to burn within. Revenge for the blood of those Jews he had never known. Sidney became a rebel.

He became a rebel against his father's house, and against a criminal world which had allowed such a large portion—both qualitatively and quantitatively speaking—of the Jewish people to be annihilated. His rebelliousness led him to seek work in Jewish organizations. At first he was adrift, he found himself in the wrong places. But after a long search he eventually found a path: he could become a soldier in the Haganah. One fine day he would turn up in one of the port cities of Europe. He would hoist the mast on a Jewish refugee ship. His passion and enthusiasm infected his phlegmatic, Bundist-sympathizing[4] father. Now he too wants to be an "illegal passenger." But Sidney is against it. He doesn't want his elderly father

4 *Bundist*: A member of the General Jewish Labor Bund in Poland (Yiddish: *Algemeyner yidisher arbeter bund in poyln*) was a Jewish socialist party in Poland which promoted the political, cultural and social autonomy of Jewish workers, sought to combat antisemitism and was generally opposed to both Zionism and Communism.

to suffer; then there is the problem of familial harmony to think of. But nothing could stop Sidney from going to the Jewish land. He knew what he wanted; he had found his calling.

Sidney asks me to say hello to his American friends who are scattered in every port in Europe, and on the island of Cyprus. He tells me to stay close to the Norwegian captain, to make sure to sit next to him on the plane. Just then the loudspeaker calls the passengers to begin boarding. We wish each other a warm farewell. We climb the stairs up to the plane as the other passengers wave goodbye to New York.

Once inside, we sit down in the deep, padded seats and fasten our safety belts. The Norwegian captain sits beside me. We look at each other and exchange a trusting smile: the start of one of those intimate acquaintanceships that arise spontaneously on long journeys.

I observe my neighbor carefully. He is a tall, thin man with gray hair. His skin is reddened, his eyes green. But he speaks with the measured tones of a cold Scot. He's been living in America for thirty years. He is retired. He spends his time tending to his garden on Long Island where he lives. In his younger years—that is to say before he turned sixty-two—he had an unusual occupation. He drove steamers across the East River, and often helped bring over dead bodies from Bellevue Hospital to Potter's Field. That was a curious job for a captain, transporting a load of corpses across the river. The ancient Greeks had the legend of Charon, who ferried the dead away from the land of the living.

My travel companion, the retired sea-captain, was the Charon of the East River.

I want to speak with him to the heart of the matter. I want to know what compelled him to take an interest in the Jewish emigration movement. The Norwegian smiles with sparse, yellow teeth. He likes to tell things in order. There is no need for haste. The trip to Paris will last eighteen hours. Six hours for eating and sleeping and twelve hours for talking. I look at him in amazement. He is a man of contradictions: the demeanor of a seasoning air traveler, merged with the unhurried, restraint of a patient storyteller.

The captain keeps his word. He begins with his youth when, at the age of seventeen, he became a man of the water, first as a Norwegian fisherman, and later as a sailor. Not long before the First World War his ship found its way to New York. He disembarked and found the New World to his liking. When war broke out he joined the American navy. Following the war he found work on the East River ferry boats and so he was transformed into the captain who transported cargoes of bodies. The destiny of the man contained its fair share of irony, and our corpse-captain dedicated his spare time to growing roses in his garden.

The ship he worked on was worth 100,000 dollars. The bodies were buried once a week. The average cargo was around three hundred bodies a week. His task did not bother him. In summer the cargo of bodies gave off a foul smell, but after work the captain could breathe in the scent of his roses. He did not mind having to deal with bodies on a regular basis. The dead never caused him any trouble—the living, yes. He was happy to do any job he could find on the water. On dry land he never earned a cent.

Who were those bodies? For the most part they were brought from psychiatric institutions, or from hospitals for the homeless, or from families that could not afford funeral expenses. But often, among the poor, homeless bodies, there wandered a prince . . .

The captain who had long ferried people from the land of the living is now ready to tell me why he has decided to work in the opposite direction, why he has decided to help transport those who have survived the European valley of death. But just then the plane's engine roar into life. The passengers become tense and attentive. From a side door emerges a tall, rugged man in a blue uniform. It is the captain of the aircraft. His eyes are joyful; there is a smile on his lips. He greets the passengers, wishes us all a pleasant flight, and requests we follow the instructions of his crew. His words are polite and warm. I follow the lead of the other passengers and fasten my seat belt. My neighbor, the Norwegian boatman, must postpone the rest of his story until our plane has risen into the clouds.

4

GENTILES WHO WISH TO JOIN THE JEWISH VOYAGE

The plane is already soaring into the clouds. The passengers experience the first turbulence, the thrill of flying in the air. Sitting beside me the Norwegian captain, discovering that a flight in the steel bird is just as calm as a train journey, continues his interrupted account of how he came to the decision, in his ripe old age, to help the Jewish sea crossings.

Back when he was leading his Ship of the Dead over the East River, he always knew what sort of people he was dealing with. He knew that they were poor. Occasionally one would find treasures while searching the rooms of the deceased. Sometimes there were even bodies in ornate coffins, with flowers even, but there was never enough money to provide for a decent burial. One time, as he was preparing to lead his boat from one side of the river to the other a Jewish woman, dressed in rags and shouting, came running toward the boat. She would not allow her relative—one of the bodies on board—to be buried without a name. She put her hand inside her basket and produced a large *tallit.*[5] She handed it to the captain for him to lay on top of the body. She sought out her relative among the dead and told the captain to be extra watchful.

The captain inspected the *tallit*, admiring the weave of the material. He was impressed by the embroidered band of silver along the upper edge of the *tallit* and promised the poor woman he would carry out her request. The incident roused a strong curiosity in the captain for the people who wore such *tallitim*. He became interested in orthodox Jews, and Jews in general, wanted to learn about their way of life. The information convinced him that traditional Jews were not just exotic, different from all other people he encountered, but that this difference in their lifestyle was a result of a painful history stretching back thousands of years. One piece of information led to another and our captain began to study the Jewish Exile. His acquired knowledge transformed him from an apathetic Gentile into a fervent philosemite. He became a supporter of Jewish nationalist aspirations. As a retiree, living off a pension from Uncle Sam, he began a reckoning of all the sins the British had committed against the Jewish people. Like an accountant he diligently recorded all the broken promises, all the trampled declarations, all the breached agreements of "His majesty's government." The demise of six million Jews also had a determined effect on his hitherto stoic world view. And our quiet

....

5 Prayer shawl.

Norwegian who had grown up around the cold fjords of his homeland, became a passionate man. He began to demand justice from those who were unjust.

A year ago, when the first refugee ships began, without Britain's mercy, to sail to Palestine, our captain became so moved by the great mission that he decided, despite his age, to offer assistance. His offer was not accepted at first. There were doubts whether his help would have any significance. But what was important was the strength of his conviction, the willingness of this Gentile to risk everything for the cause. He is obliged to return to Norway to take care of an inheritance and bring his remaining relatives back to America. Later he is determined to have the honor of leading at least one ship to Palestine under the nose of the British. The Norwegian has a connecting flight to catch in Paris and from there he will head to Oslo.

The captain turns his head away and tries to get some sleep, while I look out the circular windows. The aircraft is now flying at 150 miles an hour. Overhead; a dark sky, sprinkled with stars; below: the majestic ocean. The whole world is shrouded in night, the whole cosmos—one expanse of darkness.

Meanwhile inside the airplane—which in size and shape resembles a whale—everything is warm and bright. A smiling, blonde air-hostess distributes chewing gum and white cushions to the passengers to lean their heads on, assuring us that due to excellent weather conditions we're in for a pleasant flight. She vanishes to be replaced by an affably friendly steward boy with warm-eyes who tells the passengers a few words about how to behave during the flight. At first his words are as soft as the white pillows but then he produces a yellow jacket with belts and tassels and instructs the passengers how to use it in the event of a crash. These life-jackets work the same as a life-jacket on board a ship, or like a parachute: you just need to know how to attach the straps correctly and then, in the event of an accident, you should be ok.

The instructions, which also serve as warnings, rouse the hidden fears of the passengers, along with a boastful smile—the smile that results from forced courage. They know that the best way to stay calm is not to think about possible accidents, and the friendliness of the cabin crew succeeds in distracting us from any such thoughts. Every few minutes we are given something else: a cup of coffee, sandwiches, newspapers. The steward wheels out a stack of books—everything from classic novels to the trashiest mystery stories—and everyone can choose according to his taste.

The passengers soon enter a state bordering on monotony. Nothing new under the sun. Two hours after the initial thrill and the passengers already feel like experienced fliers. Nothing surprises them. The wonder gives way to the tedium with which every passenger is punished, regardless of whether he travels as an earth-bound mortal or whether he floats through the heavens. People read and nap. But the affable captain has no intention of letting his guests doze off so easily. He appears with the elegant and self-assured bow of a New York bandleader for whom the coming applause is never in doubt. He announces that we are flying over Halifax. He practically forces his passengers to make an inspection of his aircraft. We observe the motors, the compasses and dials. We look at the pilot who is sitting in strained concentration, holding our lowly lives in his hands. An officer with a red, muscular face spreads out a map for us and calculates with exact precision when we will reach Newfoundland, Ireland etc. The flight speed is now 380 miles an hour. The New York to Paris leg is 3,700 miles. The journey will take eighteen hours including the six hours break in two stopovers.

The interpreter, instructor and pilot have not finished their presentation when our attention is drawn to an unusual light outside even though it is just gone midnight. We all gape out the windows. Wonder of wonders! Bright beams like rays of daylight rise from the earth, though the dark skies are still thick with stars. The streams of light are coming from the sky above Newfoundland. We distinctly see the border between the brightness over Newfoundland and the darkness that envelopes the sky over our heads. The captain's overweening enthusiasm is almost enough to dampen the passengers' enjoyment of the enchanted currents of light that gush upward like a living water fountain.

Half an hour later we land in Newfoundland. It is bitterly cold. The ground is covered in mounds of ice and snow. We are dragged off for breakfast—a clue that daybreak cannot be far off. The path from the plane to the restaurant is no more than a few paces, but it is so cold that a large bus comes to take the passengers directly to the tables already set for breakfast. Who can eat in the early hours of the morning when we already had a light supper just before leaving New York? And yet we eat. You chew whether you want to or not. Without appetite. Without enjoyment, yet you chew. The plane ticket was so expensive it would be a waste to skip the meals.

It's only now as I look around the dining hall that I notice there are only eighteen passengers in all, even though the plane could comfortably hold fifty. Many of the ethnicities found in America are represented. Italians, Irish, Spaniards, Poles and an Englishman. I am the only Jew among seventeen carefree non-Jews. The Italians are talkative, and they tell us they are going to see for themselves what sort of economy *Il Duce* has left behind. The Irish are more discreet and say nothing. The Poles are snoring and the Englishman is aloof. There is also a broad-shouldered youth with a flat face and a blue beret on top of his closely-cropped hair. A Frenchman? I don't have to wait long to find out. The boy is a merry fellow, happy to talk to everyone. Finding out that I'm a newspaper man he treats me to a hail of words. I don't know how it happened, but suddenly the boy is talking to me about Jewish issues. He shows me his copy of *Life Magazine* where there are photos of the oil pipelines in Haifa after the recent explosion. He wants to provoke. I say nothing.

But being such a good conversationalist he splits himself in two and starts responding to his own questions.

He himself was an underground fighter during the German occupation of France. For that reason he feels an affinity for any nation fighting for its own freedom. The Jewish struggle is on the world's agenda. He knows that terrorism is unavoidable, but that it is not effective in deterring the occupiers. Is he against terrorism? He is intelligent enough to know, as an active resistance fighter who had himself been involved in acts of terror, that terrorism is not a tactic that can be dismissed out of hand. But he doesn't understand Jewish terrorism. The struggle for total Jewish liberation must be carried out in the open, on a grand scale, before the eyes of the world. Large-scale terror acts carried out by undisciplined groups should be kept to a minimum. The whole Jewish nation must become one legion. Jews must once again become invaders in the Land of Israel. The British are no Nazis, and now is not a time of war. Even the struggle for Irish independence cannot be compared to the Jewish situation. It is a different sort of liberation movement. The Frenchman is an optimist, a believer. He completely ignores the fact that the Jewish people lacks any political status.

Who is this young man who has such plans for how to lead the struggle for Jewish independence? Is he a former Maquis? His answer is not clear. But he tells me that during the occupation there were also other fighting groups. It was a nameless army that recruited all over France. Farmers and factory workers, lawyers and ship-cleaners, teachers and housewives. They began by taking them to the mountains to teach them how to hold weapons. When the Nazis started to pay attention to the movement, they trained recruits in their homes.

They worked in cells of three, with one commander. One cell didn't know what the others were doing. Often a brother in the resistance would not realize that his own sister was also a member. The young man was captured twice, and twice he escaped. He spent seven weeks in a concentration camp. His mission was to destroy all the documents the Nazis had gathered concerning the rebels. He would often destroy the documents, along with the building they were being kept in, by laying incendiary bombs. Fleeing the scene he would sprinkle pepper on the path behind him to throw off the search hounds.

These rebels soon grew into a formidable insurgent army. They were served by a medical corps: doctors, nurses and civilian volunteers. Their weapons were buried in the ground, and even makeshift hospitals were dug into the earth.

By the time the Frenchman had finished his story we were coming in to land in Ireland, at Shannon airport. Shannon sounds like the Hebrew word for calm, tranquility, and Ireland looks like a serene island, whose people revolted, winning their freedom from the British—the same British against whom Jewish rebels are fighting for the survival of the Jewish people. The peaceful farming nation of Ireland had raised the flag of uprising, fought, and roused the consciousness of the world in order to win their independence.

Does the Jewish nation also stand on the threshold of freedom? Will the refugee ships open a path toward total redemption?

We are led into the airport cafeteria. The meals are served in minuscule portions. A mouthful of fish, a fork-full of other foodstuffs. There isn't a crumb of bread to be seen. When we ask the waiter for bread his response is polite and stiff:

"In Ireland there's no bread during lunch."

No bread, no potatoes, no sign of milk. The coffee is as bitter as *maror*. But at least there's plenty of whisky. The Italians are outraged, but they are assured that in Italy food is just as scarce. They will need to add another notch to their belts.

Everything in the Irish restaurant is red. The walls, the chairs, the tables, and even the waiters. They hover between the tables, tense and stiff, yet at the same time, friendly. Their faces too are red. Their footsteps are heavy and loud, as though they are trying to stamp on the ground.

After the meal we hurry back to the airplane. The airport is an international fair ground. The world's roads all cross here. We pass a black wall bearing the names of people who have telegrams waiting for them from other airports all over the globe. One's eye meets a name that has become famous: Helen Friedman, the sister of Dov Bela Gruner.[6] She must be on her way back to America. A shame that our airplanes cross paths and we will never meet—the sister of a Jewish martyr who was killed not by a Nazi bullet, but by a British noose.

I board the airplane bound for Paris.

....

6 Hungarian-born member of Irgun. Executed by the British for firing on policemen and setting explosive charges.

5

At the Headquarters of the Jewish Underground in Paris

At nine p.m. I arrive in Paris, where I am supposed to make contact with the people from the Jewish underground. The mission is to be carried out with the strictest, most sacred discretion. In my briefcase I have a sealed letter from New York. I come armed with a passport full of visas, a press pass from the *Morgn Zhurnal* and identification certificates. With these weapons I am to make myself known to the appropriate authorities at the addresses I've been provided with.

In Paris the airport authorities greet the tourists with smiling faces. Luggage inspections are cursory. They waste no time looking through our documents. The only thing about the arrival that's difficult is finding a taxi. There is a green bus, an old jalopy, which brings us into the city and drops us off on Boulevard des Invalides leaving the passengers to fend for themselves. After half an hour of waiting on the street waving my hands about I finally flag down an empty taxi. I get in, along with two other passengers, and ask to be taken to a hotel near Grands Boulevards.

Riding through the streets of Paris I feel a growing sense of unease. I've taken on the responsibility of accompanying the Jewish refugee ships across the seven seas and such a responsibility demands a willingness to make sacrifices. I have to remain tight-lipped, and avoid conversation with strangers. Caution is paramount. Silence a blessing. It is like a military secret: we must not speak of it. I must keep the promise I've made to myself.

Where the taxi drops me off, not far from the hotel, a group of people has gathered, and I hear the resounding voice of a crier. It is a typical Parisian street scene, illustrative of post-war France. A crippled Frenchman in ragged clothing, wearing a stained beret, stands in front of an enormous placard which covers the whole corner of a building. The placard lists details of war casualties, nurses and graves. The man in the beret notices the crowd around him, appreciates his audience and yells at the top of his voice, rattling off the statistics of France's war losses.

"Since 1870 Germany has never ceased to represent a danger to the world . . . the Pan-Germanic ideas of Bismarck, the Kaiser and Hitler have constantly posed a threat to civilization . . . France has always been at the front-line of defending democracy . . ."

The man pauses for a moment before continuing:

France's losses in the war: 250,000 soldiers killed, 400,000 wounded, a million and a half prisoners of war . . . 120,000 civilians lost their lives, a million children and 250,000 killed or executed in concentration camps . . ."

The man's voice grows louder and stronger. His audience gets larger. Why is he shouting like this? Why does he list off the nation's losses? In whose name does he speak?

No one sent him; he's here on his own authority. Some of the people in the crowd know him. They are his loyal audience and admit that he is not all there. The war has made him lose his senses. This does not stop him winning the sympathy of passersby. He reminds France of its eternal animus toward Germany; he does so with zeal and hatred. He himself is a veteran of the First World War and he lost two sons in the second. There is justification for his having lost his mind.

It is distressing to witness this scene within hours of arriving on French soil. But something else is bothering me. My mission requires concentration and vigilance. Everything else is of no importance.

As soon as I've checked into my sixth-floor hotel room I take out my address book and call a number I was given in New York. It's now eleven in the evening and I doubt whether anyone will answer the phone at such a late hour. My sense of foreboding is not out of place. After the very first ring someone picks up and I hear a cautious, irritated voice:

"Hello? Who is this?"

"I've just arrived in Paris . . ." I begin.

"Isban from New York?"

"Correct! How did you know?"

"I was told you were coming . . . you're with the *Morgn Zhurnal*?"

"Yes."

"*Shalom*, Isban! I'll see you right away," the voice says, more confident now.

"Right now, so late?" I ask.

"Conspiracies don't follow office-hours."

"I understand . . ."

"You've come on a mission, and we have no time to lose. But you must be tired after such a long flight, and you don't know your way around Paris. The meeting can wait until tomorrow morning."

"Fine." I say.

"You have my address? And you have a letter for me too?"

"I do."

"I'll be waiting for you at ten tomorrow morning. Take a taxi."

"I'll be there."

"Don't be late."

*

By the time I wake up the next morning it's already eight o' clock. I've awoken with a mission. It's sunny outside and through the window I see cool beams of morning light moving over the cornices of the fine Parisian buildings. Nice weather has a tendency to lift one's mood and I felt energized. Fifteen minutes later and I'm dressed, washed, and sitting in the hotel dining room eating the first breakfast of my European trip. Thin, dark bread with jam, foul-smelling cheese and tasteless ersatz coffee made from roasted grains.

The meager breakfast has not dampened my mood. Out on the street I give the hotel porter a generous tip—or a *pourboire,* as the locals call it—and in one minute he's found me a taxi.

I hasten to the arranged address, eager to reach the house of a person whose every move must remain mysterious and secretive, a person who is involved in the rescue of Jewish souls, whom the British see as a conspirator, but the Jews consider a savior.

It is only as I enter the building's dark, narrow staircase that I realize I've come an hour early. The stairs are old and winding; the walls, dilapidated; ribbons of peeling paint hang from the ceiling. I knock on the door but there is no answer so I go back down to the street, reprimanding myself for coming at the wrong time. I decide to kill an hour by exploring the quiet, narrow streets of this old Parisian neighborhood.

The stripped down buildings do not inspire joy. Sorrow and melancholy radiate from the very stones. Through these dark, narrow stairwells, through these peeling three-hundred year-old walls, the Jews of Paris were dragged and sent off for deportation. From here the victims were led on their way to the ovens. I haven't attempted to look up any acquaintances here in Paris; I haven't met with a single friend, but I know that if I had someone to accompany me now he would point sadly to each building and recount that such and such a friend was taken from here and send to that place from which there can be no return. By rights I should be overcome by a feeling of despair, but I also know that from these same garret rooms come the signals to the sentries, to the guardians who wish to save what remains of European Jewry and lead them to Palestine. These narrow little rooms help conceal the network that connects Jews all over the world.

Paris, the city of poets, has always been the city of dreamers and revolutionaries. It was here that the great Polish poet Adam Mickiewicz preached for the redemption—through Jewish redeemers—of the world; this is where Garibaldi gathered strength for his uprising; here Bakunin engaged in his tumultuous feuds; the Jewish philosopher Moses Hess worked here, and perhaps here will be the starting point for the bang that will shatter the walls standing in the way of freedom, of Jewish deliverance?

Returning to the dark stairwell and knocking on the brown door, I'm met by a large young man with a mild, gentle face, smiling eyes and the demeanor of one willing to do anything in his power to help. His affability is a pleasant surprise: I had been expecting to meet someone stern and reserved with no time for friendliness. I hand him the sealed envelope. He invites me to take a seat, opens the letter, and once he has finished reading he seems somewhat more trusting of me, though still observing me carefully.

The conversation begins:

"Do you know your mission," he asks.

"I do," I say.

"Our work is being watched by British spies," he warns me.

"I know."

"They're looking for us in all the port towns of Europe."

"I know that too," I say.

"We don't want to draw any attention to ourselves."

"I won't draw any attention to you," I assure him with a smile, "though you deserve all the honor you can get."

"Attention jeopardizes our activities."

"I know."

"It can cost lives, Jewish lives."

"I know."

"Tell me, why do you want to travel on our ships specifically?"

"I want the people to know what's happening to the refugees on the seas—people are already aware of what's happening to them on land."

"Is that advisable?"

"It's effective!" I say. "It will wake up the Jewish public, rouse them to action. It will mean more aid for your work."

"Your journey's not going to be a pleasure cruise," he tries to dissuade me.

"I know. I want to follow the refugees on every step of their journey, from when they are collected from the displaced person's camps, when they are taken to the ships, until they land on the shores of Palestine."

"The British don't always let us land."

"I'm prepared for that too," I say. "I'll go with the DPs to Cyprus. I'll take on the burden of whatever happens to them."

"Such burdens are not taken on willingly," he smiles faintly.

"My commitment is what I want to prove to you," I say, "I want you to know that I'm not a passive bystander."

"If you were a bystander I wouldn't be speaking to you."

I thank him.

He pauses for a moment, rubbing his forehead. Raising his eyebrows, he continues:

"Listen, a few days from now a ship is going to reach one of the ports. You will board that ship. From there you will travel to other ports. The mission—to receive the *Ma'apilim*.[7] You will have an opportunity to see how we group the passengers. We don't yet know the date of the final voyage to Palestine. We will receive the details when the time comes. In the meantime get as many visas as you can. You will need to pass through many European countries. When you have the visas I'll send you to the appropriate harbor. Our representatives will receive the necessary information about you."

"All of that?" I stand up.

7 Hebrew term for the Jewish refugees attempting to immigrate illegally to Palestine as part of Aliyah Bet.

"*Shalom!*" he says, shaking me by the hand. "Follow my instructions."

*

Back out on the street I leaf through my passport. The only thing missing is an Italian visa. Because of my changed travel plans in New York (flying instead of taking the ship) I never managed to get the Italian visa. I must now hurry to the Italian consulate.

The streets of Paris are busy now. Among the thronging crowds there are Frenchmen with beards of all colors. The bearded Frenchmen look like they are wearing masks. Parisians don't just ride in automobiles but they ride bicycles and motorcycles as well. On a bench on Boulevard des Italiens I see a student with a red face engrossed in a book. His Jaw and chin are framed with a thin strip of facial hair, like a young Arab sheikh. On the terraces of the large cafés, people sip cups of bitter, unsweetened coffee. The whole country drinks; men and women alike.

I try to find a taxi. No luck. I feel embarrassed. Finally an empty taxi passes. I give the driver the address of the Italian consulate, but the proud driver refuses, saying he's going in the opposite direction. As I'm standing there trying to take it all in, a young lad approaches and offers his help for a hundred francs. When there are no taxis in Paris you can take the metro. He knows the way to the Italian consulate. He also knows English. Where did he learn? He was with the

English army in Austria. He also knows German and a little Yiddish—*shma yisroel* and *Sholem Aleykhem*.

I latch on to this young Jewish Parisian, who knows English, German, Yiddish, who knows the way to the metro, and together we head to the Italian consulate.

6

ON A SHIP, CUT OFF FROM EVERY SHORE

Furnished with all the necessary visas, and armed with instructions from the headquarters of the "illegal" Jewish immigration in Paris, I board a night-train that will take me to a certain port city on the Mediterranean.

In this port city I am due to meet with some Jewish underground figures who will then take me to an isolated docking point where an "illegal" ship is waiting, ready to receive thousands of displaced Jews.

All night long the train passes through towns and villages. I arrive at the appointed city at about ten in the morning. Half an hour later I knock on the door of a Jewish institution.

After putting down my heavy suitcase and showing my identification papers I ask the first clerk to put me in contact with the appropriate people.

The clerk, a large, sunburned Palestinian Jew, observes me slowly and carefully before glancing at my suitcase and smirking:

"You want to go to Palestine?"

"That's why I came," I say.

"With that luggage?"

"Is it too much?" I ask.

"It's not going to be a leisure cruise or a tourist outing . . . it's a clandestine voyage!" the clerk explains. "You may have to run, you may have to swim, and heavy bags are going to slow you down. Get rid of them! A small case with a few essentials will be enough . . . but before anything else happens you'll need to see our instructor. I'll call him now."

He lifts the receiver to his ear but is unable to get hold of the instructor. He calls a few more numbers, but no luck. In the end it's decided that I'll have to wait here in the office.

I take in my surroundings. Three large desks obscure the walls. The clerks are so overwhelmed with work they have no time to look up at everyone who comes in. And there are a lot of people coming in: refugees waiting for their weekly aid package; people from the DP camps demanding better facilities for their families; future Ma'apilim looking to find out the exact date of their departure on a clandestine ship. There are also those who come to lodge complaints about bad treatment . . .

The tired clerks hear out the complaints, the demands, the indications with the attention one pays to the unfortunate and offended. Not a single sharp word, not a grumble is heard against the claimants whose endless barrage of speech disturbs the clerks in their work. There is no tone of reproach in their responses, only apologies, gentle words and assurances that all grievances will be resolved.

I take another glance around the room. The walls are decorated with pictures of Zionist leaders, of national figures. Herzl, leaning against the balcony railing; A. D. Gordon with mattock in hand; Brenner with his rugged Bedouin beard and burning gaze; and on the wall opposite Brenner, a portrait of the late leader Berl Katznelson under which hangs his motto, which became a catchword for the whole Yishuv:

"Part the seas and welcome the returnees!"

And over the entrance hangs a line from the Palmach hymn: "*We will not bow our heads!*"

The large clerk once again tries to reach the inspector. This time he manages to get him on the telephone. From the other end of the line we learn that the inspector will arrive at the office in fifteen minutes.

Two people arrive. Two of those sea-watchmen who are nowadays to be found in ports and harbors all over the world to load Jewish ships with tens of thousands of displaced Jews, seeking to escape the European continent with nothing more than the shirts on their backs.

The two envoys greet me heartily, apologizing for the delay. They busy themselves with my suitcases, and arrange my hotel room. After I've brushed off the dust of my journey and had a wash, they invite me to have lunch.

It's hot outside. The sun is baking even though it's only late April. It's that notable tropical heat of a port city on the Mediterranean. The traffic in the streets is noisy; people pass by from every nation in the world:

Algerians, Spaniards, Moroccans, Soldiers from Tunis, sailors from Egypt, tall, long-necked guides from Sudan. Everyone is bustling in the large port-town, tinted with every international color.

My escorts lead me into a restaurant on a quiet side-street near the port. A sycophantic waiter appears and within a few minutes delicious dishes are placed before us along with two bottles of red table wine. Once we've finished the first course my escorts get down to business.

The instructor, a sedate, measured man in a pair of polished glasses, who has the appearance of a patient accountant, reads over my letter of introduction carefully.

"Your papers," he says, "indicate which ship you are meant to travel on. Unfortunately, you don't exactly have much of a choice. The ship named here won't weigh anchor for another ten weeks."

"It's not ready yet?" I ask.

"It hasn't even been converted into a passenger ship yet!" the instructor replies. "These matters aren't quite as simple as you think. We have ships of all kinds: cargo ships, riverboats, container ships—but when they come into our possession not one of them has the basic installations necessary to serve as a passenger ship. We have to have each ship refitted and equipped to make them suitable to transport thousands of ma'apilim."

"And all that takes time, I imagine?"

"Time, work and money. It depends on the size and bulk of the ship. The ship you were supposed to travel on is currently being refitted. It will take ten weeks before the process is finished, but when it's ready, she'll be able to carry six thousand passengers."

The information pleases me but the thought that I've come to this port town too early worries me. The instructor banishes my worries with his next statement:

"You're too early for this ship. For another, bigger ship that sailed through here a few days ago, you're too late. But there might be another option: tomorrow at dawn there's a smaller ship which is due to pick up between fifteen hundred and two thousand ma'apilim from various ports. That's the ship you'll travel on. Accompanying two thousand ma'apilim to Palestine is something too, right? It's a decent assignment for a newspaper man."

There is no reason to object to the suggestion. Actually it wasn't so much a suggestion so much as an order. And a newspaper man who wants to follow two thousand refugees must follow orders. I accept and the instructor says:

"Be ready by five a.m. We'll take you to the ship."

We finish our lunch. The instructor pays the bill and leaves behind a wad of paper francs as a tip.

By the entrance there is a commotion. Customers of various skin colors and clothing push past each other—some going in, some coming out.

My escorts lead me through the backstreets where British spies lurk at night on the hunt for Jewish ma'apilim ships. There are cabarets, seafood restaurants and cafés where one can buy cocaine. In the corners of the streets sit old men with the sort of French beards you only see in portraits. Amateur artists with palettes in their hands stand on the curbs working on their paintings. A watchman wanders through the neighborhood in a colorful costume from Napoleonic times. He stands watch and helps to preserve the exotic character of the quarter, receiving a pension from the city for his trouble.

The beggars, vagabonds and lurkers of the quarter represent quite a singular tribe. They watch over the neighborhood like old birds over their ragged nests. Another straw is taken, another crumb of clay crumbles away and the danger grows that the nest will fall apart entirely.

My escorts lead me through the port for many hours, speaking about the great significance of the Jewish sea voyages. The idea of "*thy children shall come again to their own border . . .*"[8] in all its historic magnitude, is being turned to reality in these European port towns on the Mediterranean coast.

I spend the evening in my hotel room preparing for the long voyage ahead.

By five a.m. I'm standing packed and ready to go. My escorts are also punctual. There is an automobile waiting for us which will drive us to a patch of coastline somewhere far beyond the city.

....

8 *Jeremiah*, 31:17

The driver is a Frenchman. His companion is also a Frenchman. Two good Gentiles helping the Ma'apilim movement.

The car moves fast. The air is cool, a cold April dawn. The sun is coming up, spreading its rich light out over the fields and orchards, growing brighter and warmer, lighting up the woods and hills, illuminating a land that stretches out so far the eye cannot keep up.

We're driving through the region of Provence.

The colorful landscape blinds us with its rainbow light. The two Frenchmen in the front of the car never cease to describe the significance of everything we pass. They point out every sight. Their presentation is full of exaggeration and fantastic overestimation, but I feel like taking them at their word.

There lies a stone where Napoleon wept for his Josephine. Nestled in those trees is a little chapel— there was once a crazy count from Paris who fell in love with his maid. The count burned down his palace, drove away his wife and children and snatched up his maid out from among the flames in order to elope and get married in that secluded chapel.

The crazy count was the grandfather of the Count of Monte Cristo.

In the middle of the road there is an old brick building. From one of the windows a half-clay figure looks out, waving a greeting to those who drive by. For four hundred years this clay figure, this French golem has been standing over that window saying "*bonjour*" to passersby. The sculpture was made by an anonymous artist, but it radiates the mastery of a Michelangelo.

After four hours on the road we come to a quiet patch of coastline. Fishing boats and tug-steamers rock on the water, and between the steamers looms a gray ship with two smokestacks.

The Frenchmen have long since stopped speaking. Our escorts do not say anything. Every word is superfluous. Our lips are supposed to remain sealed. This is a secret location. Conspiracy is afoot.

Within ten minutes I have bid farewell to my escorts. I leave my luggage in their care to pick up on the way back.

A small fishing boat takes me to the ship. With each stroke of the fisherman's oar the gray ship is pulled into sharper focus. As I get up close to the hull I read the name written on the side:

"Tradewinds."

*

All lined up in a row on deck stand the curious crew of the Tradewinds. A young blond man wearing a captain's uniform holds a pair of binoculars to his eyes. At an opening on the side of the vessel, two pairs of hands pull me up onto the ship. And once I'm standing on the lower deck I hear a greeting, shouted in chorus as though in one voice:

"Welcome aboard, sailor!"

7

THE STORY OF AN "ILLEGAL" SHIP

This is the story of a ship that has crossed seven seas—preparing to welcome over two thousand Ma'apilim and bring them to Palestine.

The ship is not very large, only about a thousand tons. It is 220 feet long, forty-five feet wide.

It could be a mid-sized steamer on the Hudson, a tug-boat on the East River, but it is a floating Tent of Israel, a fortress which must split the seas, pierce through rocks, navigate icebergs, until it reaches the promised shores.

A Honduran flag flutters on the mast, but when it reaches Palestinian territorial waters, close to the Jewish homeland, the ship will be renamed with a Jewish name. The foreign flag will be taken down and the flag of Israel will be raised.

As I board the ship, the captains are being swapped. The first captain, the Gentile who had led the ship out of Caribbean waters, across the Atlantic and into the Mediterranean, is leaving and a second captain—a Jew from Baltimore—is taking over command of the vessel.

The handing over of authority from the first captain to the second takes place in a solemn, ceremonial mood. There are short speeches for luck. They drink to the eternity of Israel and fire twenty pistol shots into the air.

Along with the first captain, an Irishman who served on the side of justice, a second Gentile crew-member leaves the ship—a Filipino who served as steward. His name is Chico Monterola, but the others affectionately call him simply "Chico." This good man served on the Jewish crew of a Jewish ship, which will carry Jewish refugees, not for financial reward. As he bids me farewell, as he sets off to return to the United States, he asks me which newspaper I write for. When I tell him about the *Morgn Zhurnal* he admits that he cannot yet read Yiddish. But on the day when the English-language New York papers carry headlines about our ship landing, or being captured, he will buy a copy of the *Morgn Zhurnal*, and ask his Jewish neighbor in Williamsburg to read my article for him.

He asks me to spell his name correctly, it is after all a strange foreign name, Chico Monterola . . . I note down the spelling as he dictates it to me. Chico deserves this small portion of recognition. It is not such a strange name, it is a combination of colorful sounds. And the bearer of that name is a privileged citizen of the colorful United States.

"Bon voyage, good, kind Chico!"

"Bon voyage, privileged sailor of the Jewish Ma'apilim fleet!"

I descend into the belly of the ship to see how the steel innards, the motors, machines and propulsion apparatus work. On the ladder I cross paths with the captain who greets me with a smile and invites me to his cabin where he will brief me with the latest information.

The captain is a thin young man, in all no taller than five feet. Light-skinned, blond, with typical Slavic features. He has a sparkle in his eyes, and a gentle smirk on his lips redolent of a high-school student. He is all of twenty-five years old, a native of Baltimore: this is Sidney Yellin.

We sit in his cabin. He hands me the key to my own cabin. I am to be his neighbor; there is only a wall between us. The captain leans closer to be and smiles. He is impatient. There's something he wants to tell me. May he speak? Am I ready to listen?

"Please captain, speak by all means! This ship is yours. The seas are yours. The two thousand Ma'apilim are yours, and now, my readers are also yours."

The self-confident captain lights his pipe. His young, blond face laughs. His teeth laugh. His eyes laugh, and he begins to tell his tale. The short history of the ship flows from his lips.

In the beginning the Tradewinds was a small patrol ship, or Coast Guard cutter. One of those vigilant sea-fortresses that stood guard over the waters of the Caribbean. It patrolled the ports of Miami, Charleston, Key West. Later it was used as a cargo-ship, transporting bananas. A gray, boring vessel, not good for much more than scrap. But on the day the Jewish underground purchased it, it received a mission, a noble calling—to part the seas and lead the Jews to the Land of Israel.

The ship was bought in Baltimore and brought to Miami where they began to fix it up, modernize it, and add all the necessary furnishings needed to convert it into a passenger ship.

The crew was recruited from various parts of America. They did not know each other beforehand, each coming from his own private, civilian life. They soon saw each other as family. One time, the whole crew was brought by plane from Baltimore to New York to be together for a celebration. During the time when the ship was being refitted it was officially classed as a cargo ship, allegedly with an intent to transport lumber to Europe.

The top part of the ship is known as the flying bridge. The ship had to cross the Atlantic in its raw, imperfect state. It was only later, in a European port, that all the necessary furnishings were added.

Though the ship is a Jewish ship, and the crew, a predominantly Jewish one, when the boys arrived in Europe they were ordered not to fraternize with the local Jews. They were not allowed to go to the Synagogue, or visit Jewish homes—all in the name of keeping a low profile, for the sake of security. This order was painful for the American boys who had strong sympathies toward, and a desire to connect with, the Jews of Europe. Even at home in Baltimore everything had to remain a secret. No Jew in Baltimore was aware that such a ship existed at all, let alone that it was docked right there in their harbor.

Word was passed via the previous owner of the ship that the crew were forbidden to bring any naval uniforms. The crew obeyed the order. The first crossing from Baltimore to Europe was hard. Sea conditions were stormy and the little ship was tossed about on the tempestuous waves. All of the sailors—most of whom had served in the fleet of the Merchant Marine—were seasick. They did not see a single sunny day during the entire crossing, only terrible winds and storms. It was like Columbus's voyage on the Santa Maria. They stopped over on the Azore Islands. Not having brought warm clothing with them, they suffered from cold and fever.

Some of the crew were first-timers. This was their first encounter with the mighty forces of nature. On top of all this they were working without pay. The only thing they got was food, work clothes and a small amount of pocket money to amuse themselves with in the port towns. Later, conditions improved. While in America they received twenty-five dollars a week, in Europe they got between forty-five and sixty dollars a week.

The first captain who sailed the ship from America to Europe was a genuine red-headed, red-faced Irishman, with a crystal clear character. He had joined the mission out of a sense of deep conviction that as a Christian he had a duty to stand on the side of those who have been unjustly wronged. Everyone respected him. He expressed his convictions with logical clarity, without high-falutin rhetoric or clichés. His confidence that the British were at fault, and the Jewish struggle was the correct one, was enough to compel this Gentile to join the fight on the side of the underdog. He led the ship to Europe, whereupon he suddenly had to return to America for a private family matter. But he wanted us to accept his offer to serve again on a future ship, which he was intent on sailing all the way to the shores of Palestine.

There were times during the crossing when lifeboats were damaged, or motors stopped working and the young, enthusiastic seamen fixed everything. These small incidents enriched their experience.

When the ship reached the European port there was a rush to finish the refitting process. Time was short. The day was approaching when they would have to leave port and they were still missing the most important thing—the furnishings necessary for two thousand passengers. Thanks to the flexibility and energy of the underground volunteers this was achieved almost overnight. They brought smiths, carpenters and painters from the local population. The work was carried out at a breakneck tempo and within twenty-four hours the ship was ready to leave port.

When the time came to leave it was a day before Passover and the crew insisted on having a seder on the ship. The departure was delayed and they pulled out all the stops to celebrate a proper seder. There was wine and matzos from America. All the matzos here were imported from America and this year there was a risk that the matzos would not arrive in time for the first night of Passover. But the crew were happy to share their supply of matzos with the local Jewish community.

The night of the first seder was a joyous one. The dining room was transformed into a stage. The walls were decorated with white bed sheets. The tables were laid with delicacies fit for a king. The crew members cast off their work clothes and dressed up like princes: ironed suits, white shirts, colorful ties. The seder was led by one of the young Palestinian Jews from the Haganah. The Haggadah was read according to the new Palestinian style. They sang Hebrew songs and American sea-shanties. Their song rang out into the air, a song containing an echo of the young Jews who were clearing a path of freedom for the People of Israel.

During the entire voyage the crew members avoided making direct references to Palestine: the code word was "Oklahoma." The entire time they were abroad, even when they were only among allies, they never once uttered the words "Palestine" or "Land of Israel"; they even avoided speaking in Yiddish or Hebrew. The code word for passenger was "Banana." They avoided words such as "refugee" and the like; there was secret terminology for everything. Caution was paramount, but no matter how careful they were, and how often they were warned, the British nevertheless began to get suspicious about the ship's movements. Legally there was nothing they could do. But using a variety of excuses, and under pressure from British secret agents, the intelligence service of the harbor began to make frequent inspections and searches, delaying the departure of the ship. The captain had even decided to leave without the necessary legal authorization, but on the final day the authorization arrived and the ship was able to set sail, to the sound of joyous singing, and make its way into the wide waters . . .

*

The jolly, blond captain, the kind Jewish boy from Baltimore has not yet finished recounting the story of the ship when the chief engineer arrives and announces that it is time to start warming up the motors, as departure is imminent. There is already noise up on deck. Some of the sailors have begun heaving ropes, others have lifted the anchor and the captain begins glancing over his chart. He spreads out his maps to decide in which direction the ship is to sail next.

8

THE CAPTAIN OF A REFUGEE SHIP

Our ship glides peacefully over the mirror-like blue waters. For an hour the captain leaves behind his charts to give instructions to the helmsman, and speak with the two radio operators after which he sets off—with me in tow—for a thorough inspection of every level of the ship.

It is now evening. The sun, which has all day heated the picturesque landscape in the distance and the surface of the water around us, has now sunk down into a fiery strip. The shore has begun to fade from view. Behind us, here and there, the flames of solitary light-house begin to glow.

"Where to? Which direction are we headed?" I ask the captain, even though I know it's indiscreet. Such questions should go unanswered.

"We don't yet have a destination," the captain smiles. "In New York they make plans, and on the shores of Europe the plans are changed. It all depends on which way the political winds are blowing over here . . . we direct our course on sea in parallel with what British intelligence is doing on land . . ."

"Are British spies very active?" I ask.

"You have no idea! They use their whole powerful apparatus against our Ma'apilim ships. They follow us with airplanes, with ships, with secret radio stations and with paid agents . . . but we outsmart them. When they're looking for us on one end of the continent, we're wandering around the other end. When they catch our scent in the south, we head north . . ."

I look around and take in our humble little ship, against which the British have to mobilize their planes, ships and paid spies. I look at our blond, youthful—and yet self-confident—captain who's showing me around every corner of this thousand ton ship, and listen to his explanation. When it comes to listing his achievements on the ship he loses all modesty. He stands by the belief that we should appreciate his accomplishments. The captain cannot remain passive regarding his truth. As soon as he took over command of the ship he made an agreement with himself that he must mold his crew into a select, exemplary team, and that his voyage must be a success. Not without pride he explains how he took a neglected, has-been cargo ship, which belonged by rights in a scrapheap and transformed it into a floating fortress. True, the setup is a little primitive and cramped, but that helps them house as many refugees as possible. And the more Ma'apilim there are on the ship—those people who've gone through hell on earth—the more it excuses the flaws and problems that the ship possesses in plentiful supply.

We continue down into the engine-room. There we hear the drone of motors. Smoke billows from an enormous boiler, and a tangle of pipes gives off an intolerable heat. Pistons are hammering, and all of it together represents the power propelling the ship forward.

"If the British come down here, they'll get some nasty burns," the captain laughed. "But they won't come. The doors will be locked. They won't get to the helm either. We won't let them touch anything—the ship is ours!"

The battle-ready captain has decided that they should put up a fight when the British come to capture the ship. He has asked the Haganah to allow him to do as he will. When he approaches the shores of Palestine he wants to use a smokescreen; he wants gas masks for his whole crew so they can make a show of resistance. It's well known that the British use teargas when they board the Ma'apilim ships to overpower the crews and refugees, neutralizing any chance of resistance. Our captain wants a counter-weapon. He plans to grab the English just as they are boarding the ship and cover their faces with rags soaked in morphium to knock them out . . . with the British asleep they would be able to lead the Ma'apilim as far as the shore and unload every last one of them . . .

Is the captain a dreamer? A fantasist? Has he been infected with a lust for adventures that other captains before him did not experience?

It's enough to listen to his logical, well-thought out words to see that he is a realist. Even his wild ideas are not impulsive, but are plans that could be transformed into deeds. By nature the captain is a mild man, a measured man. His gentle, almost bashful smile holds a good deal of charm. He takes the raillery and insults of his crew in good spirits, but when it comes to duties he is strict, almost authoritarian. He cannot tolerate when crew members undermine his discipline or break the rules. Negligence is the greatest enemy of our goals. The captain's warnings are no idle threats. At a recent port he expelled two crew members. He sent one of them back to France for being lazy, and the other he sent back to America for excessive boozing and talking too much in the taverns of the port towns.

Our captain has no more than twenty-five years on his narrow shoulders, but he speaks with the authority of a sea dog, who has been baked and beaten under sun and rain and seafaring experience. He never managed to finish his education. In this third year of high-school he dropped out to join the merchant marine. He was eighteen when he joined and served seven years. During his service he learned about the Displaced Persons camps—the DPs. No definition in the world could clarify to that Jewish American boy the significance of such words "displaced persons." His investigations caused him to mistrust the human race and how it had carved up the world. He began to move in various non-Jewish radical circles. It was only when he attended a Zionist youth meeting that he found answers to his doubts. He heard things there that rang in his ears. Two weeks later he made contact with a member of the Haganah who informed him his people were looking to recruit young men with maritime experience. He signed up and soon came to the realization that the movement had come twenty years too late. To make up for lost time they will have to send not just a few ships, but whole armadas to trample the British destroyers patrolling the territorial waters, sniffing around like bloodhounds.

The captain debunks the hypothesis that the Jewish boys, as a unit, cannot be good sailors, that their work lacks harmony and coordination. The rough Atlantic crossing put such ideas to bed. The most striking detail of all is that so far no outsider has learned that their crew is a Jewish one.

Concerning the hiding of the crew's Judaism for security reasons the captain recounts one incident which—in addition to the inherent irony—had its funny side.

When the emissary of the company that bought the ship brought it to Miami, the crew members had already started to keep their Jewish identity secret. They took pains not to say a word out of place. They keep their lips sealed. Yiddish and Hebrew were forbidden. The crew stammered in broken French—did anything necessary to confuse and mislead outsiders. The man from the company, in his naivety, began to wonder about this strange crew that didn't have its own language. They communicated in gestures, mumbled a few words of Spanish. It would have been out of place to ask questions, but he began to suspect that the sole Gentile of the crew, the red-headed Irishman, was no

Spaniard. He waited until the Irishman had gone off to the washroom, turned to the chief engineer and said:

"You know, chief, I have my suspicions that at least one of your crew—that fellow who just stepped out—must be a Jew."

The chief engineer laughed. The crewmen laughed and with renewed heart and determination threw themselves into their mission.

Walking through the quarters, which are due to house two thousand people in just a few days time, the captain stops at a large basin intended to serve the passengers as a wash-basin. It's a very primitive set-up—some tubes with holes drilled in them to supply the water. There are several identical wash-basins at various locations. There are also wooden bathrooms, a series of narrow cubicles—for women on one side and men on the other. The captain explains that these facilities, the basins and the toilets, had to be camouflaged during the voyage right up until they entered Mediterranean waters. This was to fool the British agents snooping around the ports, because the ship was registered as a transport ship for bananas.

We visit the ship's sickbay and clinic which is big enough to deal with first aid for several patients at a time. There are no beds for now, but as soon as we reach the next port they plan to build an entire hospital with beds for fifteen/twenty people in a bunkhouse up on deck.

The medical officer greets us, a large young man with red cheeks. He is responsible for medical supplies on board. He is also qualified to perform first aid. He can pull teeth and administer vaccines. The only thing he is scared of—and refuses to contemplate—is delivering babies.

The medical officer is also called the "purser," the Minister for Food on this tiny floating country. He is in charge of purchasing and distributing provisions. He ensures that there is no shortage of necessary foodstuffs. His role is the same as that of Joseph the Provider in Egypt the land of plenty.

Without waiting for me to ask anything the large, red-cheeked man produces a notebook from a drawer and begins listing statistics, in black and white, about the extent of his provisions.

He has enough stocks of medicines that he could supply the hundred thousand British soldiers defending the shores of Palestine against the Jewish immigrants . . . he also had decent quantities of insulin, penicillin and Sulfa.

His food supplies are bountiful enough to feed at least two shipfuls of Ma'apilim. He has two tons of biscuits, one ton of Dutch cheese, enough dried eggs to last two thousand passengers for two months, and three months worth of bread. Canned potatoes—two tons. Pomegranate juice—three tons. Fruit-cocktail, apples, apricots, bananas, pears and cherries. Then comes two tons of whole-fat milk, butter, jam, cocoa, coffee, tea, fish and all kinds of foodstuffs that supply all the nutrients one needs. On top of which the kitchen has a capacity to bake 250 loaves of bread a day.

And while the purser is still delivering his statistical report the helmsman approaches and asks the captain which course to take. The captain assigns another sailor the task of giving me the tour.

This sailor is a six-foot tall red-head, his figure looms menacingly above me. He is covered in freckles from head to foot; his face with red flecks. His eyes are small and narrow, like a Kalmyk's. His name is Hugh McDonald, an Irishman in blood and bone. At first glance he looks like someone from the underworld. The way he stands there half naked with a dagger on his belt, only heightens the impression that he is someone who belongs on the other side of the tracks.

But in fact the brutish-looking McDonald is a student, a Harvard College boy, who put off his studies for one impulsive reason—a desire to lead refugees to Palestine.

Hugh McDonald, whose name is now shortened to "Mac," raises his bushy eyebrows and begins to tell his story:

He was born in San Francisco twenty-six years ago. A Catholic, finished high school and studied at Stanford University in California. Later he enrolled in Harvard Law school. He worked part-time as a reporter for a provincial newspaper before quitting to study law. His father, an Irishman. His mother, from Scotland; and his only sister, a Catholic nun.

Hugh Mac grew up in San Francisco where the population is not divided into different communities, and good neighborliness is a virtue. It was only in 1936 when Mac first found out there was a group of people on this earth who were tormented and oppressed. Until then he had not quite realized that there were people of a different faith called "the Jews" or that they were at the center of the so-called "Jewish Question." Mac did not pass up an opportunity to serve in the Merchant Marine, where he witnessed several incidents. In his travels he saw many examples of how Jews were discriminated against. Mac, the future lawyer, passionate in matters of justice, was unable to fathom it. Something inside him snapped.

Having had his eyes opened to discrimination he now noticed that some Catholics were discriminated against in America. His best friend in the air force during the war, was a Jew. His best friend in Stanford, who later died in the war, was a Jew. When Mac returned after the war he was disappointed, believing that the bloody war would also result in peace for the Jewish people. The Nuremberg laws were now long in the past, and suddenly—concentration camps in Cyprus? Refugee ships being turned back at the ports? Mac decided to join the fight. He sought out contact with the Jewish fleet.

At new year's, the opportunity came. Mac was in New York with a friend who was a sailor for a Jewish ship. They went to see a Yiddish play: Sholem Aleichem's *Wandering Stars*. The actors' performance enchanted him. Later, in Café Royale, they discussed Jewish problems. The next morning Mac received a telephone call telling him to go to a certain address. A month later he traveled to Miami and became a Jewish sailor. His voyage, which led him from Baltimore to Lisbon, was a stormy odyssey worthy of Columbus or Magellan. But these bitter experiences only spurred Mac onward. He was on his way to Palestine.

Mac knows that his crew is the best one. He does not feel like a Gentile among Jews. Mac recalls too that his sister, the Catholic nun, was entirely in favor of his joining the Jewish voyage.

9

PORTRAITS OF "ILLEGAL" SAILORS

After a long night cutting through the waters, our ship approaches a strategic island. It is eight a.m. The ship floating over the deep-blue blanket of the sea—flat, and untroubled—moves without purpose, merely to kill time. News has reached us that British agents are lurking in all the ports of Italy and we must double back and take diversions. According to the schedule we should already have reached a certain port by now, but to outsmart the enemy we've had to prolong the voyage. We are constantly changing the plan in a game of cat and mouse.

The ship goes around in circles, turning hither and thither as slowly as three miles an hour—the slowest speed possible. The radio operator's finger never stops tapping. He is glued to the machine. He's waiting for an order that's due to arrive from another port with further directives about what to do next. The captain cannot make a move without confirmation from Palestine.

The world is bathed in sunlight. In the middle of the brightness, a bluish rock emerges, shrouded in fog. At first it looks like a mighty cloud, but the closer we get the clearer the contours of the legendary island emerge—the isle of the vivacious, hot-tempered Corsicans, the island that gave birth to the conspirator, the romantic, the power-hungry little despot, who is still revered by certain historians to this day: Napoleon Bonaparte.

Two hours later I ask the captain if he knows where our next stop will be. He does not know; he's still waiting for his orders.

In the meantime, between the wavering and waiting, several of the sailors come up on deck to speak with me. One by one, they approach me, talking for as long as they can spare the time. They tell me about their backgrounds, their lives up to now. Almost all of them want to appear under the spotlight of the press.

I would like to shine a light on some of the crew members here, a small selection representative of the whole crew.

There is Adrian-Abraham Phillips, twenty-eight years old. A hirsute lad with darkly tanned skin. In his greasy overalls, with a red bandana on his head, he looks like a Marseillaises opium-smuggler. He was born in New York. Does not know Yiddish. By profession he is a mechanical engineer. He worked for the Philco radio and television company. His grandmother was very religious, and his grandfather was a reverend. His role on the ship is as Second Engineer.

I would like to introduce Harold Katz, twenty-five years old. Born in Romania. Moved to America as a three month old infant. His father is a rabbi at a synagogue in Newport, an active Zionist who has greatly influenced his only child. Harold grew up in Indiana before moving to Newport. As a schoolboy he was an active member of the Avukah[9] in Boston. During the war he served as an officer on a battleship. After the war, came a period of introspection. The destruction of European Jewry, and the struggle for Jewish autonomy in Palestine weighed on his conscience, preventing him from concentrating on his studies or future career. The survival of his people is at stake, and Harold cannot sit idly by and watch from afar. He wants to move to Palestine and later become a lawyer there to help serve his nation.

Sitting in one corner of the deck, during his free time, one can always find Norman Lewis. A tall, solidly-built man with severe features and thoughtful eyes, he is always surrounded by books and notebooks. He is thirty years old. He was born in Brooklyn and educated at Yeshivas Etz Chaim in Boro Park. He is a member of Poale Zion, the Left Zionist movement. His father is a Zionist and his mother is active in Hadassah, the Woman's Zionist organization. When he arrives in the Land of Israel the first thing he will do is kiss the earth. Then he will go find his brother who lives in a kibbutz. He'll decide what to do next once he gets there: whether he will stay, or continue to serve as a sailor on the Jewish ships. He's already spent four months on board various ships. He has a mystical temperament; he tries to compose poetic verses. He is searching for

9 A Zionist student federation.

the deeper meaning of Jewish life. Norman Lewis is the product of a full Jewish Yeshiva education.

His role on the ship?—Fireman.

Shuffling forward with heavy steps comes Joseph Gilden. A native of Baltimore, his parents came from Russia. He is a high-school student. Tall, a little overweight, as hairy as an ancient forest dweller. His movements are sluggish, heavy. He served four years in the army. He began agricultural training in preparation for settling in Palestine before which he had not experienced Jewish communal life. He joined the crew with the pragmatic goal of reaching Palestine and joining a kibbutz.

In a leather jacket, with two flashlights in his pockets and a heavy pair of pliers in his hands comes Herman J. Braverman from the Bronx. With a cantankerous gaze and pitch-black hair he is whistling the currently popular "Anniversary Song" by Al Jolson.

He is the ship's chief engineer. For nine years he served as a professional machine-engineer in the navy. He has a full college education and in the navy he attained the rank of Commander of the Maritime Service. He served in the US navy right up until he joined the Haganah.

What brought him to such a decision?

Coincidence pure and simple. On one of his sailings he encountered a passenger, a member of the Haganah, who convinced Braverman to do something to help the refugees, saying the ships needed professionals. This is Braverman's second voyage. On his first trip he brought a ship as far as France.

The chief engineer intends to remain in service for as long as he is needed.

The nimble, animated twenty-one year old Mordkhe Greenfeld[10] also hails from the Bronx. He has studied two years in college, served three years in the merchant marines, and traveled America from one coast to the other. Gifted with all the virtues one could hope for, he works with the engines. In his free moments he mends the plumbing in the washrooms. If there is a hand needed in the kitchen he does not hesitate to step in. He's adept at preparing a kosher chicken, can fill a kishka, and make a fine homemade borscht.

Mordkhe Greenfeld likes to have options. He is ready to work on the Haganah ships for ten years if needs be.

Not all the sailors have joined the mission on account of their bond with the Jewish people, or awakened sentiments. Take the implacable Bernard Lerner for example, a young man constantly quarreling with everyone around him. He has low blood-pressure but the temper of six men. He is twenty-seven years old, born in Atlanta, Georgia. He worked as a sales-clerk in a department store. His parents were, in fact, Zionists but ten years ago he joined the Lincoln Battalion, which fought on the side of the Republicans during the

10 A.K.A. Murray S. Greenfield.

Spanish Civil War. All of his friends died in combat. His hatred of Fascism only grew. He always has a sharp reproach ready on the tip of his tongue for Britain which he says nurtures the Fascist snakes around the world.

His hatred of Fascism and his desire to be a thorn in the side of the British—who are, in his words, the midwives of the Fascist bastards—brought him to join the crew. During the war, he admits, he also encountered antisemitic incidents. But he is adamant to point out that these were not what fueled his metamorphosis from a department store clerk into a war-like seafarer. He will always stand on the side of the oppressed whoever they are—they could even be Arabs as far as he is concerned . . .

Bernard Lerner is the Second Mate on the ship.

And how did such an unadulterated *goy* as the Pole August Labaczewski manage to find his way onto the crew?

August is twenty-nine years old, born in New Jersey. He looks for all the world like a pirate. He wears a rope around his waist and carries a knife in his belt. Everything from the scratches on his sunburned face, to his closely cropped hair like a Russian *muzhik* contributed to the roughness of his appearance. One's first impression of him is that he looks like someone who could easily be a raging antisemite, one who listens with rapt attention to the thuggish street-preachers standing on their soap-boxes on Columbus Circle, waving their American flags and inciting passersby. But August Labaczewski is an upstanding man, honest to a fault. His simple instinct for justice is what brought him to join the other sailors.

And now I will allow August Labaczewski to speak in his own words:

"I'm from New Jersey. My mother is Italian. I've only had three years of school. I've been hopping from ship to ship for nine years now. I grew up in a Jewish neighborhood and all of my friends were Jews. All over the world I've heard tales of Jewish troubles. I can't for the life of me understand why people want to torment them so. My motto is: 'united we stand, divided we fall'. I have no intention of going back to America. From the moment I set foot on this ship I decided that Palestine would be my new home. There's a lot of work I can do. I'm a farmer, a carpenter, a smith, a welder . . . I want to work for the new Jewish homeland . . ."

These are the words of August Labaczewski, a Gentile, a Pole, brother of the Poles of Przytyk and Kielce . . . [11]

To August's credit we must add that he is an indispensable handyman on the ship; he fixes things, he cooks, he bakes bread and looks after the crew like a mother hen. The sailors call him by his nickname "Duke"—yet, despite his "aristocratic" moniker, he is

....

11 A reference to two pogroms that broke out in Poland, one just before the war, the other just after.

still upset if someone complains that the meat is too tough.

This is but a small taste of the rogues gallery of curious characters aboard the Tradewinds, but I will mention one more crewmember: a priest from Boston who has chosen to tag along as a Christian observer. He earns a chapter in his own right.

At midday the captain calls for me. He points a forefinger at the map spread out before him and confides:

"Be ready. If I drop anchor at this island you'll have a chance to come down with me ashore. We will meet with our people there, and you'll be able to pass on your letters and telegrams."

The news is a relief. Everyone at sea is drawn back to the land. I ask:

"When do you think you'll drop anchor?"

"As soon as I receive the order by radio. The radio operator picked up a signal indicating that the orders will come at 9 p.m. So, we're just waiting until then."

My impatience for those few hours to pass is great. Even the crew is anxious. Every few minutes another sailor comes by to see how things stand. Finally at 9 the order comes. The radio operator picks out the code words and makes a note. The order, emanating from an unknown port somewhere in the world, said: "Proceed immediately to H . . ."

Meanwhile a part of the crew gathers in the dining room for coffee. Meal service is long since over. People are nibbling on fruit and sandwiches. They sip glasses of schnapps or whiskey. The mechanical engineer opens up the Victrola and puts on one record after another. The sound of new Hebrew folk-songs fills the room, along with the tapping of a pair of feet, soon joined by another pair, and another until a whole group of them is dancing the Hora.

The dance begins slowly, then grows ever faster and more intense until the floor is shaking. And who do you think is dancing the Hora? The boy from Brownsville? The Rabbi's son from Detroit? The sailor whose father is a Mohel? Not a chance!—it's three Gentiles dancing the Hora: Mac the Irishman, August the Pole, and the Priest from Boston. Three Gentiles in a circle. Hands thrown over shoulders, legs entangled in legs, Hebrew melodies on their lips. They dance the dance of joy, the dance of Jewish salvation.

Meanwhile the ship is passing an archipelago of islands.

10

HAGANAH AGENTS ON BOARD

The first visitors to board the ship, after we drop anchor in a port somewhere in Italy, are a group of five people—one woman and four men—agents of the Haganah. They row up alongside us on a small dinghy and deftly climb aboard. They initially behave with the formality of harbor officials making a routine inspection on a newly arrived vessel.

But that is only the initial impression. One moment of mutual withering scrutiny between us and the Haganah agents is all it takes to break down the barrier. Their stiffness vanishes and the conversation becomes more free, though we speak sparingly and only concerning the matter at hand.

The woman speaks correct English with a strong accent. Two of the men only understand Italian; the other two speak Hebrew and Yiddish.

By her movements and bearing it is clear that the woman is in charge and she will be the one to give the captain his orders.

She is of average height, dressed in the Italian style of black clothes and black stockings. Her black, slightly graying hair is combed back. The expression on her olive face is a mixture of severity and gentleness. Her brown eyes seem troubled.

She wastes no time in carrying out a thorough inspection of the ship, to make sure that everything is in order, that there are enough beds for two thousand passengers. They check the plumbing, the toilets, the lights. They take stock of the food reserves. Then we all go to the captain's cabin and sit around the table with the captain and first officer at the head, the Haganah people on either side, and with me—a privileged witness to Jewish intrigue—taking up the space on the other end of the table.

With pencils and paper, like bookkeepers, they calculate the reserves of oil and heating material for the remainder of the voyage. They reckon that when the ship is in motion it needs 6,000 gallons of heating oil a day, and when it is docked in a port it only needs 1,500 gallons. The conclusion is once the ship sets off with two thousand passengers it will require 42,000 gallons of heating oil, giving us seven days to reach the Palestinian shore. If we have enough heating material to make it, then good. If not, a tanker will come and deliver more. If we have too much they will take away the surplus. We are not permitted to have any excess reserves. It's bad enough if the British confiscate the ship without losing excess supplies into the bargain. The fuel can be used for other ships which are already on the way.

The captain is not happy about such calculations. He is optimistic and assures them that the British will never lay hands on any part of the ship. They will not even get close. His course is set for Haifa, no less, and as captain he will lead his ship to the appointed shore.

"You realize, captain, that the British have a blockade around the entire Palestinian coastline?" one of the Haganah men asks.

"So I've heard," the captain answers curtly.

"Are you prepared to put up a fight against six destroyers?" the woman interjected.

"I don't care how many destroyers there are, my ship will slip past the blockade."

"You're quite the optimist, captain!"

"That's the goal." the captain says, speaking rashly and impulsively. "My men didn't give up their civilian lives, leaving behind college places and good jobs . . . we didn't go to all that trouble to fix up the ship, putting in so much effort; or weather the storm during the Atlantic crossing—we didn't go through all that just to let the British take our ship."

"That's the truth of the matter, unfortunately," adds the other Haganah man. "We bring in the Ma'apilim, and the British take our ships."

"That has to change!" the captain exclaims. "I've heard that by the shore in Haifa there's a whole fleet of confiscated ships. If it were up to me I'd launch an assault to take back the lot."

The young captain's steady tone, his determination, and his spirit impress the Haganah agents. But between the captains spirit and the British destroyers are 2,000 lives that hang in the balance. We cannot put Jewish lives, those who have survived the gas chambers, at risk. Our goal is to bring living Jews to Palestine. Nevertheless the captain's speech is received with muted applause; we drink a toast.

Once all the details of the onward journey have been discussed, once the Haganah have explained why it was necessary to avoid a certain strategic island and come instead to this quiet Italian port—the British spies are on our tail—the woman, who reminds me somehow of Vera Finger,[12] orders the whole crew to be brought in, and makes the following declaration:

"You all know that our work is a conspiratorial one. And as conspirators we must be discreet. Enemy agents are lurking, even in this quiet port. We are under strict orders not to let anyone go ashore. The village here is small, but it is bustling with locals. We cannot be sure who is an innocent passerby and who is a spy. Our work requires 100% discretion. It is strictly forbidden to allow outsiders onto the ship! It is forbidden to trade with them, or show them hospitality. Remember the position we find ourselves in. Bear these rules in mind!"

Everyone solemnly swears to follow orders. The Haganah commander greets this show of loyalty with a smile which contains everything:

Faith, determination and sadness.

Her military tone elicits respect from the sailors. As we part ways I hand the commander several letters

12 Vera Finger was a renowned revolutionary in Tsarist Russia.

that need to be mailed. she takes the letters, scrutinizes them and places them in her bag, saying:

"We will need to begin censoring your letters and descriptions."

"Censoring?" I ask in surprise.

"Yes. We have experience with newspaper men. There are Jewish writers for English newspapers who have trouble with restraint and responsibility. They were with us, observed our work, and when they went back to America they wrote such fantastical things about us we could hardly believe our eyes. None of it was accurate. We were red in the face when we saw those descriptions."

"No doubt they were sensationalized stories," I say.

"But written by Jews!" she protests.

"Jews sure, but not *our* Jews," I say. "Those are Jews who write in a foreign language, superficial Jews who only see what's on the surface."

"You Americans are too fond of chasing after sensation!" she continues with annoyance.

I try to explain to her the difference between the interest in the Ma'apilim ships shown by a representative of a Yiddish newspaper, and the curiosity shown by a non-Jewish newspaper. For us it is a profoundly important issue: a matter of life and death, the only way to save the Jewish refugees of Europe. While for them it is all just material for exciting stories. And wherever there is a desire for excitement and sensation, exaggeration necessarily follows. I attempt to explain more clearly:

"In America we call them '*human interest stories.*' But I feel a duty to give an accurate description of the Ma'apilim, their path, their pain, their suffering and joy, their successes and failures."

She scrutinizes me again, and says in a strict, determined tone:

"Your letters will be redacted."

"Will they?" I ask.

"Yes. You must avoid using too much detail in your descriptions. You must not give the names of places you pass. Keep in mind that this could make our work more difficult. Incidentally, if you are so confident in your ability to remain careful and discreet, why would it bother you if we read your letters? You don't trust us?"

"I trust you."

In order to gain the confidence of the Haganah commander I hand her my "letter of introduction," the paper I brought with me from New York for emergencies. It is essentially a kind of certificate given to me by a Haganah representative in America for me to use if I come in contact with high-ranking Haganah officials in Europe.

She reads over the document carefully. It seems the letter has an effect, as her over-cautious tone immediately softens. She hands the letter back and says:

"This means something. We will supply you with information to the full extent permissible. Stay close to the captain. We'll call for you."

This newfound confidence is exhilarating. This will open doors to the secret rooms where operations are planned. Later, when the Haganah commander leaves the ship, I read, for the first time, the letter that she handed back to be, in its now unsealed envelope.

In the letter, written in Hebrew, I read:

To our friends, *Shalom*!

The bearer of this letter, Sh. Isban, representative of the *Morgn Zhurnal* newspaper in New York, comes to you to accompany the persecuted and oppressed Jews of Europe, to participate in their struggle and share in their destiny . . .

It is particularly important that there be a person from the Yiddish press in America to act as witness to the Aliyah of the Ma'apilim and give expression to these events. Because up to now this has not happened. I therefore request that you do everything permitted to grant him passage on one of our larger ships. Naturally this will not entail financial costs on your part: he represents the *Morgn Zhurnal* and the newspaper will naturally cover any expenses involved . . .

```
    I  am  confident  that  you  will  do
everything  in  your  power  to  facili-
tate his needs. For us it is a matter
of  great  importance,  particularly  in
the  struggle  to  win  over  the  hearts
and  minds  of  the  average  Jew  on  the
street. This  will  help  mobilize  aid
and support for our operations . . .

    (signed:)
```

I imagine that from now on this letter will be the key to opening locked doors for me, allowing me access to the labyrinthine hiding places of the Jewish underground.

That same afternoon, standing on deck, taking in my surroundings, I look at the green hills, home to a single village, and I notice a group of rowboats, filled with curious Italians heading toward us. It isn't long before the boats have reached the bow of our ship. There is a commotion. Several Italians—young girls and boys, even small children—fall upon our ship with outstretched hands begging for food, chocolate and cigarettes. The Italians somehow know that the crew is American. They also know something else they aren't supposed to know—that the ship is bound for Palestine. We hear pitiful voices: "Mister! Mister" and their boats are soon rained upon by a shower of cigarettes, chewing gum and chocolate. The Italians are grateful. Their cries grow louder. They row back to shore to spread the news that American guests are handing out gifts.

The ship is anchored in an enchanted bay, surrounded by mighty hills. Mountains decked in cotton-like vegetation. The thick sheets of green are as soft on the eye as plush, as velvet carpets. Here and there the red roofs of the local houses poke out like poppies. Our ship is anchored in the middle of the bay, a mile from the land. Near the shore, a little uphill, we see the ruins of two tall buildings, which the Germans had used as barracks. There are also foxholes and pillboxes here.

Around this bay, and other bays like it, American bombers hammered day and night until the enemy had been smoked out. The water is so tranquil here, the harbor so quiet as though passenger ships never landed on these shores. In the late evening hours the silence only grows more pervasive. The crescent moon in the sky and the silver nets in the water make the crew uneasy; they are looking for distractions. Everyone gathers in the dining room. A hot-headed lad is constantly changing the records on the Victrola. He's playing songs sung during the Spanish Civil War. Some of the crew served in the Lincoln Battalion. The captain himself likes to remind us that the singers of all those records were killed in the battles around Barcelona and Madrid. Many of the dead had been his friends. You stand there for a moment, and you have to wonder: where do these Spanish songs fit it, on a ship that will carry refugees manned by a crew preparing to defy the British Empire?

But you forgive the eager young warriors. Freedom is their motto. The urge for freedom is what brought them together on this ship. Freedom drove them to this daring enterprise. And it is entirely in keeping with the spirit of their mission for them to play freedom songs, even if the melodies are those of other nations. Suddenly, in the middle of a song, August Labaczewski, the Polish chef emerges from the kitchen. On his head he wears a round fur hat; around his neck, the red scarf of a hooligan, and from his belt hangs a pirate's knife. Both of his arms are tattooed up to the elbows with snakes, daggers and leaf patterns. He claps his hands to the rhythm, throws back his head, kicks his feet—not feet, but springs!—and dances a Polka, a *Kamariska*. He is a crafty fellow in every way; he is a singer, a dancer, an actor. The others are enjoying the spectacle, clapping and whistling. The noise grows so loud the captain comes down and warns us that the crew of a Ma'apilim ship must behave like smugglers: quiet and hidden.

The warning is effective. The singing becomes more subdued; the dancing, more reserved. The crowd disperses; some go to work in the engine room, others go to bed. The engines hum steadily, and the dim lights of the ship wink over toward the village on the shore.

11

A SECRET HAGANAH MEETING

One foggy afternoon, a few hours before our ship will set off in an undetermined direction to pick up thousands of refugees from various shores, a small dinghy rows over to the ship. Two tall, tanned boys from the Haganah climb up the rope ladder to the top deck and seek out the captain.

Two minutes later the captain knocks on the round window of my cabin door.

"We're going down to the shore for a conference with the *shu shu* Boys . . . you ready?"

"Shu Shu boys" is a popular term on our ship. It is a secret name for members of the underground. It's a term current only in our crew. For Palestine too there is a code word: "Oklahoma." Nobody says "I'm going to Palestine,"; they say "I'm going to Oklahoma." Instead of calling the passengers refugees, migrants, DPs etc, they call them "bananas." The reasoning? In normal times our ship was a cargo ship carrying bananas bound for Oklahoma. Naturally every ship is a world unto itself with its own special regulations and code words.

The captain's invitation to join the secret meeting tears me away from my writing desk. I throw on a coat and a French beret. The captain is waiting for me on deck accompanied by the chief engineer. We set off together with the Haganah boys on a narrow dinghy and row toward the shore.

On shore a tangle of pathways leads off in every direction. The hilly landscape is covered in green, prickly shrubs; and, where there are no shrubs, copses of trees gather, as dense as small forests. Here and there we see the red roof of a cottage emerging from the landscape.

If it weren't for our escorts from the Haganah we would soon get lost. The wild landscape around us is like a jungle. The pathways, which spread like arteries over the green hills, beckon seductively, calling us toward disparate hidden spots—each one seeming to imply the existence of secret encampments.

We walk in silence. The Haganah boys, high-spirited lads by nature, hold their tongues in our presence. Silence is key, and when they do speak they carefully ration the words and fragmentary sentences. Conspirators don't gush with talk. Good discipline in the underground army begins and ends with holding one's tongue.

Our chief engineer cannot handle long periods of silence. The wrinkles of a smile form around his lips and he asks the captain:

"How d'you like these green hills?"

"I like them."

"What do they remind you of, captain?"

"It looks like Central Park in New York . . ."

After another fifteen minutes walking through the ordained back-ways, we turn and realize that, without us having noticed the climb, we are on the summit of a mountain several hundred feet above sea-level. Below us lies the calm sea, topped by a light fog, waveless and flat as a sheet of glass.

A paved road leads us into an inhabited village. Following the Haganah boys we avoid the main road and take side streets. Evening is already beginning to set in. A sharp wind batters the branches of the ancient trees. Despite the wind some boys are waiting for us in an empty square up ahead, and when we pass they try to sell us revolvers, watches and cameras. As payment they don't want money, but American cigarettes. The magic word "*Americano*" has held the villages along the path in its grip like a psychosis ever since our ship entered the nearby waters. For several days already boats have streamed toward the ship. The elderly *Paisans* want alms. Girls ask for chocolate and chewing gum, while poor mothers with infants display pots of cooked food.

The Haganah boys don't allow us to try any of the wares on display. We head down a small alley where we stop in front of a two story building with old fashioned balconies and windows behind grates. Above the iron door of the house hangs an iron hand.

The task of knocking on the door with the iron hand belongs to the Haganah boys. The iron door opens and we enter. It is pitch black in the stairway, but our feet seem to find their own way up the wooden staircase until we find ourselves in a dimly lit room which appears to be a long oval chamber.

In this room I meet a familiar face. It's the female Haganah commander, the one who reminded me of the revolutionary Vera Finger. Here she is known as Signorina Maria.[13] She is dressed in black, as before. Her eyes contain the same smile of faith and sadness. She invites the arrivals to sit at a round table which is covered in an enormous map of the Mediterranean and surrounding lands. There are three men already sitting around the table, two of whom I've seen before on the ship. The third man is unfamiliar to me.

In Jewish underground circles there are no introductions as the usual custom would dictate. Instead one looks at one another, exchanging confidential glances and one begins to talk straight to the point.

Signorina Maria moves a couple of rickety chairs over to the table for us to sit on. She switches on the electric lamp that hangs over the table, which casts a faint shine over the map, and she says:

"The purpose of this meeting is to decide the future route for your ship. Our plans are changed even before we get a chance to decide them ... This is not our fault. The enemy has increased the number of its patrol ships across a wide stretch of sea. We received information that indicates your ship will be intercepted at the port

13 Real name Ada Sereni (1905–1997) one of the principal organizers of Aliyah Bet operations and its chief commander since 1947.

we had planned to send you to. Spies are also active in Balkan waters which will lead to a delay in collecting the passengers in the various ports."

"Does this mean we're going to change course?" the captain asks.

"No. You will delay departure by two days. We have a new plan. It will be a surprise for the British. It's going to be a bold move, but without bold moves we wouldn't be where we are today."

"The plan is ready?" the captain asks.

"Everything is in place," Signorina Maria replies. "Our drills have shown that isolated ships are a good bait for the British destroyers. We will now send out several ships at once. Two days later your ship will then leave port in the opposite direction. This will fool the British . . . on the way to the first port you will rendez-vous with another ship, two days later you'll meet a third ship. This one will be coming from Greek waters. Aboard that ship will be thousands of Ma'apilim. You'll need to load up on passengers along the way. The location of the port will be communicated to you by radio."

Signorina Maria began moving a pencil over the surface of the map. Like a magic wand, that pencil traced the route, jumping from port to port, cutting through seas and paving a way for the sea caravans leading tens of thousands of refugees, the People of Israel, toward their freedom.

The captain follows the moves on the map. He listens to her explanations like a diligent schoolboy, making here a comment, there a suggestion, and once the strategic course has been laid out in all its details he stands up from his chair, glancing uneasily around the table and speaks:

"I'd like to stick to my original plan: give me gas masks—enough for the crew at least—so that my men can defend themselves against the British tear gas and continue to pilot the ship after the fight has begun . . . get me some smoke canisters so that we can release a curtain of smoke near the Palestinian shore, and you'll see, I'll bring the passengers ashore and turn right back to Europe to pick up a second load."

Signorina Maria admires the captain's enthusiasm, but she cannot follow his demands. There are no gas masks or smoke canisters to be found in the ports of Europe. Such supplies could only be sourced in the United States, only after which they could begin to estimate whether it would be a fair fight. Could the captain of a Ma'apilim ship afford to start a fight with a British warship?

Signorina Maria does not fail to remind the captain that our Ma'apilim are the most hunted and oppressed group of people under the sun . . . their lives must not be put at risk under any circumstances. They must be brought to Palestine alive.

She does not forget to add:

"Our greatest weapon is vigilance and caution. The British spy network is an exemplary one. And they have a bad influence over other countries. They ordered France not to allow our ships to leave their ports. They asked the Italians not to let us through. They send notices to Yugoslavia, threats to Albania . . ."

The captain slams his hand down onto the map:

"Who do the British think they are? The rulers of the world? Do they think all the nations of the world will be their servants?"

The captain's rage subsides when one of the Haganah members shares the latest news that two ships have succeeded in breaking the blockade and the Ma'apilim have landed. Two other ships were captured and the passengers deported to Cyprus.

"That's what I'm talking about!" the captain ranted. "We need to send whole flotillas of ships. That way two out of three will get through the blockade."

It takes a long time to convince the captain that, in the sacred underground work of the Haganah, impulsive outbursts are one thing, and sober strategizing is another thing entirely. The Jewish underground army always chooses the latter. The head must keep the heart in check. And the results are positive.

It's already pitch dark by the time we set off back to the shore. We trudge back through the same pathways as before, passing thick copses and cotton-like shrubs. By the shore, after we have parted ways with the Haganah boys and climbed into the boat that we would row back to the ship, the captain says:

"An interesting woman, that Signorina Maria. Do you know anything about her past?"

As it happens I do know something, though it is forbidden for me to say anything to the captain. There's not a lot I can say in public about this woman, an exemplar of Jewish refinement and heroism. To ensure the security of the work to which she dedicates her life, she cannot be identified. Her identity must remain a mystery.

It is however satisfying to note that a Jewish woman, a daughter of the Yishuv, is not just the leader of the Haganah in a particular territory in Europe, she is not just the chief commander who gives orders to the ships ferrying refugees to Palestine, but she is also the widow of a great Jewish figure, one who fought like a hero and died as a hero.[14] It was he who, during the critical years of the war when the Jews were facing their worst crisis, smuggled out large numbers of them right out from under the noses of the Nazis. He brought them out by airplane, by submarine, by cargo-ship—he brought them over every sea until they reached the promised land. On one of his air missions he landed as a parachutist in a country occupied by the Germans. The Nazis captured and executed him.

His name, his heroic deeds represent in and of themselves a chapter of the history of the new Jewish Yishuv. But his work, cut short by the enemy, has not been undone. His work is being continued by his wife, Signorina Maria, who is now the commander of the

14 Enzo Sereni (1905–1944) an Italian Zionist, co-founder of kibbutz Givat Brenner, celebrated intellectual, advocate of Jewish-Arab co-existence and a Jewish Brigade officer who was parachuted into Nazi-occupied Italy in World War II, captured by the Germans and executed in Dachau concentration camp.

Ma'apilim ships drawing nearer—week in, week out—to the shores of Palestine.

As we row back toward the ship we notice a number of boats filled with Italian women and children laying siege to the Tradewinds, blocking every opening, waiting with pots in their hands. The ship's cook, the good-hearted August "the Duke" has brought out on deck two full buckets of soup, along with bones, vegetables and fruit and has begun filling the pots of the gathered Italians. Cries of gratitude ring out. A sailor approaches, a hot-head who's always going around day and night ranting about discrimination against Negroes, about Fascists in Spain. He grabs one of the buckets of soup and hurls it into the sea, screaming:

"They want to eat American food, do they? Where were they when Mussolini was in charge? Why didn't they fight against him then? Eh? They want something to eat? Fuck all is what they'll get!"

"How d'ya know they didn't fight?" another sailor calls out. "Lot of Italians were partisans who fought the Nazis!"

"Nonsense! the hot-head responds. "They helped the Nazis! They also helped the Spanish Fascists with their planes."

"You're certain that these people here begging for food are the ones who helped the Fascists?"

"I'm certain of nothing; and since there's no way to find out I'd rather throw the food into the sea than to feed the suspects."

The hot-headed sailor, who plays the Spanish Civil War songs every evening and carries the grievances of the world on his shoulders, looks around, sees the circle that has gathered around him on deck and cries out:

"I'm fighting against Fascism! I'm no Zionist! Palestine and Spain are the same to me. In both places we fight the same enemy—Fascism and imperialism!"

12

THE LONELY CASTLE

The harbor is located in a land where the women are mountain climbers and the men are fierce hunters. In this country the people are hospitable to visitors and tourists. To enemies, however, to invaders who seek to take their land and conquer their nation, they are merciless.

I go to visit an abandoned castle which was used last year as a hiding place for scores of refugees as they made their way from the camps to the Ma'apilim ships. The refugees smuggled themselves across borders, sleeping in makeshift nests along the way and here, in this old castle belonging to a king-hearted christian landowner, they found a way station in which to gather before continuing on to the ports where ships were waiting for them.

It is a seven mile journey from the sea to the castle and I had no choice but to travel there by automobile. My escort from the Haganah has arranged the trip in such a way that the locals will not notice our arrival.

Our usual caution is well justified. No one must learn about the location of our anchored ship. The port authorities of the coastlines our ship passes must not see us, and must not find out in which direction we sail. A tightly-guarded secret.

It's evening when I arrive at the castle. The building, constructed like a fortress, sits atop a rocky hill. The sun's last rays slip across the cornicework of the roof towers, and the castle in its solitude looks for all the world like a deserted monastery.

The path leading up to the castle is winding and paved with sharp gravel. My escort, a seasoned hiker, hands me a long, gnarled walking staff and shows me how to take the first steps. He stretches out his own arms like wings and begins taking large strides uphill. I climb after him.

Up above, at the hill's summit, the castle loses something of its charm. The play of light that seemed to envelope the building when seen from below has vanished. The brick-red color walls, and the white plaster pillars have been weathered by dust and age.

But the surprise comes when, standing before the iron gates by the entrance, we see a man with long gray hair, and a long sculpted beard resembling an image of the Canaanite god Dagon. The man is wearing a black suit with a white flower in the buttonhole. His tie is pedantically arranged. His cheeks are fresh and red as though they've just been pinched.

It is the owner of the castle. My escort whispers to me that the man stands there like that everyday, waiting for visitors to come and see his castle. He is only too glad to recount the tale that gives his building renown.

The man bows to us slightly, with a smile, greeting us with a booming voice:

"*Willkommen! Willkommen!*"

My escort takes me by the arm, leads me through the doorway with an air of familiarity, and whispers in my ear:

"You'll enjoy your visit. Don't speak to the *goy*. Of the seven languages he jabbers you won't understand a word. What interests us is the Jewish side of the castle, and that requires attentiveness."

I'm already inside when my escort closes the door behind him. I ignore the castle's owner, who is still standing outside, and obediently follow my guide. He turns on a bright flash-light which lights up the walls like a spot-light. my escort says:

"Notice the graffiti on the walls: every inscription tells a chapter in the history of Jewish misfortune."

My guide is correct. I look around and see that we're in a tunnel. The tunnel served, not as a passage-way for migrants, but as a place to rest for refugees who had escaped from the camps in Germany. Here they would wait until the storm passed, waiting for the signal that it was safe to head to the coast where the first Ma'apilim ships were waiting.

And so they set off for the coast, but not before in-scribing their names on the walls, and their messages. Each message was a reaction to a post-war event, a protest against the apathy of five continents to the crime that was committed against the Jewish people.

The Christian proprietor of the castle where the tunnel is located is obsessed with preserving the graffiti and inscriptions on his walls. He considers it historically valuable. He is convinced that in time the castle will be transformed into a museum, a sacred place which will attract pilgrims, and so he stands every day by the iron gate like a watchman, greeting anyone who turns up.

As I walk I stay close to the walls which glisten a brick-red color. My eye is drawn to a short note written in red paint.

"Here marched the last battalions of the Warsaw Ghetto."

The beam of light from my guide's torch moves on to the next inscription, also in red paint.

"The fight for the ghetto has not ended; it continues on the barricades in Cyprus."

A third message, carved on a pillar with a nail, reads:

"All our important battles were fought on walls: the walls of Jericho, the walls of Yodfat, the walls of Betar, and the walls of the Warsaw Ghetto."

It seems the memory of the Ghetto uprising left a deep mark on the hearts of the Ma'apilim who stayed in this tunnel. Their many notes speak with intense piety and reverence about the Warsaw battles which served as a signal and catalyst to revolt for tens of thousands of Jews in the camps, who decided to endure whatever it took to break out and reach the shores of freedom.

Here, a typical military slogan:

"The fight for the Ghetto endures. The walls have not fallen. They have expanded as far as Cyprus . . ."

I'm now standing deep inside the tunnel. Every inch of the walls here is covered in writing, carved slogans, Biblical citations, and verses of national poets. A procession of nameless legions, seeking to express the state of their spirit as they marched through the dark tunnel toward freedom.

Suddenly I come up against a pillar which is covered not in slogans and verses, but in the outpouring of a young soul encapsulating the tragic wandering of his generation. It was written in Hebrew with ink on a scroll that looks like parchment. The young man's hand had taken its time to write in an ornate, pedantic style. It is a piece of graphic art. This credo is a Jewish cry for help, where belief conquers despair, and faith defeats resignation.

This is what that anonymous Jew had to say to the world:

"We have gathered here in this tunnel from every corner of Europe. We are what remains in the wake of the storm. We are the remnants of an old and tragic nation. In the depths of our souls the memory of the conflagration lives on, the memory of pain and suffering. The roar of exploding bombs still rings in our ears and the murmur of leveled cities.

"Our childhoods have been washed away by a deluge of fire and brimstone. We are chased and hunted by the agonized screams of those who were burned and gassed, preventing us from ever knowing peace again ...

"No one can understand it who has not lived through it. Who can grasp what it means to take a lamented, hunted beast and turn it back into a man? We will no doubt never again be normal children of men.

"We have beaten a path here through sleepy Czechoslovakia, through the steppes of Hungary, through the frozen Alps and sunny Italy. We walked across borders and through fences. We defended ourselves in the darkness of night. We have used every means conceivable to reach the sea whence we will be taken to the Promised Land.

"We know there are long days of disappointment ahead of us, days of wandering in strange, noisy harbors until the longed for day arrives.

"We will probably travel on a small ship, on one of those ships that sail with a false name under a foreign flag. For days on end we will be pressed together in the lower decks, suffocating on the stench of mice and seawater. We will have to hope that the British birds of prey will not see us from above. Eventually the day will come when the coast of the Holy Land rises out of the fog. Our eyes, which will be bloodshot from so many sleepless nights, will fix on those white shores, and our hearts will pound as with hammers ..."

The vision of the young migrant does not end when he sets foot in the Promised Land. His imagination keeps going. He sees things that will happen to him and his companions even after they have fought through seven circles of Hell to get to Palestine.

"And we will arrive, young in years, but old in experience. We will become a burden for friends and educators. They, the people of a quiet life, will shake their heads complaining about how difficult and complicated we are . . .

"We know that the education system of our youths will no longer be fit for purpose. A new approach to a new reality will be needed. The work of our educators will be an arduous one. They will need to find a way into our hearts and psyches which are so different from those of normal people, for in our travels over the world we have believed no one, have trusted no one . . .

"The most simple and self-evident things have been distorted in our understanding as though reflected in a crooked mirror. The clearest things we have approached with suspicion. Each person awakens mistrust and animosity in us. We were like beasts of prey, locked together in one cage. We were overcome by wild, primitive instincts. We have suffered from hallucinations and nightmarish flashbacks . . ."

And the hand that wrote such melancholy words on this sheet of parchment, dripping with mistrust of the degenerate world, ends with the following paragraph:

"But there in the Promised Land we will begin to rebuild the web of our lives. The degenerative manifestation of our souls will vanish. The skin of exile will be shorn off, our will—hard as steel—will overcome all obstacles and create something out of nothing.

"We will pave the road for those who will come after us. The yoke of responsibility will ever weigh down on our shoulders."

The contents of the document, this manifesto of a young Jew who belongs to the Majdanek-generation, buzzes in my ears for a long time, even after I have exited the tunnel and come back outside. The magnanimous Gentile, the owner of the castle who had offered hospitality to so many wandering Jews on their journey to freedom, once again accompanies us politely as we descend the crooked, trailing path.

As we return aboard the ship, several sailors approach to inform me that, while we were ashore, something has happened that broke the crew's routine monotony and may serve me as material to report.

I do not attempt to resist as they descend upon me as one man and recount in unison that a crew member has been sentenced by the captain to two days in the brig. They add, also in unison, that the man thoroughly deserved his punishment.

The perpetrator is the ship's fireman. He is the one they mockingly refer to as "The Mystic." He reads Schopenhauer, writes verse and only listens to Rachmaninov. Some crew members cannot tolerate his oddness. It's been four months since leaving Baltimore that the humor-starved crew have been waiting for a chance to trip him up. The opportunity arose. The deck officer asked him to perform a task that was outside of his normal duties, but that he should nevertheless perform because there is a shortage of hands, and because all the others have taken on roles outside of their official eight hour shifts.

The fireman refused. To back up his argument he quoted Schopenhauer. The deck officer, a strict realist, was in no mood for philosophical exegesis and so he complained to the captain.

The captain's judgment was quick: two days in the brig with only bread and water. They led the fireman to a cell barely big enough to sit or lie down in. The prisoner served his sentence with stoic calm; all he asked was for a copy of Nietzsche's book *Ecce Homo*.

In the report the captain wrote that the prisoner was punished for deserting his duties.

The crew decide that a first arrest, on this ship's maiden voyage as a refugee ship, is cause for celebration. They go down to the dining room where they drink and dance merrily.

After dancing and drinking his fill, one sailor wants to know how much sacrifice one needs to demonstrate on a refugee ship mission. Another sailor asks:

"How big is Palestine?"

"250 miles long, forty miles wide," the deck officer answers.

"Is that all? That's what all the fuss in the world is about?"

"It's bigger than that, what are you talking about?" someone says. "Did you forget to include Transjordan?"

"Yeah, did you forget to count it?" a third interjects, "and the neighboring lands that belong to us according to the Bible: Syria, Egypt?"

"Such a scholar! What kind of Bible did you study? You're talking like a conqueror, an aggressor!"

The captain enters. He has overheard the conversation. His face lights up in a smile and he claps his hands and rubs them together:

"Give me 250 miles long and forty miles wide. I don't want a single inch more land than that! Syria! Egypt! No thank you. 250 miles long and forty miles wide! That's how much space my ship is after."

13

THE BRITISH SEARCH FOR THE SHIP

Late at night the radio operator intercepts the alarming news that the British fleet commanders have ordered our ship to be chased. We have become the center of attention for the commander who rules over the Mediterranean. British patrol ships are on duty. British surveillance airplanes are flying fast and low over the most strategic European port towns. The British intelligence service has tripled the number of its spies and paid informants. They are looking for us in France, in Portugal, they track us in Corsica, they head us off in Italy. They watch from the British fortress of Malta. It appears that every department of His Majesty's Royal Navy has nothing better to do than to race to see who can catch our ship first, while we remain in our successful hiding place somewhere in a lost, quiet harbor.

What is the explanation for such a concentrated chase? What caused the sudden scorn of the British naval officers? Have they been informed that our ship will not sail alone, but will form part of a Ma'apilim convoy? Are they afraid the convoy will break the blockage, evade all obstacles, and slip into Palestine unhindered?

The sailors are discussing the matter. The captain attempts to guess. The chief engineer proposes a hypothesis. The answer comes suddenly the next morning. Just after breakfast there is a commotion on deck because, unannounced, without warning, the stern Haganah commander Signorina Maria has arrived in a row boat. She climbs the rope ladder like an able mariner. She has only one escort with her. She goes straight to the captain's cabin and orders the whole crew to be gathered. She wishes to speak to them.

The crew assembles in the dining room in a matter of seconds. Everyone's ears are pricked; they are attentive. They have a premonition that they are not here to listen to compliments for their bravery. They are not mistaken. Signorina Maria lets loose like a furious school teacher:

"Sailors, you have done something which jeopardizes our entire operation here in this country. You distributed American cigarettes to the villagers who rowed up alongside your ship. You did so out of generosity, but your generosity could cost you your freedom . . . you drew too much attention to your presence. There isn't a town or village along this entire coast that doesn't know about your ship now . . . those American cigarettes are the perfect breadcrumbs for the British navy on your tail. You're now in an uncomfortable situation. Staying here is dangerous, and moving to another port is also dangerous because the enemy is waiting. There are dozens of British patrol ships looking for you. This situation has me rattled. It should not have happened! All foolishness must be avoided! You are sailors on the way to smuggle Jews into Palestine!"

Signorina Maria falls silent for a moment, her mild, brown eyes burning in rage. She is trying to control her anger, but is failing. Her face is contorted in a grimace. Her formal severity has gotten the better of her feminine mildness. Her words were hasty, full of reproach and fear:

"Sailors! Discipline is something you cannot escape from. We warned you not to let any of the locals come near the ship. You must concentrate on your task. You have each signed up for an important mission. You must follow orders and respect the rules! Do not forget that we are at war with a more powerful enemy . . . I will have to send a report about your actions to America! It appears you were not sufficiently prepared for your mission. You do not understand the gravity of the undertaking. You will go on your way and we will remain here. We must continue this difficult mission, but, sailors, your negligence will cost us dearly! I apologize for my sharp tone, but it had to be said. It had to be."

Having finished speaking, Signorina Maria slips gracefully out of the dining room. The sailors are ashamed, full of regret. Mutely, they curse their foolishness. Exchanging glances, they cannot fathom how such a trifle—handing out chocolate and cigarettes to hungry Italians—could have such repercussions, that it could have alerted the entire British navy.

I go back up to my cabin. There is a knock on the door and at the threshold stands the young priest from Boston.

The priest is an outlandish specimen on the ship. He is not a passenger, and not a crewmember. Neither is he a newspaper man driven by ambition to join the underground expedition. He is a priest, an active member of the "Christian Palestine Committee." His task is to see with his own eyes the march of the Ma'apilim to Palestine in order to later tell the story to the Christian world of the Way of Suffering traversed by the remnants of the People of Israel, those who have not been consumed by the flames of Majdanek and Auschwitz.

The priest is fond of restating his mission. During our many discussions he tries to convince me that the urge to become an illegal passenger has plagued him for over a year, since he first heard that the Haganah had begun its branching sea voyages. It is an honor for him to reach the Holy Land as such a pilgrim.

The priest likes to over dramatize his mission. He is by nature an enthusiastic man, and if you look closely into his eyes you'll come to the realization that there's an element of theatricality about him. He plays too much with clichés; he manipulates with oratorical phrases as though he were not sitting and chatting, but standing on a platform looking out at a large audience.

None of this detracts from the man's charm however. Despite the calculating effects which he wraps in his priest's clothing, one can believe what he says. He is honest and upstanding. The fact that he took it upon himself to play the role of the uprooted wanderer to travel through various ports on various ships—that alone is hard not to respect. He has already changed ships several times along the way. He seeks new experiences at every turn. Thanks to his contacts with the Jewish underground he manages to reach people and places that other men—with less ambition and stamina—would never be able to reach. It's five months already since he left America. He has already visited the refugee camps of half of Europe. His notes, which will form the basis of the lectures he intends to hold once he returns to America, are hidden somewhere in France. He does not want to risk letting them fall into the hands of the British. And he is still only getting started. He is waiting for the ship to be loaded up with thousands of refugees.

The priest stands in my cabin. He has, he tells me, a new plan and he wants me to hear it. He wastes no time:

"What have you, as a journalist, decided to do when we reach Haifa? Give yourself up? Or allow yourself to be deported to Cyprus with the others?"

"I'll go to Cyprus," I say.

"That was always my plan too," says the priest, his youthful, ruddy face wrinkling into a grimace. "But now I realize that it would be better if I gave myself up in Haifa . . . my task will be completed after all, once I've accompanied the thousands on their voyage. I have enough material for my lectures. The Christian Palestinian Committee which authorized me to travel on this ship will be pleased when I travel across America explaining, to the Christian world, as a Christian, how Britain is treating the people who gave us the prophets, civilization and religion."

I look at the young, passionate priest, a man prone to falling into oratorical tones mid conversation. He is blond, tall and hairy. His family background is Swedish. He has enough strength in his shoulders that he could have been a coal miner, and enough patience to be a New York subway conductor. And yet, he is a priest. A priest with a mission. The sailors make fun of him, thinking he is a little mad. After all, what madness is it to take on the burden of Jewish troubles when his position as a Catholic priest offers him money, respect and an easy job?

The priest's reputation also took a hit when he volunteered to work in the kitchen. He became a dishwasher and now serves the crew during mealtimes. This gesture gave the crew even more opportunities to play jokes at his expense.

But the ambitious priest ignores gossip and ignorant prejudices. What worries him now is the British hunting our ship. He comes to the conclusion:

"They will catch us eventually. If not at sea, then in Haifa. And what then? Most of my notes are safely hidden in France. But I must still take notes. New things happen every day. These tumultuous experiences are an inexhaustible source of inspiration . . . what have you done with your articles?"

"I've sent them all off in the mail," I say.

"I'm going to hide my notes in my shoes, and in my laundry. I'll bandage my hands and hide them in there—anything to keep them out of the hands of the Brits."

The priest looks around, as though paranoid that someone is eavesdropping, and speaks in a low voice:

"What do you think of how strict these Haganah people are with the crew? A little too harsh, don't you think? The trouble is that both sides misunderstand each other. The lifestyles of the Europeans are alien to our boys, and vice versa. The American seamen don't understand the constant dread and terror the Haganah feels carrying out their daring enterprises . . . I wouldn't really call it fear . . . precaution is the word. And if it's true that handing out those cigarettes caused such a commotion, then the sailors deserve their reprimand. Our boys seem to think they're still in the Merchant Marine on trading missions . . . they feel safe . . .they seem to forget that the refugee ships are sailing under false names with borrowed flags."

The priest would gladly say more, but just then the captain enters. He sits down with a smile as though he had heard the whole conversation.

"What's the latest, captain?" the priest asks.

"No news," the captain says calmly, "apart from the fact that there's something I need to tow at the next stop."

"Tow?"

"Yeah. One of the Haganah ships ran aground a while ago. And seeing as how I have a few days to spare according to the schedule, we're going to stop there and tow it into the water. After that we'll tow the ship all the way to the next port. It's a valuable vessel, too valuable to be left to rust. It's big enough to take on four thousand passengers . . ."

"Has that been decided?"

"Nothing is decided. Every few hours the strategy changes . . . My commanders are the radio signals . . . I wouldn't be surprised if an hour from now a new set of orders will come in that changes the whole schedule."

As it turns out, it does not take a whole hour for this to happen. True to his word the captain is not surprised when two Haganah messengers arrive on deck to inform us that we should proceed without delay into open waters. The sailors gape. The deck officer asks three questions in rapid succession:

"What's the reason? Has there been a change of plan? What is the situation?"

"The situation is that your ship could be intercepted at any moment. Harbor officials and police from the nearest port are looking for you," one of the Haganah men explains.

"Are we to set sail?"

"I give you three hours," comes the answer, "I want all unnecessary motors, machinery and pipes to be unloaded from the ship so that the scrap should not be seized by the British. I have several Italian dock workers. There's a tug-steamer waiting for us. It must be done quickly, without a hitch."

The crew throw themselves into the work with enthusiasm, and two hours later the material has been loaded onto the steamer.

They calculate that by removing the scrap they prevent 27,000 dollars worth of material from falling into British hands.

The Haganah men seem satisfied, but also on edge. One goes to find the chief engineer and asks:

"How long does it usually take for the motors to warm up?"

"Three quarters of an hour," the chief engineer replies.

"Shorten it to half an hour," the Haganah man orders.

The engineer agrees and, as he heads down to the engine room to give instructions, the second Haganah man gathers the rest of the crew in the dining room. He regards them for a moment in silence. His gaze is clouded, his thick brows furrowed. Then he begins to speak in a low, labored tone:

"Sailors! You are now leaving the harbor where you were unwanted guests . . . The Italian police under pressure from the British wish to seize your ship. Hurry away from here. Your captain will lead you to ports further away. You will pick up drinking water in the nearest port of call. You have enough fuel to last you until you reach your destination. Tonight you will receive the passengers aboard your ship. Treat them well. They are suffering, traumatized, and therefore sensitive . . . when they board all lights on the ship must be turned off. Remember that the port is not a desert. The slightest noise can awaken the inhabitants. You must behave like obedient soldiers. Do not speak amongst yourselves during the operation. Work in silence. Do everything in your power to make the operation a success. I wish you all good luck and *Shalom!*"

"*Shalom! Shalom! Shalom!*" a chorus of voices responds.

Climbing down the rope-ladder to the boat, the Haganah man waves me goodbye, and then calls out in a voice both stern and polite:

"I cannot give you any orders. You are a civilian passenger. But I beg you: forget the country you are about to leave, forget the ports you have visited and the people you have met. Forget my face too . . . do you promise?"

"Do not worry, commander," I say, "everything I write will be cryptic."

"*Shalom!*"

"Peace and blessings!"

Fifteen minutes later, the smokestack begins to roar. The anchor is raised. The engines hum and the ship sets off through the water in full haste.

14

MUTINY

The illegal mission is one of great responsibility, and the determination of the sailors to watch over the Jewish sea-caravans is unwavering. But there are moments in the life of every individual when petty, egotistical characteristics gain dominance over cool reason and self-interest takes over even those who have answered the most noble calling.

The sailors on the Jewish Ma'apilim ships are not immune to such weaknesses.

After sixteen days of wandering from one port to another, crawling from one shore to the next, when the orders finally come to *rendez-vous* at a series of ports to gather almost two thousand refugees, certain dissatisfied voices begin to be raised from among the sailors.

On the surface, the complaints coming from a section of the crew are petty and trivial.

The first sailor complains to the captain that he does not receive his fair share. One complains that his work at the anchor is the hardest. Another complains that his bed is a hard bench. A forth complains that the voyage is unplanned and interminable. The list of complainers includes a cook, a deckman, a motor operator, and a bridge guard.

Jealousy plays no small part in the affair. Greed and resentment are rife among the unsatisfied. Contemptible, unimportant whims, rise to the surface. In the confusion of emotions, the malcontents seem to forget the purpose of the voyage.

Furious, the captain listens to the complaints and says that whoever wants to leave the ship should disembark at the next port. He isn't going to stop anyone.

The first officer protests. He criticizes the captain, saying he should show a stronger hand, and not permit anarchy. He scolds the first mutineer, the motor operator:

"What did you expect this voyage to be? A picnic?"

"Picnic or not," replies the motor operator, "if we have to put up with hardships we should each get our fair share!"

"You don't seem to have it so hard."

"Hard enough, and without the slightest comfort."

"Who asks for comfort on a cargo ship that used to transport bananas?"

"Your bed is soft enough!"

"I sleep on a makeshift bunk we cobbled together back in Portugal!"

The first officer has nothing else to say. Taking his place in the duel of words comes the chief engineer who has just arrived. He fixes on the second mutineer, the deckman—a blond, broad-shouldered youth, hairy as a bear.

"You want to run away too?"

"It's time to head home. I have a wife, and a kid to raise ..."

"You know someone who runs away from a battle is considered a deserter? Our ship is prepared for battle."

"You'll have enough fighters without me!"

"You're a deckman; we'll need you to organize the resistance in position when the British attack. And what kind of commander abandons his battalion in its hour of reckoning?"

It is difficult to respond to such a reproach. The chief engineer pins the mutineer against the wall. The deckman withdraws. The chief engineer seeks out another mutineer, the bridge guard. He wants to break the resistance of the mutineers one by one. The guard, a thin, bony man with a head of curly hair, is at that moment standing on the bridge with binoculars raised watching for signs of British surveillance ships. The chief engineer asks him:

"What do you think about the voyage?"

"It's taking too long. We're wasting time and burning too much fuel ..."

"Don't worry about fuel, we've got more than enough. And this isn't Columbus's days either, time is not an issue."

"This long, drawn out wandering is an issue for some of our men. Don't forget our boys have their own responsibilities ..."

The chief engineer, his muscular face full of smiles, leans over the bridge guard—who now appears child-like and helpless—and asks him:

"What's bothering you, sailor? Have you left your sweetheart behind in North Carolina?

"You'd better believe it."

"What is she: a brunette? A red-head? A blonde?"

"She's blonde."

"Write her, sailor, and tell her you've got a post on an illegal ship. You guard the captain's bridge, a captain who does not know the name of his ship, or the color of its flag . . . write and tell her you keep watch so that the enemy's spy-planes don't find us. You have a mission, sailor . . . She'll understand. She'll forgive you. And when you get back to North Carolina she'll throw flowers at your feet . . ."

The chief engineer quashes the quiet rebellion one mutineer at a time. He takes the wind out of their sails, sometimes with a gentle word, sometimes harsh, stinging words. The mutiny melts away. The rebels waver; their decision to leave the ship is not definitive. As long as the ship can still dock in a European port, the path for deserters remains open.

But, that same day, when the captain comes to his crew with news from the radio signalist that they must plot a course to two Italian ports to pick up the refugees, because the British are about to crack down on the whole operation, the men are silent . . . faced with the hour of need, their desire to complain vanishes.

The crew is informed of how, for months, the British foreign secretary has been putting pressure on the French government for showing too much leniency toward Zionist activities in France. A year ago the British Foreign Office requested the French authorities indicate to certain Zionist activists that their continued presence on French soil was not welcome. To France's credit the official response was that there was no legal justification for harassing people against whom no charges had been brought. More urgent were British demands in relation to the Ma'apilim ships in France. Britain claimed that the "illegal migration" to Palestine used French ports as transit points. The British even attempted to warn France that Jewish terrorists were preparing large-scale criminal actions on French soil ... France always responded that there was no evidence to suggest plans for such terrorist atrocities. Now the British have changed tactics and are lobbying the French authorities to curtail the movement of Jewish displaced persons within the French occupation zone in Germany. There was even a deliberation in Paris between representatives of France, America and Britain, about the movements of Jewish refugees from one zone to another.

The campaign has had some effect. France—at the last minute and under pressure from Britain—imposed measures to curtail the "illegal" sea-crossings. The problem is that France is the only country in Europe that serves as an exit to other seas further afield. If someone has a visa for America and wants to travel from a French port, there is no legal grounds to hinder the passage. But is the same not true of a passenger with a visa for Chile or Paraguay who has no intention of going to those places, but who wants to go to Palestine?

Such complications stick in the throat of the British. How can the French keep an eye on passengers whose papers show they are traveling to Brazil but who turn around midway and head east instead?

Throughout the night the ship glides past various Italian islands. Light-houses call from the shores, winking with secret messages. The blond captain is hopeful, his optimism grows. He is now certain he will break through the British blockade. All that's missing is gas-masks and smoke canisters. If his current ship lacks the necessary equipment he will ensure that his next ship will be different. He does not ignore the fact that there are three ships moving at one time; if two are captured, a third can slip through the blockade— and the captain is determined that that third ship will be his!

The radio signalists have locked themselves in their room to listen for secret instructions. It is the hour when we await the definitive order telling us which port we will reach tonight to pick up the first group of refugees.

Ten minutes later the radio operator announces the name of the port; its name is "Khara." The word casts the captain into a state of confusion. He searches for a similar name on the map and finds nothing. He flips through the atlas and country maps, he consults the weighty sea-book which records all the names and information of every port in the world, even the very smallest. That name is nowhere to be found.

The code-language is Hebrew. The captain calls me to help. For half an hour I strain to find an explanation for the word Khara. In the Bible there is a Harran, a difference of only one letter in Hebrew, but Harran is far inland, not a port. I add up the letters, attempting some *gematria*, but I come up short.

It is nine p.m. In an hour our radio operators must speak in code to a station somewhere in the world. It would be an opportunity to ask for clarification about the name of the port. For now we are cruising in no particular direction. But the clock is ticking. An hour passes and the error has been cleared up. It was all a simple spelling mistake. Two hours later an order comes to dock somewhere to the north, between two large ports. The coastline is quiet, surrounded by rocks. A flaming lighthouse, like a pillar of fire, will call our ship in.

On the captain's bridge stands a tall, bony man, his face ravaged by the elements; it is the pilot who has accompanied us from a port in Southern Italy. It is he, not the captain, who is currently leading the ship. He knows these stretches of waters as well as he knows his home village. He knows every inch of water. He can spot a mine, or a piece of floating debris from a sunken rowboat.

The tall Italian pilot is now the guide. Under his guidance the ship will avoid dangers and bypass the areas not yet cleared of mines.

Coffee and sandwiches are brought in. The pilot passes the helm to the deck officer, telling him to keep going due north, and sits down to drink his piping-hot coffee. Between one sip and the next he says:

"Too many British agents here in Italy. If not for the spies the British would never find our whereabouts."

"Are there Italians who work for Britain?" the deck officer asks.

"Italy is a poor country. And the British always dominate the poor . . . paid agents circulate in Genoa and Milan. The Italians keep an eye on them, but the British pay off the informers . . . there are those Italians who serve the British for money, and there are those who work against their own government. But overall there are more Italians who help the Jews than hinder them . . ." the pilot smiles. Out of respect the deck-officer calls the pilot "captain."

"Captain, when will the British cease being in our way?"

"When you flood the seas with ships . . ."

"Flood the seas?

The pilot grows angry. "What is one ship a week? Why not seven ships? Your goal is as good as won anyway. Your ships carry homeless passengers. We are in peacetime. The British are not able to shoot. When the ships are caught the passengers are sent to Cyprus. Cyprus is a stepping stone to your land."

The chief engineer beams, the deck officer is excited. The captain's eyes glow. It is his dream. Smoke canisters to make a smoke screen. Gas masks for the tear gas and armadas of ships filling the seas. That is how one conquers an enemy. That is how one takes a country.

Abruptly, the pilot puts down his coffee and moves to the railing. He takes the binoculars and gazes long and hard at the dark horizon before calling the captain:

"See that red light in the distance? That's our rendezvous point."

The pilot takes back the helm. In that moment he becomes a partner in the Ma'apilim movement. He does not trust anyone but himself to guide the ship into port, where thousands of uprooted Jews are waiting with all their worldly belongings.

15

SMUGGLING REFUGEES

It is midnight. The big night. The night when we will smuggle the first refugees onto the ship. The sky, which by rights should be dark on a night like this, is bright and filled with stars. The moon—not a sliver, nor a crescent, but a full moon—lights up the way.

On a night of clandestine activities these conditions are against us. The moon is too bright. The spies on the shore, too alert. Only the sea bubbles in a quiet storm.

Our ship, which usually goes nine miles an hour, is now clipping along at a speed of seventeen miles an hour. On shore, hills stretch out on either side of the bay. Small lighthouses blink and beckon in the distance, but it is not for us that they beckon. We are waiting for the enormous searchlight that will lead us into a secret cove. The captain does not leave the bridge. The pilot orders the ship to speed up. The deck officer passes on the orders through a speaking tube which leads down to the engine room. The bow of the ship bites through the waves like an incisor.

The faster the ship glides, the more land surrounds us. The land—the Italian soil—spans the coast in a desolate, raw state, bordered by cliffs: the last stretch of neglected land.

There is an uneasy atmosphere on board. The sailors pace around the ship, whispering, waiting for the captain's orders. The hour of expectations: this is the hour they left their homes for, in Georgia and Texas, in Virginia. For this hour they crossed the Atlantic, traversed so many ports, and drifted over endless waters.

The dishwasher from the kitchen, a religious boy from Brownsville, a lively soul and a disciplined sailor, emerges on deck with a wet cloth and joins the growing circle of sailors. He speaks joyfully:

"I'm happy we've finally come so far!"

"You're happy?" another says, "I'm feverish with excitement!"

"There'll be something to see," a third says.

"A great spectacle!"

"Boys, don't dramatize things! You're not actors. We have a mission and it must be done!" an earnest crewmember calls out.

"We have to work fast."

"The ship has to be gone from here by daybreak."

"Get your skates on, Joe!"

"Abe, don't fall asleep at the anchor!"

"And you, Al, don't think this is like washing dishes!"

The deck officer hurries over from the captain's bridge with a light in his hands. He knocks on every cabin door:

"Lights out!"

One by one the lamps are extinguished, not just in the cabins, but also out on the main deck, the promenade deck and the captain's bridge. It's now as dark as in a forest. Only here and there one can make out the glowing red circle of a cigarette.

Light in hand, the deck officer tracks down every crew member, with the exception of those working in the engine room, and calls them together for a briefing in the dining room. Once the crew has taken their places around the table the deck officer begins:

"Sailors, we will reach our destination in an hour's time! It will not be a usual docking. The ship will remain anchored a hundred meters from the shore. The passengers will arrive in fishing boats. The process of bringing them up on deck must be fast and smooth. It's a bright night. But water conditions are against us. We'll need your complete concentration and fast action . . . remember, we are being observed. We have friends in Italy, but there are also those who are working against us . . . Sailors, be prepared to take aboard eight hundred passengers!"

"And the rest?" someone asks.

"Tomorrow night we will pick up another seven hundred passengers from a different port. It is possible that in the open sea we will rendezvous with a small ship and pick up a further four hundred passengers. That will be once we're close to the Palestinian shore . . . Tonight is our first opportunity. Sailors, this is a great moment! We all feel the same feelings. This is what we've wanted. When the time comes each of us will take our places, above deck, or below. During the operation—no smoking and no speaking! Keep in mind that we are operating outside the law. Sailors, listen carefully! I will call out the names of each sailor and the job he will fulfill."

After the deck officer reads out the names from his sheet and their assigned tasks, the sailors return to the upper deck.

The ship proceeds at a quick pace. The shores are covered in thousands of lights. Searchlights, spotlights and lighthouses cast beams of light that cross paths in the night sky.

Our ship does not allow the lights to lead it astray; it continues its forward course.

The pilot, the good Italian, who holds the ship's wheel in hand, is full of stories of the sea. In the darkness his tongue does not cease recounting tales of daring maritime exploits. The tall, gray pilot is Genoese, but he is not interested in his compatriot Columbus. He is more taken with the Portuguese fisherman Magellan, who in 1519 undertook a perilous expedition in the name of the king of Spain.

The pilot tells his stories at the same time as he navigates a path through the mines. He steers the floating ark toward a safe harbor. Next to him stands the captain, chain-smoking cigarettes. He smokes like a chimney. The radio operator picks up a signal from the shore.

The latest order: come to a certain spot. Searchlights will guide the way, lighthouses will send signals.

The ship swims like a whale. Another mile. Another. We are arriving closer. Large, coarse rocks come against us. The pilot, impatient, orders a northward turn. He hands the binoculars to the captain. The captain passes the binoculars to the other bystanders in turn and points:

"See that bright light? The Star of David."

I take the binoculars and look. In the distance, a large bright light hangs from a pole in the shape of a Star of David. A large picture has been placed in the centre of the star: a portrait of Herzl. Every corner of the Jewish Star is set with blinking lamps, like diamonds.

The light shines like the sun. The image cries out in a thousand voices.

A Jewish Star on the Italian coast marks the rendezvous point. Herzl's face is calling in the Ma'apilim ships to him.

The picture represents a reminder, a comparison. In a Jewish institute in a French coastal city I saw a portrait of another Jewish leader. A leader from the Yishuv—Berl Katznelson. And under his portrait, the slogan: "Part the seas and welcome the returnees!" And here, on the Italian coast under a bright night sky, the portrait of Herzl shines like a pillar of fire, calling directly to our ship:

"Come, sailors, and welcome the wanderers to the Land of Israel! What a journey from the shores of France to those of Italy. There you were called, and here are the deeds. There, the slogans; here, the actions."

The ship picks up speed, heading in the direction of the Star of David. We reach the spot faster than expected. Some sailors stand ready to drop anchor, others stand ready to welcome the oncoming fishing boats. The ship circles left, circles right, and we hear the clatter of the chain as the anchor drops and the ship comes to a halt.

There is only a hundred meters between the ship and the shore. Terrible silence reigns all around. Large cliffs dominate the view. Behind the Star of David, a hill looms. On the hill is a stately house. The windows are lit up and the doors are open. This is the place, the station for eager Ma'apilim.

On the darkened ship the entire crew waits in anticipation.

Suddenly, searchlights burst into life from the shore, coming from many different positions at once. They communicate in the language of fire. In a matter of minutes the sound of a motor rings out. Something as big as a river boat is approaching. The closer it gets the more details come into view: the boat from the illegal outpost comes to greet the ship. Subdued voices in Italian and Hebrew follow the rhythmic hum of the motors, and, when the boat comes to a stop, barefoot fishermen begin to climb onto the ship. Greetings are made silently through hand gestures. The crew and fishermen make themselves understood via sign-language.

The half hour wait stretches out like an eternity. I look once again toward the hills. There is movement near the house. Binoculars reveal columns of people making their way down the hill. Dark figures in gray clothing, like soldiers, with rucksacks on their backs. The columns of people stretch longer and longer as though they are endless. One line after another. One column behind another.

Somewhere there is a loud splash.

Suddenly caravans of fishing boats begin to stream from all sides. The boats come from the right and the left, they come out from the rocks, and the cliffs. Barefoot Italians, and daring Jewish sailors, row with all their might and the water barely makes a sound. The stars, it seems, have gone out. The moon appears to have hidden itself, deliberately, behind a cloud—wanting to aid the conspiracy on Italian soil.

O, have you ever seen how a nation—the remnants of a nation—smuggle their way out of a whole continent? Not from the continent of slavery, but the continent of extermination?

For the remaining Israelites the continent has become a land of graves. And from the graves those who survived by miracle or by chance emerge to save themselves. They stream toward secret ports. Their destination is unfamiliar shores where ships are waiting to ferry them to safety. The small fishing boats cut through the water with a gentle lapping sound. The refugees sit huddled, as mute and unmoving as statues. Everything is going according to plan.

On the shore stand some Italian police; they are not there to hinder the flow of refugees, but to keep away curious locals and informants who seek to prevent the migration.

And from the shore the burning Star of David still shines, with Herzl's head inside. How differently that visionary must have imagined the return of his people to their land!

Suddenly, amidst the tension and held-breaths, the sound of a baby crying rises from one of the boats. The baby cries grow louder and stronger. A Jewish child crying in the middle of the sea.

The childish cry does not stop. Such crying could ruin the clandestine action. It could draw the attention of a lurking plane or an enemy search boat.

Do not cry, child of Israel, do not cry! You are a Ma'apil child being smuggled across the border, to board a ship bound for a safer place ...

The child's voice cries on. Someone takes the child by the hand, snuggling it, coddling it until the crying gradually subsides.

When the first boat reaches the ship the loading begins. The sailors work fast and efficiently.

Stretch out an arm, pull, and a refugee stands on deck. A second sailor leads the refugees below deck to their places.

The sailors remember what the Haganah agent said to them in the last port: "be good to the refugees!

They have suffered a lot; they are victims of terrible savagery." The crew treats the passengers with care and kindness. They pull them up from the boats as they would pull up drowning people from the water.

Coming aboard the refugees look around them, gaping and bewildered. They carry bundles and rucksacks. They eye the sailors with suspicion. But once they have been taken below deck and been given a bed where they may rest their heads, they regain their confidence, the confidence of being among one's own kind.

In the confusion mothers look for their infants who strangers had carried on their laps in the boats. Children wait for their parents to show up. Families reunite; people seek out their loved ones. There are congratulations all around.

An old woman, wrapped in half a dozen scarves, shawls, coats and overcoats cries out for joy:

"We're starting off on the right foot, may we all get off the ship on the right foot too!"

The uprooted, expelled exiles stream aboard onto every deck. Sailors accompany them to their places. The last fishing boat is emptied. The captain looks at the clock. It is 1:45. He is triumphant. The operation lasted exactly an hour and forty-five minutes. The good news that they had loaded 800 passengers so quickly spreads like wildfire through the ship. The night is far from over. The water swills in the pale moonlight.

The Italian pilot asks for a cup of hot coffee. The captain consults his map. The deck hands raise the anchor. The helmsman retakes his post. Thirty-two sailors return to their positions and the dark ship slips quietly away from the clandestine cove.

16

PARTISANS, GHETTO FIGHTERS AND VETERANS

The tumult and clatter of the newly arrived passengers lasts into the early hours of the morning.

The noisiest culprit is a red-haired Jew with the beard of a traditional school teacher. He is so delighted to be surrounded by his siblings, cousins, and in-laws that he never stops kissing his relatives, shouting:

"Oh, who could have expected such a gathering? All of us on the same ship to boot!"

"What gathering are you talking about, *landsman*?" a lively young man in a pair of Cossack boots shouts over.

"What do you mean, 'what gathering'?" the red-head bellows. "These people have all been found! One was in Italy, another in Holland, a third in Germany, and now? Here we all are traveling on one and the same ship!"

A youthful mother leading a small child by the hand puts down her suitcase, her bundle, and seeing her bed, says:

"It's a lot better than I expected! This ship will lord it over the seas. We could travel for three months on a ship the likes of this."

A Jew with a disheveled blond beard paces through in a hurry. He does not allow the sailor to accompany him as far as his bed. Whatever meagre possessions he'd had with him have long been abandoned. Eyes closed, he throws himself down on his knees and kisses the ship's cold floor.

"God in heaven! I've lived to see the day! How great is your glory, Heavenly Father!"

The passengers are still marching to the lower decks to locate their beds. Boys in leather jackets, in boots like Cossacks; girls with flaxen tresses, tied with peasant-like head-scarfs; old men in rabbi's hats; Hasidic wives in wigs; tall lads with tousled hair; older women in heavy frocks.

In one corner, standing over his open luggage, an old Jew, as white as a dove, removes his outer kaftan, then his vest. He takes off his hat, and stands there in his velvet yarmulke, rubbing his red eyes. He sighs:

"Why do I remain? Why such an honor, Merciful God? My dear children! Why did you have to go to the ovens, why?"

Joy in one corner, sorrow in another.

On the other side of the deck stands a boy, all alone with a lonesome bundle. No one is glad to see him. His presence does not console anyone. No one speaks to him.

That wicked devil: irony, which men of refined taste like to consider charming, played such a demonic prank on that boy—He was born in Palestine. How does a child of the Yishuv end up becoming a refugee?

Listen, and hear his sorry tale! In 1925 his parents came to Palestine from Poland. In 1928 the boy came into the world. In 1929 there was a crisis in Palestine.[15] But those Jews who knew how to weather a crisis in Poland, Romania or France had no patience for weathering a crisis in Palestine and they returned in haste to the land of Grabski.

In 1943 his parents went to Treblinka. In 1947 the orphan set off alone for Palestine.

If, over the course of the voyage to come, I do not encounter a worse drama, then this boy will go down as the saddest refugee on the ship.

This first short night is so momentous that most of the passengers go from being complete strangers to close friends, united in a desire to do their part and share the troubles of the wandering ship.

Soon people are back on their feet. Women are prepared to do laundry for the crew; young men, experienced waiters and cooks from their army days, volunteer to help in the kitchen. Locksmiths and mechanics want to work in the engine room. Carpenters try to make themselves useful by building huts and bathrooms on deck.

Not everyone's helping hands can be put to use, but those that can are happy.

Next, a great exodus begins on board the ship.

---

15 A reference to the 1929 Arab riots in Palestine.

The passengers begin to arrange themselves into smaller groups, each with its own representative, based on political and religious factions, and begin to rearrange their sleeping quarters accordingly. This is helpful for the crew as each group's representative can negotiate with the captain, the cook and or with the agents from the Haganah on behalf of the others.

The three Haganah agents, who turned up the night before the first group of Ma'apilim came on board, have, for all intents and purposes, taken over the running of the ship.

The task of navigating the ship over the waters still belongs to the captain and his crew, but the inner workings of the ship's economy, the distribution of food and supplies, the issuing of instructions, and defensive preparations in the event of a British attack—all these tasks are now in the hands of the Haganah.

As emissaries from the Land of Israel the agents exercise their authority to the fullest extent possible, something which pains the captain who would prefer to be in charge. These tensions are but minor disputes which melt away before anything ever comes of them.

The first day of ship-life for the Ma'apilim begins with a commotion.

The Aguda[16] passengers gather on the upper deck for morning prayers. When they first begin to put on their tallitim there are barely enough people to form a minyan, but by the time the prayer-leader reaches

16 Members of the ultra-orthodox political party Agudat Yisrael.

the eighteen benedictions, there are a full six minyans present. The group's praying collectively on deck under the open air, the choral song, and the fluttering of dozens of tallitim lends the ship a ceremonial atmosphere.

Nearby the Mizrachi[17] passengers also gather together for morning prayers. The Mizrachi faction is mostly made up of younger people, who have gathered in two large groups. They lack the old-fashioned gilded tallitim with the heavy embroidered edges, and one can see the *shel roshes* protrude more visibly over their hats, likewise the leather straps over their bare arms, and their tallitim are short like scarves.

Long tallitim, short tallitim—the morning prayers are a colorful spectacle which draws the attention of the other passengers, bringing all dealings on the upper deck to a halt.

Breakfast is late on the first morning. The bustle, the chaos, and the fact that every group, every faction is elbowing their way to the upper deck makes the punctual serving of the first meal all but impossible. This could have given the impression that food is scarce, whereas in reality provisions are plentiful.

The representative of the Mizrachi, a nimble young man with a thin beard, runs to the captain, to the Haganah agents, to the deck officer threatening to resign if they did not give him the very upper deck, the promenade deck, for his people.

---

17 Members of Mizrachi, a religious Zionist movement.

"It will be like a rudderless ship!" he warns "I have two groups under my supervision. Over 180 people, with families, with children, and we must concentrate them in one place. If they are scattered all over the ship, I won't be responsible for keeping the order!"

"We are responsible," the Haganah agent says.

"And who will give them instructions? Who will distribute their food?"

"Their representative."

"I must have organization!" the representative says, "I can't lead if I don't have my two groups together."

"If you can't lead, we'll choose another representative to lead in your place," the Haganah agent says, becoming more stern.

"Does that mean I can resign?" the representative asks.

"It's up to you. And don't forget that this is a Ma'apilim ship. Tonight we will pick up another seven hundred passengers. As a representative you need to show that there will be days when not a single soul will be permitted on the top deck. Everyone will be hidden below."

The warnings and insinuations clearly convince the stubborn Mizrachi-representative, and with the knowledge that this is no "Queen Elizabeth," but an overcrowded refugee ship he goes back to carry out his responsibilities as circumstances dictate.

The quietest and most unassuming passengers on board turn out to be the Aguda Jews. They do not complain, even though they occupy the darkest corner in the belly of the ship. They stay where they are put. They follow all the rules. They have not even complained that they will have to endure a somewhat sparse, dry diet during the trip, on account of their principle of eating strictly kosher, though they have been given every assurance that all the food on board was supplied by Jewish firms and is all guaranteed kosher.

Particularly active and visible from the very start have been the three groups of Hashomer Hatzair.[18] Well trained, with an exemplary education, they are prepared to tackle all obstacles and have adapted remarkably quickly to their new surroundings. Regardless of where on the ship they are, whether together or separated, they know that they are on the way to Palestine where the Yishuv is waiting for them. In the meantime they have no intention of remaining passive bystanders, but active Ma'apilim.

Their contributions to the running of the ship are visible wherever one looks.

The most silent and low key faction are those of the Betar movement,[19] though they are numerous: around 250 members. These most militant of the Revisionists, normally so eager for controversy, so vocal in their every venture, are quiet here on the ship. They loaf around like gatecrashers at a wedding. Perhaps this is down to a feeling of defeat for having to travel on

18 Socialist Zionist youth movement.

19 Right wing Revisionist Zionist youth movement, founded by Vladimir Jabotinsky.

a Haganah ship, but their modesty begins to feel distracting or suspicious. There are even rumors going around that their silence is nothing less than the calm before the storm.

It isn't just political parties and movements that make themselves heard in the bustle of the ship, but also everyday Jews unaffiliated with any party lines, programs or colors.

There are Jews from Czechoslovakia, from Hungary and Bulgaria. There are Jews from Russia, from Romania, from Austria and Italy, but the majority on board are Polish Jews: the remaining Jews from that land sowed with the bones and ash of annihilated European Jewry.

Standing out from the crowd: young Jews in Cossack clothes, in Hungarian or Romanian soldier's uniforms.

There are many partisans and veterans from Poland who had fought on every battlefield against the Germans. The partisans fought bravely in the forests. They burned down bridges, blew up trains, decimated dozens of enemy battalions. There are Soviet veterans of Stalingrad, of Sebastopol, of the liberation of Warsaw. The bodies of the partisans still bear unhealed wounds, like branded marks. The bodies of the veterans are bent. They carry pockets full of medals and awards, the highest prizes for heroism. But none of the victorious countries for whom these veterans fought were able to offer them a safe home, and so now they find themselves on an illegal ship bound for Palestine.

But their morale is not broken. They still have their humor. They even have time for word games.

A boy in a soldier's jacket with no buttons, a flaxen mop of hair, and a face that looks anything but typically Jewish, brings his hands together for joy, and says:

"One thing I'm glad about is that I won't have to be a displaced person."

"You don't like the term?" another asks.

"Displaced disk more like, what with all the troubles we've had to bear on our backs."

But after humor, comes earnestness in all its tragic honesty. The partisans are the frightful exemplars of Jewish uprootedness. They sacrificed their blood to foreign altars and were then cast aside. To the saying: "there are no atheists in fox holes," we can retort, "the partisan trenches give birth to the profaners of man."

There can be no worse indictment of mankind for its apathy to the atrocities all around, than the accusations that come from the mouths of the Jewish partisans. At every turn one hears casual and cynical comments about civilized man and his world order. To justify this bitterness the partisans provide examples from their own experiences, the histories of their own sufferings. They have wrestled with death on countless occasions. They survived all manner of hellishness until they reached the rescue ships waiting for them at the shore. It is visible in the faces of their wives who devotedly followed them over every steppe, traversing every forbidden land. It is visible in the children who were born in the forests to the noise of bombs, and in border-crossing stations.

These children are a particular post-war phenomenon. They are half-baked, malnourished and yet large. One seven year old child weighs as much as three. Their eyes are as naive as infants, yet their lips exhibit the shrewdness and wisdom of old men.

Every partisan mother sees her child as a Kaddish, which, thanks to a thousand miracles, broke through the light of the world. Hannah, the wife of Elkanah, who wept for Samuel at Shiloh in front of Eli the High Priest did not weep with as much joy for her newborn prophet as the partisan mothers do for their infants.

There are mothers among the partisans, and there are expectant mothers. The expectant mothers are a problem on all Ma'apilim ships. The regulations permit pregnant women as passengers only if they are no more than five months pregnant. Whether it is because the medical examinations are so flawed and perfunctory, or whether it is because the women succeed in flouting the rules, over half of the pregnant women on board could conceivably go into labor at any moment.

This leads to complications as, on any given ship, there are not always enough midwives or gynecologists to deal with delivering babies. On top of which it almost always happens that the children decide to come out when the Ma'apilim are defending the ship from the British. The last birth pangs of the mother coincide with British troops launching tear gas canisters at the passengers.

But the expectant partisan mothers seem not to be aware of this. Logic has no hold here, and calculations have no place. They rush aboard the ships because they do not want to spend another day in the camps, or in the port towns. There is one calculation that is not insignificant—any woman who gives birth on the ships is allowed to stay in Palestine, along with husband and child. They are not sent to Cyprus. What greater prize can there be for the Ma'apilim than to be spared a further edict of expulsion?

17

MA'APILIM SHIPS ARE COMING!...

The illegal passengers' first day on board is filled with change and enthusiasm. Everyone is overwhelmed by that special kind of agitation that comes from too much joy. The curious wait for interesting events. The unhappy seek distraction. The enemies of boredom try to find ways to pass the time. All day long people bounce from one source of excitement to another.

The evening draws many curious passengers to a part of the lower deck between the kitchen and the dining room which is normally reserved for the crew. They have come to watch the forty infants, sitting on their mothers' laps waiting for the third of their daily milk-portions. Preparations in the kitchen are so slow, and the waiting diners are so curious that this has become the evening's attraction.

Izzy, the Minister of Food, supervisor in the kitchen, a chubby, blond lad with red cheeks who's barely had time to wipe his own mother's milk from his lips, comes in carrying a crate of forty baby bottles. The fat, blond eighteen year old was born in Atlanta, Georgia. He is a university student and active in Habonim. He did not have time to go around with girls. He's too young to get married. But he is well-practiced in handing out the baby bottles, having worked as a nurse in a maternity clinic.

He attaches a teat to each bottle, checks if the milk is flowing by pouring a drop onto his arm, and then places the bottle into the baby's mouth. He shows the baby's mother how best to hold the bottle and gives her instructions on how to prepare the feed herself.

The mothers, whose children were born in the camps, listen attentively to the instructions of the good natured young man. They thank Izzy for his attentiveness and do as he shows them.

Izzy gazes over "his" forty infants and smiles like a proud father.

A short bystander, clearly a father of one of the infants, who is observing the milk feast, opens his eyes wide and calls out scornfully:

"That's how it is, is it? That's how you feed babies in America?"

"Yes."

"And that's American technology, is it?"

"Yes."

"If you think that's an American achievement then America is more backward than I thought!" the unhappy father decides.

"Don't insult America!" intervenes a second father.

"I don't hold much store by that kind of technology!" the first father grumbles. "Call me old fashioned, but I think our grandmothers had the right idea. Babies should be fed the way nature intended."

"Nature's way mustn't be all it's cracked up to be—Look how you turned out!" laughed the second father.

The two fathers descend into a quarrel. The first explains his position:

"Do you know what milk means to a child?"

"I know well enough."

"Milk is the main source of nutrition for the first six years of a child's life; milk is what the body is built from. Milk makes the bones grow ..."

"I know all that!" the second father interjects, "I'm as much of an expert as you are!"

"And you expect me to believe that the milk in those bottles holds up? It's a cheap imitation, is it not?"

These last words are enough to offend Izzy under whose supervision the babies find themselves. He's not impressed with the small man's interpretations. Compared to Izzy the man is a shrimp, a runt. Izzy is sure that the man was breastfed, while he, Izzy, was brought up with a bottle. And who is the healthier specimen?

Izzy slips off his leather jacket. He rolls up his right sleeve and flexes his muscles. He pushes his way toward the short man and shouts:

"See these cheeks? See these shoulders? See these muscles? That's what I got from four year's worth of drinking imitation milk!"

The bystanders applaud, enjoying the young American's bravado. The young mothers scold the short father, who always finds fault in everything.

From the row of bystanders an elderly woman in a wig steps forward. She straightens her headscarf, wipes her lips in embarrassment and says:

"Honestly, there's no appreciation for what the American boys are doing for us. It's a disgrace to complain about them!"

"We're plenty appreciative, we are!" someone else calls out. "What do you expect us to do, lift them on our shoulders in celebration?"

"Frankly, they deserve as much!" the elderly woman says stubbornly, "They're putting their lives on the line for us! Such dear boys! They find ships and take us to the Holy Land!"

"And where were they when we were being put into concentration camps?" says a voice.

"You're talking like a real jack-ass!" another interrupts. "Those boys were in the army; they fought for victory."

"A bitter victory!"

"Tell us, if you're so smart," the elderly woman says, "are you so sure that if you were in their position you'd be so willing to leave your rich father's house, and a good job, to go work on some illegal ships?"

"I'd go if I was paid."

"They should do something to help their brothers!"

"But they're not even being paid!"

"You should be ashamed of yourself!" an elderly orthodox Jew scolds him. "If I had anything to say about it, I'd have you sent off the ship! Interloper!"

"What I'd like to know . . . " another voice enters the fray, "What I'd like to know is how you'd behave on a goyish ship, with a goyish captain and goyish crew—would you speak about them the same way?"

The argument, which has up to now been escalating in hushed tones so that passing crew members will not catch the insults, explodes entirely.

Debates break out in every corner. Arguments drag on. Every little thing on the ship is subject to heated discussions. Kibitzers and complainers have a mountain of axes to grind.

A young husband, father to be, embraces his friend, a Mizrachi, whose wife is on the verge of giving birth, and congratulates him in a loud voice:

"Baruch, congratulations, all credit to you!"

"What do you mean, Saul?" Baruch asks naively.

"I mean that before this journey is over, you'll be a father."

"That's in God's hands, Saul!"

"I'd wager that I'm right!" Saul insists.

"If it's in the stars," smiles Baruch, the lucky father-to-be.

"Stars, luck, God! You know what's in store for you? You'll be recognized as a citizen of Palestine. You, your wife and your child."

"And?"

"And you get to avoid Cyprus? You gain a year at least!"

Baruch smiles, pleased by Saul's prediction and assurances. But just then another man joins in, a tall, thin fellow with a sour grimace on his face as though plagued by precautions. He says:

"I don't consider it such an achievement. By rights you shouldn't have let your wife travel in that condition."

"Why not? Don't listen to him!" a bystander adds.

The tall, thin man explains himself:

"Because you never know what'll happen along the way. And that's not even considering the British, or the weather."

"What's the weather got to do with anything?" asks Saul.

"You think it's always going to be as smooth as a river? Just wait until we get out into open waters, you'll see what the weather can do out there in the Mediterranean . . . "

"Pipe down, preacher-man!" Saul interrupts, "no one wants to hear it!"

But the preacher is not yet ready to pipe down. The argument looks set to continue, but in another corner of the ship, near the iron barrier, several rows of passengers have gathered to watch the sea.

The ship is far from the coastline. There is no sign of land on the horizon. The sea lies stretched out like a blanket of glass. Overhead—a deep blue sky; underneath—gently lapping velvet waves.

Enchanted by this beautiful spectacle someone began to sing Yehuda Halevi's Songs of the Sea. Other voices begin to join in and the melody resounds around

the ship—a powerful choral hymn to the azure sky and
the blue waters below:

> I have forgotten all I love,
> I have left my own home;
> I gave myself up to the sea—
> Carry me, sea, to my mother's lap! . . .

> The sea grew angry,
> Twisting and wriggling.
> Suddenly it roars out,
> And it sways and growls.

The voices of the Ma'apilim increase in volume and
intensity. It feels as though the sky, the sea, the soaring
sea-birds, and all of creation have a part to play in the
song.

Yehuda Halevi's song, the powerful poetic ode to
the sea which he composed while sailing to the Land
of Israel eight hundred years ago, now feels prescient
and prophetic:

> And here they come,
> Wild, enraged, with white foam,
> Waves of lions, waves of snakes,
> Growing out of the abyss.

> Here a valley opens up,
> Here stands a tall mountain—
> Quiver, sail, bend, O mast,

While you my heart remains steadfast.

You have a mighty God in heaven,
Who splits the seas with his bare hand;
On his wings with this storm,
He carries you to your dear Land.

When the bell rings calling for the evening meal the passengers make their way to their places, rejoining their groups or factions. The representatives and kitchen helpers bustle up and down the stairs, carrying enormous pots and ladles, hastily distributing the cooked food. The hungry passengers pounce on the food as soon as it is served. They eat their bowls clean and swallow bread without chewing it. They lick every last drop of compote from their fingers. Some of the young boys raise their voices:

"A free trip to Palestine, and a fine meal like this to boot! Who needs visas!"

"Don't think it's going to be free lunches forever."

"The trip is twelve days, right? Then that's twelve good lunches!"

A youth rubs his hands together, "due to all the waiting it's been eight days since we had a warm meal on board."

"Yet we can't gorge ourselves, boys. I can't stand excess," calls out one particularly difficult individual, a dour, humorless fellow.

"Glutton and drunkard! Complaining about the food? You're not talking to a UNRRA[20] official!"

"I'm talking to you!"

"You can talk like that to me, sure. But don't open your mouth like that to the Haganah men. They can send you right back to where they found you."

As they speak, a pale young man with a scar on his face approaches. He does not speak Yiddish, does not speak Hebrew. Nevertheless he has something to say in this argument, and so does his best with shrugs and hand gestures. It transpires that he is a Hungarian Jew. Someone finds him another Hungarian to interpret.

All he wants to say is that the bread is good, the soup is hearty and the meat is delicious. What a sin it is for people who come from a breadless continent to complain about the food! It was a miracle that he'd made it to the ship at all and if someone had told him he would have to fast during the whole journey he would not have complained. "I swear it, or my name isn't Endre Pardosz!"

And how had Endre Parsosz, the estranged Jew, ended up on an illegal ship?

It is a story far removed from the monotonous.

Endre Parsosz went through three concentration camps and was left as little more than a shell of a man. His wife and children were turned to ash in Auschwitz. After the liberation of Hungary, Endre Pardosz became a tram-driver in Budapest, traversing the streets of the

20 United Nations Relief and Rehabilitation Administration.

liberated capital. One day he noticed his tram filling up with people—men and women burdened with back-packs and bundles. Out of curiosity he asked them:

"Where are you all going?

"We're going to Palestine!"

"Where is Palestine?"

"Several thousand miles from here."

"And could I also go to Palestine?"

"If you want to you can also come."

"What do I need to travel there."

"A rucksack and a bundle."

"Is that all?"

"That's all."

"Wait for me, I'm coming with you!"

Pardosz dropped them off at their stop and asked them to wait for him. He then drove his tram to the terminus and joined the Ma'apilim. That same evening he reached the nearest port.

With the coming of night tension on board once again begins to rise in preparation for welcoming the remaining seven hundred passengers, from another port this time. From which? The radio operator is still waiting for the signal.

The signal comes. The captain is asleep so the signal is passed on to one of the Haganah agents. When the ambitious captain—who had wanted gas-masks and smoke bombs—finds out that they did not want to wake him to give him the message, he begins to shout, accusing the crew of conspiring against him. What kind of captain can he be after all, if he's not even trusted with knowing the name of the port he's supposed to drop anchor in. All attempts to calm him down are futile.

Later, when the stars are out and the lighthouses begin to guide the ship ashore, the captain regains his composure.

Transgressions are forgiven. Hatchets are buried.

The loading of the remaining passengers takes place amid howling winds and uneasy clouds.

It is the second night of the clandestine activity. The Ma'apilim arrive in rubber dinghies. The dinghies bob up and down on the waves like balloons. Silence reigns. All of creation seems to lend a hand in the operation: the moon is hidden away. The stars are out of sight.

The icy winds blow the refugees toward the ship.

Later, when our ship—packed with over 1,500 passengers—reaches the open sea, it sails with pride and grace, as though it were king over the waters.

The elated crew members break out into a song, which reaches the waves, as far as the heavens:

"Clean up the waves, Britannia, Ma'apilim ships are coming!"

18

THE BIRTH OF THE FIRST MA'APILIM CHILD

I record everything that happens on the ship with the vigilance of a barometer recording changes in air-pressure, or a seismograph picking up the tiniest movements of the earth's surface. Sudden events break the monotony which hangs like a lazy cloud over the decks. Every passenger is an enemy of monotony and a disciple of surprising, even fantastic, news.

In the pursuit of entertainment there are already various rumors making waves as they circulate over the ship. The passenger who seeks excitement tends to spread these rumors in order to pass the time and amuse others.

This is how on the third day of the voyage the news proliferates that the Revisionists, who represent a large number of the passengers, are planning to seize control of the ship. These rumors keep 1,500 Ma'apilim bewildered for hours. How can a group of passengers organize a mid-sea putsch and take over a ship that is the property of the Haganah? It's hard to fathom.

It is difficult to grasp for the ordinary folk, but not for those adept at theorizing, speculating and hair-splitting to transform the unbelievable into reality.

The plot is the hot topic of the day. There is no faction on the ship that doesn't have its own opinion or position on the matter. Speaking in hushed tones in small circles, they gather in every corner, in every doorway letting their voices be heard.

Learned men from Aguda and from Mizrachi, Marxists from the leftish parties, all discuss the issue aloud as though it were the most important event in world history since the atomic bomb.

"Nonsense! Pure nonsense!" bellows a Hungarian Jew with a Russian-style goatee, "they haven't the slightest chance of success."

"Success or no success, they're going to give it a shot!" his opponent cries.

"Let them try! They'll get their hands burned!"

"Burned? They'll have them blown clean off!" screams a man, whose hair is tied up in two bristly bunches, which protrude from his head vertically like horns.

"Do you know what it would mean for the Revisionists to try and start something with the Haganah? They'll be wiped out!"

"You think there'll be a civil war on the ship?"

"If it can happen, it will happen!"

"That's the thanks they get for welcoming them onto the ship?"

"They should never have been allowed on board!"

"Let them find their own ships!"

A middle aged man approaches and holds out his hands with fingers outspread.

"Tell me, Jews, I am naive about such things. How exactly does a conspiracy happen on a ship?"

"Like any conspiracy!" comes a curt reply.

"And the captain has nothing to say about it?" wonders the naive man.

"The captain's got a gun to his head."

"And the crew?"

"The crew will be overpowered."

"And after that?"

"Then the conspirators will take over all the positions and lead the ship in the direction they want."

The naive man does not yet follow:

"Tell me, Jews, what's the sense in wanting to take over the ship? Revisionists or not, the destination remains the same: Palestine."

"The sense is the Revisionists want to take all the credit for taking a shipload of Jews to Palestine."

This last explanation does not help ease the tensions. The situation looks bad. The misunderstanding grows. In the heat of the discussion the consensus conclusion is that the best thing to do would be to perform a thorough search of the Revisionists quarters and confiscate any weapons thereby avoiding the danger by rendering them harmless.

Before the suggestion reaches the captain's ears the rumors had already made their way to him. The captain, who is ready to fight with the English battleships, is not afraid of the Revisionist conspiracy. Plots are of no importance, but as the father-figure of the ship he feels responsible for his passengers. If the rumors are true that the Revisionists have weapons he is worried that if the British do succeed in taking the ship, and some of the Revisionists use their revolvers, it will provoke the British to open fire, putting Jewish lives at risk.

Such a danger, such a risk must be avoided at all costs.

No sooner does the captain share his concerns with the Haganah agents than they reassure him that the strictest safety measures had been taken back in the port towns.

The Revisionist passengers were searched three times before they were allowed on board.

The sound of guitars and mandolins drifts down from the promenade deck. A circle of ghetto fighters are singing religious songs, while behind them two dozen enthusiasts dance a hora without rhyme or reason.

Behind the captain's bridge several women are sitting with their children, listening to the melodies of the guitars and mandolins, to the tapping of the hora, sharing tragic tales of the past. The dark nightmares of the past do let up even on this escape ship. One life will not be enough to tell all the horrors they have witnessed.

The most tragic thing to happen to the Ma'apilim families was being torn apart. A father sent to the gas chambers, while a mother remains in a concentration camp with their child. The child—the lucky one—is entrusted to the care of a good-hearted Christian until the storm passes . . .

The good-hearted Christian could give the child only what she had to give, and so the child grows up alienated. Not being a freethinker, the Christian takes the child to church, and the result was fatal.

When the mothers returned to find their children they had to fight with tooth and nail. A fight that cost them rivers of tears, prayers and fantastic sums of ransom money. And when the ransomed children finally made it home they were drawn to the outside world, to the pulpit and the church.

One mother recounts how, after the liberation, when she was telling her neighbors about her tragic experiences, about the Holocaust in her village where the Jews were expelled and the synagogue was burnt down, where the rabbi was hanged—when she began to cry her alienated daughter was unable to comprehend her mother's tears and called out:

"Mama, why are you crying about the rabbi? The priest is still alive!"

A second mother tells a story about her last Seder, in a camp in Italy. The first night of Passover was celebrated in full style: decorated tables; a holiday mood among the guests; bottles of wine on the table; silverware sparking, the plates, the pristine white table clothes, the kiddush-cups, the decorated walls—all lent the seder an exceptional holiday atmosphere.

The cantor, a tall, beaming man who was there to lead proceedings, sat at the head of the table. He wore a high velvet yarmulke with a golden Star of David, a white kittle with a silver trim.

In this story the girl, the uprooted Jewish child, was so enchanted by the set up that she said, in Polish, to the guests around her:

"In our church there was also a priest, but this one if far more elegant ..."

One final illustration of the effect a couple of years estrangement can have on the lives of the tragically few child survivors in Europe:

A minyan of mourners visits the home of a bereaved Jew during the seven days of Shiva. A nine-year old girl is wandering around, a former hidden child. She watched the men wrap themselves in tefillin. The prayer leader prays in front of a lectern. A torah is opened and the girl stands there gaping. Someone turns to the girl and asks her in Polish:

"Hanke, why don't you pray too?"

"Give me an idol and I'll pray to it," the girl answers.

Someone hands her a little statue of Herzl which happened to be on a nearby desk. The girl grasped the little Herzl in her hands, dropped down to her knees and began her prayer ...

Those estranged Jewish children, those returnees from the Gentile households from the churches and from the conversion chambers ...

Suddenly the ship begins to rock. Waves splash onto the upper decks. In the evening, the sea had already swayed with the storm. Sea-sick passengers begin to knock on the doors of the clinic. Here and there, passengers have begun to throw up their lunches. Those who were afraid go down underneath to lie in their beds. Those with more experience walk briskly on the top deck, breathing in as much fresh air as they can.

The rocking ship and the swelling waves however are not concerned with the movements on deck. In the bustle, the passengers do not neglect their hygienic duties. They wash themselves by the open taps and take showers by overturning basins of water.

Men shave in front of tiny mirrors hung on pipes and chimneys. Volunteer hairdressers, bored of idling, offer to cut people's hair for free.

An old Galician barber reports to the captain's bridge with a letter of recommendation, saying that in Vienna, in the old days, all the members of Franz Josef's court would come to him. He offers his services to the whole crew. He requests the privilege of being able to use his tools on the heads of the sailors. The honored job is his. Within minutes the small deck of the captain's bridge is transformed into a barbershop. The chief engineer is the first to receive a haircut, followed by the others.

The captain does not submit himself to the scissors, for fear that cutting his hair will bring bad luck. Superstition gains the upper hand. He makes a pledge with himself not to cut his hair until the voyage is over.

The Galician barber, coiffeur to the Austrian court, evidently knows his craft, as soon candidates start appearing from the ranks of the passengers, with towels around their necks, all ready for their own haircuts.

The tired barber glowers at them with a look as though they had lost their minds, and growls:

"Your audacity, gentlemen, is unbelievable! You want me to cut your hair on the *kapitanski most* (the captain's bridge)?"

The closer it gets to nightfall the stormier the sea becomes. The waves rise up like walls, raining down over the upper decks, spraying the promenade deck, and the sailors begin to forecast a nasty night ahead.

Amid the commotion, amid the rocking of the waves, comes the news that a child has been born, a boy.

The first-born child of the refugee ship. The passengers have known for three days of a woman on the verge of going into labor. They knew she was in pain, that they may need to perform a cesarean section. But here between the sky and the water they did not know if the doctor could be trusted.

The concern for the mother and the mistrust of the doctor were so great that women were praying to God for the birth to be delayed until they landed.

Now that the boy is born the surprise has turned to joy.

Women whose babies were born in the forests, while stealing across borders to the sound of air-bombings, are envious of the new mother. People are saying that a child born on a ship is like a prince: all borders, all countries are open to him. No frontiers for someone born in the bosom of the sea. Every flag will protect him. He is a citizen of the world.

Know-it-alls on board say that because we are sailing under a Honduran flag that the newborn infant is a Honduran citizen. But he will also become a citizen of the new Jewish Homeland, Italy, France, Egypt and all the countries that border the Mediterranean.

Partisan mothers who had gone through their labors in fox holes, in the caves of death do not envy the boy his destiny. But they regret the bitter lots of their own children. The first undrunk milk will never be regained. The first food, which they lacked, cannot be gotten back.

Night washes away the envy. The raging waves wash away the resentment. The ship rocks between mighty waves and stormy winds.

19

THE START OF THE SABBATH

The passengers' curiosity to know the ship's location, and the direction it is going, began on the very first day, ever since we passed the Adriatic sea and entered deeper open waters.

With each passing hour the tension mounts. The further we get from any sign of land, the greater the excitement and anticipation. There is an agreement between the Haganah and the crew that, at any given moment, the passengers must not know what country's territorial waters they are passing through, how far they are from the shore, or which day the landing will take place. They must not know these details, just as they must not know the names of the captain and crew.

These things must be kept secret for security reasons but the Ma'apilim are impatient. Anything that can break the monotony is a good way to pass the time.

After five days of endurance, and suppressing their excitement, groups begin to gather on deck to speculate: where in the world are we? The ship has to stop somewhere. What stretch of water are we in now?

A Hasidic Jew from Krakow, with a light, scruffy beard and bi-focal lenses on his nose, is the most boisterous debater among those groups.

He holds his tangled beard in his hand and begins to rant:

"Listen up, you won't pull the wool over my eyes. You want to know where we are?"

"Let's hear it then," someone cries out.

"What difference does it make to you? It's a military secret. But I know!"

"If you know—talk!"

"You can rely on me. I know my geography . . . I knew when we passed the Strait of Messina. I was awake the night we sailed past Corsica. I didn't sleep through the Sardinian islands either . . ."

"If you know so much, and you're such an expert in geography," a young Mizrachi shouts, "then where are we now?"

"When we see land, I'll tell you."

"There's land over there," someone says, pointing a finger.

The gathered people turn as one to gape in the direction indicated. Far in the distance, barely visible through the fog, the contours of the shore emerge. The Jew from Krakow squints. He removes his glasses, wipes them and puts them back on his nose. He stares, squints and eventually shrugs:

"It's too far away. I need binoculars."

"I don't need any binoculars," cries out a skinny bald man. "I'll tell you where we are. How many days have we been at sea now? This is our sixth day? When did we leave Italy? A week ago? What day is it today? Friday?"

His calculations continue for some time. He stares into the sky like a stargazer, even though it is broad daylight.

He measures up the water with a half-closed eye as though trying to ascertain the distance between the ship and the shore, before announcing solemnly:

"We are in the area of Greece!"

"And you don't need to prove that somehow?" someone comments.

The skinny bald man takes his opponent by the hand and answers him in a low voice:

"Do you see that strip of land? That is Greece! I recognize it a mile off! I could recognize it over a whole ocean. I fought there in the First World War. I was a German soldier.

Someone bursts into laughter. The circle divides. Those who believe stay where they are, while those with doubts back away a few steps.

The Irish sailor Hugh McDonald is passing on deck wearing blue trousers and sandals, naked from the waist up.

Mac is as strong as Samson, and as red as Adam.[21] Mac is the most popular sailor among the passengers. He laughs when he should be serious. He smiles when

....

21 The idiom is based on the etymological link between the Biblical Adam and the red clay from which he is said to have been formed.

he should be stern. From him—they are sure—they can get, if not complete information, then at the very least a clue.

A black-haired boy from the Ihud faction plucks up the courage and asks Mac:

"Tell us, sailor, whereabouts are we now?"

"I don't know," the red-skinned sailor says.

"You mean to say they're hiding the ship's course from you too?"

"That they are!"

"You're joking! Any sailor can read the maps, and any mariner can interpret the charts."

"True enough. But it is in the interest of our work to know little and understand even less."

"Honest to God, that's the right answer," shouts a Czech Jew, wearing heavy clothes like a mountain-climber. "Why is it so important to you all to know the position of the ship? Why do you have to know what's cooking in another man's pot?"

Another Jew seconds the objection:

"That's how it is! The less you ask the less you know, the better the chances of us landing."

"Oh, if only we could be sure of landing!" an elderly Jews says, holding both hands up as in prayer.

"Our ship will land." the Irish sailor assures the crowd.

"And the British blockade?"

"There won't be a blockade!"

"There won't be a blockade?"

Two women, hitherto silent listeners to the conversation, smile sweetly and say:

"We're under no illusions; we know we'll be taken to Cyprus. And we're ready for it."

"You mean Cyprus is unavoidable?" someone asks.

"We can't avoid it. It's the seventh circle of Hell we have to pass through to reach Palestine!"

It is already afternoon. A few hours before the ritual lighting of the Sabbath candles, and the territories of the Aguda and Mizrachi Jews are already abustle. A dilemma presents itself. The mitzvah of lighting the candles is of utmost importance, but how to proceed?

Down below, among the wooden perches, among the bunks, fire is not allowed. There is not a spare inch of space to be had. It is a wonder that such a small cargo ship could overnight be transformed to carry over 1,500 passengers. And it carries them obstinately. On legal passenger ships there are smoking rooms, dance halls, rooms for card games, cinemas, even a synagogue with Torah scrolls. While here on this floating Tent of Israel?

But one must not be held back by the circumstances. Two representatives from Mizrachi and two from Aguda come to the captain asking for a place for the women to perform the benediction of the candles.

The captain is aghast. His fear of fire is so great he seeks consultation with the chief engineer who is responsible for all things fire, light and water. The Haganah agents intervene. A newspaper man, who has been recording all events on board over the last twenty-four hours, approaches.

The discussion is short. The ruling—favorable. Permission is granted to bless the candles with the condition that all possible precautions are taken to prevent a fire.

The crew's dining room is requisitioned for the task. Every woman wanting to light a candle must provide a half-candle with a trimmed wick. Empty cans of fruit are placed along the table instead of the missing candlesticks. The iron doors are shut. Two volunteer guards stand at either end of the table, surveilling that the wind does not catch the candles and blow the flames as far as the wooden walls.

One by one, the women proceed down the steps leading to the dining room, in order to welcome the Sabbath.

The women come in their weekday headdresses, in head-scarves and in silk bonnets. They come in Sabbath clothes, in floral shawls. One after another they light the candles, piously place their hands over their eyes, and with awe move their lips. The women who will invite the Holy Sabbath into the belly of the ship.

A quarter hour later a few hundred Jews gather on the top deck to greet the Sabbath by praying *Maariv*. Observant Jews come and secular Jews, the extremely pious, and apostates. People stream across every ladder. There is a great urge to demonstrate the transition from the workaday six days to the sacred day of rest.

The melodic voices of *Lechu Neranena* mingle with the lapping of the waves.

Afterward, the leader of prayers climbs up to the captain's bridge to thank the ship's father-figure.

"Bravo to you, captain. Do you know what it means for our Jewish women to bless the candles on the way to the Land of Israel?"

"I know."

"No evil powers could contend with such a Sabbath. Captain, the mitzvah is a great one!"

"The mitzvah might be great, but in the meantime, the ship is at risk!"

"On account of the mitzvah the ship will evade the British, captain!.

"Let's hope it will!"

The solemnity of the Friday evening does not end with the prayers. All groups and factions on the ship retire to their corners to seek amusement. The promenade deck fills up with the lively youth from Hashomer Hatzair. It just so happens that this Friday coincides with the second anniversary of the war's end, a war that annihilated millions of innocents and martyrs. The survivors prepare to celebrate the date on the open deck of a refugee ship.

An enormous circle of human bodies, intertwined threefold, fourfold sixfold, forms around the barriers. Reflectors glow on either side of the ladders; overheard, a sky full of stars. And at the center of this circle of spectators stands an emaciated Ma'apil, recounting the years of the *Umschlagplätzer*, the ovens, the systematic extermination of the Jewish people.

The emaciated Ma'apil begins to go through a horrifying inventory. He weighs and measures the extent of the destruction. How dreadfully unequal the difference is! Hundreds on ships to freedom, and millions of dead turned to ash, spread over desolate fields and forests!

His memorial is the bloodless interest paid by the living to the dead. It is the Ma'apilim's kaddish to the scattered graveyards of Europe.

Guitars and violins play, their cords containing the reblossoming of Zion. The sorrowful dirge holds the echo and the warning that the things done to the Jewish nation will never be forgotten.

Girls declaim poems with melancholy voices—sad, mournful verses. They lack the elementary power of song. Not one of the screamed poems reaches a high poetic standard, but they make the hairs stand up on your neck nevertheless when your ears capture their gloomy syllables.

A young refugee girl declaims a poem in Polish: "It is quiet in Europe." So goes the sorrowful refrain, repeated on the lips of a pale girl who, that evening, looks for all the world like a Biblical Rachel, a weeping mother . . . "It is quiet in Europe . . . no Jews there anymore. No traders on the markets, no one selling bagels, no herring-mongers . . . no traveling salesmen, no factory owners, no students, no scholars . . . it is quiet in Europe, oh how horribly quiet!"

In another corner of the ship, the Revisionist camp gather to remember the celebration of the recently ended Lag b'omer. Some of them put on the uniform of Betar. The organizers want to add color to the occasion and celebrate historical heroes: Bar Kochva, Reb Akiva, the uprising against the Romans.

A speaker stands up. His speech is a military one against the British occupier. It contains—to everyone's surprise—no negative words about the opposing Jewish factions. Instead the speaker calls for unity in the hour of reckoning against the enemy, recalling that civil wars brought on the destruction of the temple, and the destruction of the Jewish people is what the enemy wants.

The terror of the Holocaust inspires a deep silence. The silence infects the hundreds of listeners. It infects the ever jolly crew who are here as part of the crowd. The silence even infects the sea, which becomes flatter, swallowing its own waves, and rocking as tranquilly as a river.

20

PREPARING TO RESIST

For three days now the ship has been following the Turkish coast without sign of anything suspicious. No surveillance planes pass overhead. The optimists among the crew are feeling hopeful. The captain is confident that his strategy—his plan to take the ship on a detour and approach through the Turkish back door to evade the British—is working; this causes him to turn his mind back to his revolutionary plans for future sea crossings.

He does not forget to reiterate his demands to the leadership of the underground fleet: smoke canisters, gas masks, and iron spikes to ram English ships if they should get too close.

The captain is full of enthusiasm. This does not stop the Haganah agents from beginning to prepare their defense plans for a British attack. First, all the loose or insecure materials on deck are removed. The makeshift toilets, the wash-rooms, even the wooden cabins full of bunks are dismantled and taken away. The demolition work is carried out at an unprecedented tempo. The noise of sawing and hammering is relentless. In little more than an hour the ship regains its appearance as a regular cargo ship.

There is still a long distance between the Turkish shores and Haifa. They calculate that, without British interference, the ship will reach Palestine in two days' time. Feverish preparations are underway on the Palestinian coast for our arrival. The radio picks up one secret message after another. Contact is maintained in an almost unbroken flow or information, with new instructions coming on the hour. Groups of people gather on deck. The optimists have the floor:

"The time is coming!

"All of Palestine is waiting for us!"

"We were orphans in the concentration camps," one man says, "we were step-children in the camps, but here, near the shores, we will become a part of the Yishuv."

A thin woman with a pockmarked face wrings her hands with a groan, "please let the landing succeed!"

"I dunno, I don't believe in superstitious humbug," an excitable man shouts, "but my heart tells me this time it's gonna happen!"

"Why shouldn't it happen?" the first man says, with an expression on his face of one who knows secrets. "Look, it's the first time a Haganah ship has approached from the opposite direction. It won't even occur to the British to go sniffing around in this area."

"Let's hope so! From your mouth to God's ears!"

"What do you mean—in the opposite direction?" another asks.

The knower of secrets takes him by the arm and points to the shore:

"You see that land there?"

"I see it."

"It's safe to let the secret out now: we are sailing through Turkish waters . . . instead of taking the short route from Italy to Haifa, we've taken the long way around.

"So?" asks the naive man.

"So we've lost five days, but the route is safer. There are no British ships in the area."

The circle hangs on the man's every word as though he were privy to all those secret communications. He feels elevated in his position and with a conspiratorial grimace he continues:

"There's something else I know. On the shores of Tel Aviv, Haifa and all over Haifa Bay the whole population is waiting for us . . ."

"How can the whole population wait?"

The knower of secrets makes use of his two large hands to explain the situation further:

"Do you understand how a landing works? The captain is waiting for a signal telling him where to go . . . let us say for instance that a signal comes from Palestine telling him to turn toward Tel Aviv. It happens to be Saturday. The beaches are full of people bathing . . . we drop anchor and we all run ashore, removing our clothes and mingling with the bathers . . . people in bathing costumes are hard to tell apart."

"And what if we have to land somewhere else?" someone asks.

"In that case someone will be waiting for us with trucks. The whole Yishev waits for us . . . the whole nation is waiting . . . they'll load us onto the trucks, we make tracks and spread out all over the country."

"That sounds like a more logical plan."

"As long as we make a landing we're winners!" assures the knower of secrets.

In the middle of this heated discussion, the Haganah agents arrive and begin organizing resistance groups.

The carpenters among the refugees are occupied. The locksmiths are put to work. Installers and mechanics have their hands full. Wood is being cut, sticks are transformed into clubs. Pipes and iron bars are turned into blunt defensive weapons to use against the enemy.

The chief engineer emerges from the engine room accompanied by several sailors and begins to set up barriers and fencing around both sides of the ship. The stairs leading to the lower decks are blocked off with barbed wire. The ladders leading to the promenade deck, the searchlight tower, and the captain's bridge are smeared with oil and grease. All conceivable pitfalls are put in place to hinder or at least to slow down the British in the event they board the ship.

In every corner of the ship resistance groups begin their training. The Haganah agents, like commanders, give instructions on how to use the weapons if the struggle escalates. The rehearsals are in full swing.

The resistance groups, made up of many partisans, ghetto fighters, veterans of Stalingrad, Sebastopol, and Warsaw are enraged by the mere prospect of having to confront the British. Voices are raised:

"Let's break open their skulls!"

"We'll throw them into the sea!"

"Such brigands, pirates that they are!

Down below in the engine room, all the walls, and even some of the machinery, are covered in insulting anti-British graffiti, with furious protests and nationalistic slogans.

Everything is set up so that the arrival of the British should be as unwelcoming and painful as possible.

Alongside the preparations for defense, the passengers are ordered to go down to the lower decks and to wait there until the time comes for the ship to land. To compensate for the fact that the lower decks are stuffy and uncomfortable the passengers receive extra rations of cigarettes, chocolate and chewing gum.

In this mood of preparation the ship continues along the Turkish coastline, a wasteland where hills peak out of the green fog, an expansive hinterland in a world where wars are waged over small stretches of land.

The same night a signal is intercepted from Palestine with orders, including, for the first time, a name for the ship: The Lord James Balfour.

Each ship sails with a foreign name, under a foreign flag for most of its journey. But a couple of days before the end it receives a Jewish name, decided by the Haganah commanders in Palestine. A Jewish flag is unfurled and thus the ship arrives on the shores of the Promised Land.

This time the ship receives the name: Balfour.

Though it's already past midnight, this news spreads throughout the ship. The crew and Haganah agents are dissatisfied. Almost everyone joins in the dispute: Why "Balfour" when the heirs of Balfour are right now blocking the borders of the country? Now as they sabotage the legacy of Balfour?

Over an hour the discussion lasts: Why Balfour? After the White Paper, and Cyprus?

But orders from Palestinian headquarters are orders which must be obeyed. Two painters are told to paint two large "Balfour" banners to be hung from the Captain's Bridge. Simultaneously a message is sent back to headquarters voicing the crew's dissatisfaction with the choice of name.

Suddenly screams ring out from down below. Some women are running around, wringing their hands. The closed doors of the clinic burst open. A sixteen year-old boy is led out of the engine room; he has severed a finger. The accident happened to a helper in the engine room. The Ma'apilim always want to make themselves useful when they come aboard. They help in the kitchen, on the captain's bridge, and in the engine room.

Leybl, an ambitious orphan boy from Warsaw who was helping out with the oil furnaces, got his hand caught in the machinery. His recklessness cost him half an index finger, which is still dangling by a piece of bone. The panicked doctor does everything he can to give the boy the illusion that he will be able to keep the finger. He applies a splint, bandages the hand and supplements the treatment with a few words of encouragement

The operation to amputate the finger is postponed until Haifa.

It falls upon the nurse to calm the young patient. She holds his hand and strokes his brow, brushing his disheveled hair and comforting him.

She puts every ounce of tenderness and pity that she has into her words of solace.

"Don't cry, Leybele, it's only a wound. You're a soldier and you've been wounded . . ."

"I'm going to lose the finger, aren't' I, nurse!" Leybele cries.

"Only half a finger, Leybele," the nurse said, not wanting to mislead the boy, "and they won't send you to Cyprus because of it. You'll get to stay in Palestine . . ."

The boy continues to cry.

"Are you crying, Leybl? A Ma'apil crying? A soldier on his way to Palestine crying?"

They lay him down on a bed. The nurse sits beside him and speaks to him as to a younger brother:

"Is it not worth half a finger to be allowed to stay in the Promised Land? What's a finger, Leybele? I'd give half a hand . . . remember the oath, Leybele, *If I forget thee, O Jerusalem, let my right hand forget her cunning.*"

The boy dries his tears.

21

AN ENCOUNTER WITH BRITISH BATTLESHIPS

Another day passes. On the second day the ship enters Lebanese waters. That hilly land shimmers in the sun, mountain ranges, like giant camel humps, extending into infinity. Lebanon seems to have taken on an immense expanse, whether because the dread of unseen enemy ships is rising, or because the present hour is stretching out for an eternity. Either way, the whole crew is poised between worry and anticipation.

The sailors are standing at the very edge of the deck. Arable land, divided and cut-up like a chess board extends between chalk hills and orchards. In the valleys shepherds lead their flocks. White houses and tents are scattered over wide areas. Cars the size of ants drive over the roads that snake through the mountains.

Both the crew and some of the more daring passengers are standing ready in swimming costumes, ready in the event they will have to swim a few miles to shore. The captain and the Haganah agents do not leave the radio for even a moment. They wait for instructions from the Palestinian shore.

At nine a signal comes saying the name of the ship has been changed from Balfour to Hatikva—Hope in Hebrew. The two painters set to repainting the banner without delay. The banners will be ready, when the time comes, to cry out the name Hativka from both sides of the captain's bridge.

The deck officer, who is standing guard with the binoculars to his eyes, suddenly turns around and calls out:

"An airplane!"

The eyes of two dozen sailors gaze up to the clouds. It's a plane—the first dismal harbinger indicating that they are on our trail. The plane approaches from the south very high up. The noise is muted at first, like the buzzing of a bee, but the closer it gets, the louder the buzzing becomes until the sound is as loud as a cawing crow. The plane circles high above the ship's smokestack, before coming in lower, banking to the left, then to the right, and performing a hasty somersault. The daredevil whimsy of the plane infuriates the sailors watching from the deck. With balled up fists they scream threats:

"Deceitful British!

"Albion!"

"You won't have it easy from us, pirates!"

Amid the spirals and loops of the agile aircraft it becomes apparent that the messenger from the skies is a piece of American engineering. The sailors who served in the navy recognize the iron bird's form and grace as that of a B-24.

"Can you believe it?"

"It's one of ours!"

"Good old Uncle Sam's been giving out presents . . ."

"Arms for sea-bandits!"

The plane's maneuvers last for many minutes, buzzing around like a wretched fly before finally vanishing into the clouds. Ten minutes later it's back and circling the ship again. Clearly it is taking photographs to be sure it's found its prey. The sailors console themselves that the plane might leave them alone: the decks of the ship have been cleaned up and it looks just like any old cargo ship.

But the consolation is a false one. After a full twenty minutes of circling the plane leaves once again, but half an hour later the consequence arrives. To the south of the Syrian coast,[22] the first British warship makes an appearance, cutting through the water with such speed as though afraid to be late for something.

The sailors are surprised. Even the first ship to chase the Ma'apilim is an American vessel—manned by British pirates. The sailors, the veterans of Uncle Sam's navy are now in their element. They are able to make calculations, judging the distance and speeds that this war ship is capable of. A ship like that can do thirty miles an hour. A swift little devil. What an unfair

....

22 Translator's note: The author seems to be using the words Lebanon and Syria interchangeably, I have maintained his usage throughout.

fight! The top speed of our Ma'apilim ship is seventeen miles an hour.

Soon a second war ship appears behind the first, also bearing down at speed. Then a third, a fourth, a fifth. We count up to six. The ships move in formation as a convoy. The tension among the crew all but gives over into quiet resignation. No one exchanges words. Questions and answers make no sense in moments such as these. The Haganah agents exchange glances with the captain, the captain with the crew. Their glances express mute rage. The deck officer approaches the captain:

"Should we hang up the name?"

"Not yet."

"Should we raise the flag?"

"We'll wait."

They wait. The six warships surround us in a circle. Two of them are close enough for them to observe us through binoculars. Their crewmembers, from the cooks to the captain, are dressed up as though for a parade. They look at us the same way they'd look at Zulu tribesmen. The captain gives the order: it's time to make the ship Jewish, it's time to raise the Jewish flag.

In a matter of minutes the refugee ship is displaying its Jewish name: Hatikva, visible from both sides of the captain's bridge. The flag on the mast heralds the Jewish Homeland as we approach its shores. From the lower decks, from their hiding places, over 1,500 Ma'apilim begin to stream. They flood the decks.

The first warship on the right moves another step closer in our direction. Suddenly a voice calls out. The first cry of our foe—a voice through a megaphone, ringing our over the sea like a bad song:

"Attention! Attention! We sympathize with your suffering! But not one of you may set foot in Palestine illegally! You must understand . . ."

The Ma'apilim on deck prick up their ears. The expression of sympathy draws a mocking response. The warning elicits a shudder. The voice through the loudspeaker speaks in English, but they are soon interpreted into French, German, Yiddish and Hebrew. Not five minutes later a second warning arrives from the enemy's loudspeaker:

"Attention! Attention! We know your ship's course. But the way will be blocked! . . . we invite the women and children to come on board our ship. They will come to no harm . . . we will take them to Cyprus . . . they will receive food, clothing and shelter."

The British ultimatum—which is part invitation, and three quarters threat—is met by the huge audience of Ma'apilim with peals of laughter. But this does not stop the British circling the ship again and giving a third warning:

"Attention! Attention! When our troops board your ship you must not resist. All resistance will be futile . . . it will only cause innocents to suffer . . ."

For a long time the voice from the loudspeaker remains silent. Both ships continue at one and the same stride, the same tempo and rhythm.

The voice from the loudspeaker takes on a pained tone. The voice asks how long we have been at sea. Who the crew is. Where the captain is. They want to speak to the captain!

How logical the words of perfidious Albion sound in this moment! It is only right that when two captains meet in the middle of the sea they should have a little chat . . . A twelve year-old boy grabs a megaphone in his hand like a shofar. He springs up onto the captain's bridge, climbs onto the railings facing the British ship and calls out:

"I'm the captain! I'm the captain! Talk to me!"

Laughter ripples across the deck. But the British loudspeaker does not ignore the twelve year-old Ma'apil's call. The voice continues with suppressed reproach:

"We want to speak to the real captain!"

The real captain of the Ma'apilim ship of late May 1947 no longer exists. The crew no longer exists. The only thing that exists are 1,500 Ma'apilim, full of stamina, and an unwavering determination to reach the shores of Palestine.

The ship is moving along the Lebanese coastline. From up close we can see the fertile land, divided like a chess board. We see the chalk hills and orchards, the houses and white tents. We see the green valleys and the shepherds tending to their flocks.

The six warships follow us. Suddenly a new warning cuts across the water:

"Attention! Attention! Your crew and captain will be arrested and put in prison! We know who you are! We have your photographs! Your good friends the Italians have given you up!"

This is a lie and a provocation. An attempt to instill defeatism in the hearts of the brave Ma'apilim. And when the provocation does not work, and the 1,500 passengers are not prepared to give themselves up with their ship, that is when the British decide to use terror to inspire panic.

All night long the warships shine enormous spotlights on top of those Ma'apilim who, due to the cramped conditions, are sleeping on deck.

The disturbance causes people to move *en masse* to the other side of the deck which disrupts the balance aboard the ship, causing it to lean several times to one side. Clearly this is something the British want. The calculation is a brutal, devilish one: if the refugee ship with its 1,500 lives tips over and begins to sink, the passengers will call for help and then the British ultimatum will become:

"Give yourselves up!"

The sleep-deprived captain runs between decks. 1,500 lives have been entrusted to him. 1,500 people he's promised to lead through all obstacles to safely reach landfall. Now the time for trial by fire has come. The hour of truth. Will he keep his promises?

The captain stands on the bridge. He is calm and confident. In the darkness he addresses the frightened passengers who fill every deck, looking to him for consolation.

As captain he should give orders. But his words are gentle and pleading:

"I would like all passengers to quietly go back to their places. There is no danger. There's no reason to be afraid. Stay calm and be brave, Ma'apilim!"

These words are like a tonic for the bewildered passengers who now obediently return to their beds. The words "be brave, Ma'apilim!" rouses the resolve and buoyed up the nerve of those few hundred Ma'apilim who are not prepared to give up the ship without a fight.

By dawn we have drawn closer to the Syrian coast. The further south toward Palestine our ship reaches, the more audacious the British warships become. They are no longer our escorts, but would-be captors, lying in wait for the right moment to pounce.

22

THE BATTLE BETWEEN THE JEWS
AND THE BRITISH

With each passing mile the appetite for plunder increases. Two of the six warships are moving parallel to our ship, not falling behind for a second. The other four ships follow at a distance.

Though the pincers around us grow tighter and tighter, the crew remains in good spirits. The appetite to tease the enemy grows. Our ship moves with panache, making circles and spirals. The warships think we are pulling back, hesitating over which course to take. Judging by the position of the ships it often appears as though we are the ones chasing the British.

In preparation for the moment of resistance this cat-and-mouse game provides satisfaction and encouragement for the crew.

The British look over to our ship. Resistance groups stand at the barriers, ready to meet the enemy. We look over to their ship. At the front of their deck, behind the barriers, their troops line up, armed from head to toe, as though preparing for a serious battle.

We eye each other up, challenging one another, a moment of the very highest tension.

Smoke is pouring from the captain's cabin. They are hastily burning the maps, charts, documents and strategic plans.

A ladder is attached to the wide smokestack. A sailor quickly paints two symbols there. On one side, a blue Star of David. On the other side, the national emblem of Ireland, a green shamrock.

The deck of the ship looks like a battlefield on the eve of battle. Two doctors stand in front of the clinic. Two dozen or so nurses with red Star of David armbands stand ready at their posts.

A sailor hangs red hospital signs at the entrance to the clinic, and the door of a cabin where a pregnant woman is awaiting labor—a warning for the British not to attack these rooms.

The ship is still following the green Syrian coast. In the distance you can see Beirut.

It is 1p.m.

The ship is twenty-two miles from the Palestinian coast.

Up on the captain's bridge, the helmsman hastily turns the ship south, seeking a way out of the predicament. The captain in his room stands bent over his charts. The radio operator has stopped sending messages and cut the lines with the outside world.

Suddenly a roaring splash of water is heard cutting through the silence.

The British warships are sending dark clouds toward us. A hasty clap on the wall, a resounding crash against the protective barriers and the confrontation has begun. Their troops swiftly begin to climb over the barriers of our ship. They are armed to the teeth with steel helmets on their heads and metallic gloves all the way up to their elbows. They have rifles and clubs, as well as heavy loaded pistols hanging by their sides.

From the moment they start climbing they make use of their clubs. The resistance groups begin banging their sticks and iron bars and move to protect the barriers from the invaders. A few British troops manage to make it over the barriers, while others fall into the sea. There are a series of bangs—the British fire warning shots into the air. The defenders take a step back. Afraid that they are being fired upon, they begin beating the intruders without mercy. Bloody faces are seen on both sides. The nurses begin seeing to the wounded; friend and foe alike are led to the clinic.

The air is filled with enfeebled voices, women screaming.

The British, fearing a long, drawn-out fight, begin launching gas bombs. A white cloud rises, enveloping everything in a thick fog.

People become breathless, their skin and eyes begin to sting. It's impossible to see. Refugees, reminded of the gas chambers of Poland, start beating the enemy with increased ferocity.

Cries ring out:

"Oh, I can't see!"

"We're going blind!"

"Don't rub your eyes!"

"Put wet cloths over your eyes!"

"Go up for fresh air!"

"Everyone out!"

From below deck, streams of women and children begin to pour out with damp cloths over their eyes, pushing and shoving to get to fresh air, where the smoke dissipates faster. Every now and then a defender succeeds in throwing a gas bomb back into the faces of the British who are as powerless to resist as their victims.

Row after row of British troops arrive, one by one gaining ground on the ship's deck. They secure certain positions on the deck and begin to bring aboard small machine guns which are placed at strategic positions: on the roof of the captain's bridge, on the promenade deck.

In sight of the oncoming British the defenders increase their resistance. The more ground the enemy is able to take, the harder the defenders fight. Every punch falls like a hammer clap.

The commotion grows. The British tighten their hold on the positions they have taken and with the butts of their rifles begin to smash the wooden decks. The cries of the women and children rise up to the heavens. The orders coming in from all sides drown out the cries for help:

"Don't let them gain another step!"

"Push them back!"

"Don't forget, they are the aggressors!"

"Women and children back down below!"

"Defend the ship, Ma'apilim!"

"Beat the enemy!"

"Sailors, advance!"

"Freedom for the People of Israel!"

"We will reach the Promised Land!"

The resisters protect the upper cabins like an iron wall. The fighters—some of them veterans of Stalingrad, defenders of Moscow, uprisers from the ghetto—use their bodies to block the entrances to the lower decks. Passage to the captain's bridge and the engine room is also blocked.

The resisters fight for every inch of the ship, as though it is not a ship, a floating refugee tent, but the Promised Land itself. Such zeal, the likes of which was demonstrated by the guards of Yodfat, or the heroes of Masada, or the defenders of Betar.

From below deck the Irish sailor, Mac, rushes out in a state of agitation. He jumps up to the promenade deck and with his bare hands tears down the wire netting on which a small machine gun rests. In the blink of an eye he slings the machine gun into the sea, along with the British sailor to whom it belongs.

The captain's bridge is protected by a group of partisans, under the supervision of the Polish sailor, Duke.

The Duke enthusiastically beats back the British boarding party. With each blow to the helmet another boarder falls back toward the barrier whereupon a partisan is there to take over and throw him overboard.

Gas bombs are falling all around, and those who launch the canisters receive a merciless thrashing from Duke whenever he gets his hands on them.

Cheering him on are a group of bruised and battered sailors. They shout out:

"Lay into 'em, Duke!"

"Make goulash out of him!"

"Beat that lousy Limey!"

"Get those pirates!"

"That'll teach them to attack a refugee ship."

Duke does what he can. The Irishman Mac arrives and distributes new sticks and pipes to the defenders.

Jewish nurses continue to bandage the wounded on both sides.

The British run as though under cannon-fire. They're looking for the stairs that lead to the engine room and stumble around the tangles of barbed wire. Suddenly gas canisters are falling on all sides. A thick cloud spreads out enveloping the bridge, the smoke-stacks, and the resisters who flee in all directions, rubbing their burning eyes, seeking cover from the gas.

Nurses rush forward with buckets of water and cloths.

Once the cloud has dispersed and the 1,500 passengers regain their bearings the resistance has been broken.

The ship is still outside territorial waters. British sailors with weapons are posted on both sides of the deck. The captain's bridge has been occupied. The promenade deck has been captured. A few officers, running through the conquered passengers, seek out the entrance to the engine room but do not find what they are looking for.

The ship and all 1,500 refugees has been taken. A young nurse, a Hashomer Hatzair member, with a half-torn armband runs over the deck though every step is blocked by armed British guards. She manages to slip through far enough to come up close to a British guard and scream the few English words she knows into his face:

"I hate you! I hate you!"

These are the first minutes of the British victory. The guards; unsure whether they are deserving of the young girl's respect or animosity, hold their tongues and continue to wield their loaded weapons in the passengers' direction. Some of them regard the girl with annoyance, others smile as one smiles at the whims of a child.

One of the wounded resisters, a disheveled, sweaty youth who refused a bandage for his bloodied brow, stands opposite the entrance to the clinic. He was captured there in the moment when the resistance was broken and there he is being watched by a British soldier whose revolver is aimed at the man's belly.

The wounded resister does not see the barrel of the gun pointed at him, does not see the danger. His face is contorted in pain and he screams at his captor:

"Do you have a home? Tell me, do you have a home?"

The angry guard does not respond, and moves the gun closer to his prisoner. The young man continues:

"Do you have a home? Tell me, do you have a home?"

"Yes," the guard growls.

"Then why can't I have a home too? Why can't my people have a home?"

This simple human question, which under such circumstances should not by rights receive a response, did receive one. The blunt British guard regarded the boy for a moment and then spat out an answer:

"You deserve a home alright, six foot underground..."

Nearby stands a second armed guard. He is talking to another prisoner who is interrogating him about the moral justifications for capturing an illegal refugee ship.

This guard is far from being blunt; he is a flexible man, a man of compromises. His face is mild. He says to his interlocutor:

"I see you're a cultured man. You are a Jew, but you must understand the British position on letting the Jews form a state in Palestine."

"And what about the Balfour declaration? the Jew demands.

"That was thirty years ago ... nowadays there are political compilations ..."

A group of English officers approaches the passengers and asks, almost pleadingly:

"Where is the engine room? Do you know where the entrance to the engine room is?"

The seamen from "His Majesty's" Royal Navy have taken the ship, but they have not managed to take the engine room because the signage on the doors is misleading. Our sailors and engineers have locked themselves in and are in the process of dismantling the machinery, carrying out their sabotage. The engines are ruined. Later the electric lights go out. The plumbing is destroyed. This destruction brings some measure of vengeance and satisfaction to the saboteurs.

No furnished passenger ship will fall into the hands of the British, but a just about seaworthy wreck of a vessel, without light or water. A dead ship, a floating scrapheap.

23

THE CAPTURED JEWISH SHIP IN HAIFA

For two hours the sailors and engineers remain locked in the engine room. As the battle raged on deck, and long afterward they sat in the suffocating heat and humidity of the boilers and furnaces, preventing the British from taking control of the ship. As time passes, and the boarding party is still unable to break down the door, it is the sailors themselves who blow the hinges off the doors to let themselves out.

A rope is thrown over our captured vessel, and the British warship begins to tug it, tugging its pillage, in the direction of Haifa.

The sea is still. A bright blue color. The tranquil waves stride like fixed quilts of ice. The floating warships have already passed the Syrian border. The northern shores of Palestine open up before us.

As the passengers gaze out toward the shore, doctors slip past unnoticed transporting some badly wounded patients to the clinic. Leaning on the shoulders of two nurses is the tanned, broad shouldered sailor Michael. Michael is a war veteran. He fought for the British Empire, serving in Singapore and Burma. He received a wound to the head and they put a metal plate in his skull. During the fight on the Ma'apilim ship he caught a blow to the head. Blood pours from his wound. The same blood he spilled in service of the British Empire.

Two British sailors arrive in the clinic carrying a British officer on a stretcher. He is in a bad state and in need of a blood transfusion. An English sailor volunteers to donate his blood and the doctor performing the procedure is also English. He was called from the British ship, but the doctor is not up to the task: he is drunk. And so the Jewish doctor, a refugee, is enlisted to take over. The tension between the British and their prisoners abates. The initial mistrust gives way to confidence. The British guards feel relieved. They set down their rifles and holster their revolvers.

Hostilities ended, I take a look around the ship where every deck is covered in captured passengers. I go to the promenade deck where many crew members are and my eye falls on the Duke, who had thrown the British one after another into the water, and so heroically defended the Jewish ship. The Duke is now sad.

I see Mac, the Irish volunteer, the brave sailor of the Jewish fleet, who flung a British machine gun—operator and all—into the sea. Mac too is melancholy.

The heroic sailors, those courageous guardians of the sea, have been captured.

In the crowd I catch the eye of our captain. He is standing like a mourner, dejected and beaten. My gaze lingers on him, unable to break away from his expression of despair. And Heine's poem comes to the surface of my mind.

Heinrich Heine, the estranged Jew among the poets of the world, once wrote a poem about two grenadiers, two French grenadiers. The last of Napoleon's defeated armies in Russia who were marching a retreat, beaten, battered and hungry. Nothing concerned them anymore, nothing disturbed them. On the ruined byways of Russia their world had gone under.

"For wife and child what do I care!" sing the last grenadiers, "As hungry beggars let them fare . . . My emperor, emperor—is fallen!"

This is the defeated mood I see in the eyes of the captain, our conquered, our beaten captain.

His ship, his ship—is fallen!

By now it is evening time. Hundreds of passengers are standing with their faces to the shore. The ship is passing the stone city of Acre. The old town with its prison, like a fortress, is bathed in a fiery evening glow. A small steamer approaches our ship, loaded with food and provisions. They have come to offer food to the hundreds of hungry passengers. It is enough for the British to see the looks on the passengers' faces for the ship to be sent back to where it came from. Food is offered again an hour later and the passengers decline. The drinking water facilities have been dismantled on board, yet the thirsty Ma'apilim do not ask for a drink. The lighting is broken, yet they choose to remain in the dark. This does not discourage the cheerful among the English crew from going around the ship offering chocolate, cigarettes and biscuits to the women and children.

A young sailor approaches a Jewish girl and offers her a block of chocolate.

The girl takes the chocolate, examining with surprise the colorful packaging which bears the Hebrew logo of the Palestinian firm "Elite." She then returns her innocent gaze to the friendly Englishman and hurls the chocolate into his face:

"I don't take gifts from plunderers!"

In the spirit of relief that reigns on deck, an old Jew fusses with his bags. He opens his trunk, rummages about inside for ages until he takes out two Torah scrolls, which he has brought for his sons in Palestine.

The old man calls over a couple of British sailors to his trunk and joyfully points to the scrolls:

"I saved these treasures from Buchenwald."

From the deck hospital a midwife arrives, announcing the news that the second pregnant passenger has just given birth. Another boy born for the new Jewish Homeland.

Night is setting in. The ship slides over the smooth velvety waves. A fire from a lighthouse calls from the shore. Hundreds of passengers stretch out their arms in the direction of Haifa city, which has begun to shine with thousands of lights.

The passengers begin to jostle each other. Someone says:

"Look at Haifa, what a city!"

"A city? It's an empire!"

"Who could have dreamed we'd come this far?"

A Jew with a knotted beard joyously turns from one group to another.

"I see they're preparing a fine welcome for us!"

"The entire British navy is waiting there for us!" another says.

"They don't have anything better to be doing?"

"No doubt we are such a mighty force that the British have put their empire aside for a moment and sent all their sailors over here for us!"

Someone points to something:

"What kind of ships are those?"

"Where do you see ships?"

"Over there! Four ships like fortresses."

"Those are deportation ships."

"To take us away to Cyprus?"

"Where else would they be taking us, to Ophir?" a cheerful lad says.

"I hope I'll give me a nice cabin at least."

A young man in a pair of high boots and a leather jacket shoves the last speaker:

"I see you're in a funny mood!"

"What more do I need? The British will treat me to a free cruise. So many miles spent at sea already, a few more won't kill me."

"For me Cyprus is the Promised Land." someone suggests. "The way I see it, Cyprus is a corridor to Palestine."

"You'll have to stand in the corridor a whole year!" consoles the cheerful lad.

"But I won't have to go back to the German camps?"

"No."

"Then the wait will be worth it!"

Motl—a jolly fellow from Romania, a dancer and singer who used to play Gypsy-romances and rhapsodies every night on his accordion—sits down on his baggage by the entrance to the clinic. He hangs his head and begins to groan.

"What's wrong with you?" a passing woman asks him. "Do you not feel well?"

"I feel like I'm at death's door," Motl says, his eyes glazed over.

"Is it your head?" the woman asks, laying a hand on the boy's forehead.

"My stomach, my belly, my appendix, everything!" Motl groans.

The woman looks at him with a twinkle in her eye and says:

"Are you playing theater, Motele? Trying to convince yourself that you're sick? You're as healthy as a horse!"

"Hush, woman!" says Motl grabbing her lips in his fingers. "Shhh, I want to get off in Haifa . . ."

"Then what are you doing sitting here, get into the clinic and lie down on a bed."

"You won't denounce me?" Motl asks for reassurance.

"Denounce you to the British? May my enemies never live to see such a thing!" the woman swears. "Let one Jew at least make it down to Palestine."

Motl proceeds to an empty cabin and lies down on the bed.

A Polish Jew with a worn, angular soldier's hat pushes his way into the circle, and speaks in a low voice as though he has a secret to tell:

"They say that the deportation ships waiting for us are old, worthless wrecks . . ."

"Don't worry, mister," someone responds, "They have a good uncle, those British, he'll find them some new ships."

"You mean Uncle Sam?"

"Who else would I mean?"

"And why doesn't the uncle send ships for the refugees instead?" a naive man asks.

"Who are you that America should send you ships? An uprooted, homeless person? We're talking about wealthy Britain here!"

"But Britain is a defaulter, let's not forget! They still haven't paid America back for its debts in World War I."

"The rich always get credit, even defaulters!"

It is quiet for a moment. With a pair of pointy elbows a Jew who has hitherto remained silent makes his way to the front of the circle. He does not speak to anyone, only stares a British sailor in the eyes muttering a list of grievances, one after the other, in Yiddish:

"And with the ships they get from the Americans they chase our ship half way across the sea! And with the planes they get from the Americans, they spy on us! Oy, what a world! God in heaven is that any kind of world?"

The ship edges closer to the Port of Haifa. A thousand lights shine over the enormous hilly city. The captured passengers break out into loud song.

The armed British guards standing at their posts are agape: This is how the prisoners of Zion, the Jewish captives sing? No! This is how 1,500 Ma'apilim sing to mark their arrival in their homeland.

Suddenly the chimneys of the six warships whistle. It is a signal from the British ships that they are bringing ashore a captured Jewish vessel.

24

ON THE WAY TO CYPRUS

Over the next six hours, the ship—breathless, shattered and crippled, its motors extinguished like dead entrails—is tied to a warship and slowly tugged ashore. At eight p.m., lit up by searchlights, it finally arrives at the Port of Haifa.

The city of Haifa, scattered over Mount Carmel, spread out over the neighborhood of Hadar, twinkling with a thousand lights, beckons to the refugees, calling them to its shores. The lights speak in letters of fire, and the Ma'apilim break out a spontaneous oath as though they can read the message in the flames: "*If I forget thee, O Jerusalem, let my right hand forget her cunning.*" The chains drag the ship to the port's wooden pier, while the powerful voices of 1,500 refugees belt out the Jewish national hymn.

One by one the singing voices trail off. The passengers, filling the deck with all their bundles and baggage, are preparing to disembark.

The entire length of the port is occupied by British troops, sailors and port inspectors. Military men in their thousands, from the airborne division with their red berets, guard every building and street from the inner city to the port, yet here and there in the distance people can be seen waving their hands and flying makeshift flags: it is the daring children of the Yishuv who have slipped past the patrols to greet the arriving Ma'apilim.

On the pier, near the guard-posts, there is a gathering of correspondents from the Hebrew press, notebooks and cameras at the ready. Soon there is a barrage of flashes as the photographers begin to take pictures.

The work of unloading the passengers begins. Military men in red berets climb aboard on ladders. Once they have taken up positions on deck, the British sailors who captured the ship disembark. It is a changing of the guard.

Minutes later two British doctors arrive followed by medics with stretchers, ready to transport the sick and the wounded.

The medics are helpful and respectful. They knock on one cabin door after another looking for patients. A nurse who serves as a midwife comes. The doctor who serves as an obstetrician came. Sick patients with weak hearts are carried off the ship, as well as the two women ready to give birth. Leybele, the boy with the severed finger is also taken off the ship. The sick, the wounded, the pregnant—they are all spared the banishment to Cyprus. They have earned the privilege of going to hospital and staying in the country.

The first passengers begin to move over the bridge. Their luggage is taken and thrown over to a group of soldiers who perform a feverish search. The passengers, for whom the Promised Land has now become a forbidden land, proceed to the place where the four British deportation ships are waiting for them. The ships destined to return the Jews to their exile bear lofty, imperial names: "The Empire Lifeguard," "The Empire Shelter," "The Empire Comfort," "The Empire Rest."

From the promenade deck Ma'apilim shout down to the journalists, seeking to get in contact with their relatives:

"I'm looking for my relative Zalman Binder!"

"My brother, Chaim Tamari, in Atlit. Let him know!"

"My uncle Yisroel Finkelshteyn doesn't know I was coming with the Ma'apilim . . . send him a greeting! I'll be waiting in Cyprus!"

British guards push the journalists aside, hindering the exchange of information with the passengers. Down below the passengers' pockets are thoroughly searched, after which everyone is led to a military tent where they are sprayed with DDT. From there, the path leads to the deportation ships. Alongside the passengers I slip through the British control. My one suitcase burns in my hand. The British grab my suitcase from me and I proceed swiftly past the spot where the press representatives have gathered. Only a thin barbed-wire fence separates us. It is so hard to keep silent in this moment and so dangerous to speak. I see a few familiar faces. Someone waves at me. The passengers behind me shake their heads at the journalists. What are these signals? Who is waving? Why are they shaking their heads? One careless word and I'm a prisoner of the British. It's good that my notes are hidden, and that I've entrusted my documents to others.

With bated breath I edge forward. Passengers in front of me, passengers behind me. One step followed by another and another and before long we are standing in front of a ship, The Empire Shelter. The first deportation ship is already full, and the second is filling up fast.

In the propaganda the British are spreading against the Jewish sea-crossings, they accuse us of running ships in dangerous and unsanitary conditions. It is enough to take one look at the Empire Shelter to throw those same accusations back in their faces. If lies and swindle are the diamonds in the crown of the British Empire, then hypocrisy is the crown itself. The refugees are packed in like cattle. Mothers with children on their laps. The old, the weak, underaged— everyone crammed together in rooms separated by thin wire divisions. The whole set up resembles stables for livestock. The air is stuffy. In every room a British soldier stands, armed and armored, in a dome-shaped helmet. Each soldier, each "Tommy" sweats like a beaver, but his face remains severe—a steel mask. He does not complain. He is a humble subject of His Majesty's government. Whatever is asked of him, he performs his function like a robot.

The passengers on the other hand *do* complain. They are rebels wherever they go. They agitate in the camps, on trains, in ships. Four young men, as strong as Cossacks, dressed in threadbare gray uniforms, push their way to the front to make their grievances heard. Their complaints are wrapped in scorn and gallows-humor. One man points to the room divisions and asks:

"What's with the cages?"

"You expect us to endure fourteen hours here?" asks a pregnant woman.

"We're not enduring, we're enjoying a pleasure cruise to the Promised Island," interjects a voice with a hearty laugh.

"Compared to this death-trap the Hatikva was a luxury Yacht!"

"You can say that again, we might as well have been living in a palace!"

The deportation ship is spick and span on the outside, but a pig-sty on the inside.

"A plague on Britain's house and a pox on the Empire if this is all they have!" comes a groan.

Instead of stewards, soldiers go from one cage to the next distributing tea and dry rusks. It is the first meal provided by our new British hosts. The passengers sip the tea and nibble the rusks in silence. All is quiet, the stillness that comes from resignation, from apathy, from making peace with the enemy. After tea some of the refugees doze off on their feet. Those who have seats slept like emperors, dreaming and forgetting that they are due to be banished to an unfamiliar island.

It is a starry night. The sea is dark. Even the light-houses on shore have ceased their shine. The ship glides at a brisk pace; the motors hum. Another mile, another wave conquered. The passengers are calm.

How silent they are now, those exiles from Zion! They no longer sing Yehuda Halevi's Songs of the Sea. No liturgical odes fill the air.

The faster the ship cuts through the waves, the more distance it traverses, the stronger memories emerge of those tales from Jewish history that speak of the ancient Island of Kafrissen: Cyprus.

These Jewish stories light up the memory like flashes, demanding to be told.

Cyprus as an island of exile is no mere coincidence in the long lineage of Jewish history; it is no innovation on the part of the British usurpers. Cyprus has a place in Jewish history: it was a base for Jewish rebels after the destruction of the Second Temple.

Cyprus is the third largest island in the Mediterranean. The island is located sixty miles west of Lebanon and Syria, and two hundred miles north of Egypt. The area of the island is about three and a half thousand square miles.

The Cypriot shores are mostly rocky, with hills scattered around the bays and ports of the island. Between the hills are wide expanses of woodland, home to tropical fruit trees.

The three principal ports are Famagusta, Larnaca, and Limassol. The capital is Nicosia. The lakes of Larnaca are salt-water and unusable as drinking water. In Famagusta, where the main refugee camps are located, there is a freshwater lake, which dries up in summer and overflows its banks in winter. Transportation is provided by a rail and road network. The local population are mostly Greeks, Turks and other Muslim ethnicities. The three vernacular languages are English, Greek and Turkish.

To understand how this fertile island fell under the rule of he British it is necessary to look at a few historical details because Cyprus and the Jewish people had certain things in common in the period when Judea lost its independence, and the Roman Empire conquered all the East.

In 1450 BC, Cyprus was captured by the ancient ruler Tutmosis III. The Phoenicians—ancient Syrians—and Greeks who inhabited the island were conquered. Over the course of the next 900 years the Phoenicians, Egyptians and Assyrians tried to gain control of the island, but without success. It wasn't until around 500 BC that the Egyptian Pharaoh Amasis finally destroyed the island's defenses. But ten years later, a Persian leader annexed Cyprus.

Many bloody battles were waged over the island. Conqueror and conquered took turns in switching roles. Kings and princes, small kingdoms and mighty empires fought over the territory, at one point it even fell into the possession of Alexander the Great. It was only in the first century AD that Cyprus became a Roman province. Sergius Paulus became the first proconsul of the island. The famous philosopher Zeno was born on Cyprus 2, 500 years ago, and the great Roman orator Cicero served for a time as governor where he passed important legislation.

The histories tell that in 115 AD a group of armed Jews, resident in Cyprus, rose up against the Romans. The rebels destroyed the city of Salamis, killing 250,000 Roman troops over a period of two years. It took the Romans a very long time to finally put down the rebellion. In the aftermath the senate decreed that no Jew would be allowed to live on the island. The defeated Romans' revenge was so harsh that whenever they found a Jew living on the island they would sentence him to death by burning. For many generations Jews avoided the island. As late as 1911 the census recorded only two hundred Cypriot Jews.

But Cyprus did not remain with the Romans. The island continued to change hands from one conqueror to another.

In 1184 a Syrian ruler came to Cyprus named Isaac Komnenos proclaiming himself emperor. Arab invasions took place regularly. One invasion was led by the Caliph Harun Al-Rashid. Later Cyprus was freed and for a while things were quiet.

In 1191 King Richard the Lionheart of England landed in Cyprus. His landing bore more the characteristics of a personal adventure than a military undertaking. He came to rescue his fiancée Berengaria of Navarre and also his sister, the dowager queen of Italy who were both taken captive by Issac Komnenos. Richard defeated his foe. After the victory Richard married his betrothed in the city of Limassol making her the Queen of England. Richard did not exhibit any great interest in Cyprus as a year later he sold the island to an Italian prince, who styled himself the "King of Jerusalem." This prince's last heir gifted the island to the Republic of Venice.

Venetian rule lasted until 1571 when Cyprus became an Ottoman province.

The British flag was raised over Cyprus the 12th of July 1878 as a result of a treaty between the Ottomans and the British. The agreement stipulated that the British garrison troops there and use the island as a springboard for protecting the Ottomans in the event of a war with Russia. When the Ottomans, under the command of the sultan, joined the first world war on the side of Germany, Cyprus was annexed and became a British dominion. Now the island is a British crown colony, ruled by a governor who is assisted by a council of twelve members, elected every five years.

For a long time Cyprus has been a forgotten point on the map. But in the early part of this century Jewish pioneers began to explore the idea of establishing Jewish colonies there. They wanted to cultivate land in areas near the Jewish Homeland. To this day you can find signs of these attempts, traces of the failed colonization efforts. You can also find the remains of Jewish orchards, the futile labor of Jewish planters who believed they could stake a claim on borrowed land.

David Tritsch, the dreamer among the hard realists in the Zionist leadership, continued for many years to harbor utopian dreams of a mass Jewish colony on Cyprus. Whether it was because he had a prophetic intuition, or whether it was because he possessed a higher poetic imagination, but decades ago he had the great desire to turn the island of Cyprus into a safe haven for the Jews on their way to Palestine.

His desire—a twisted interpretation of it, in a brutal form at any rate—came to be realized.

When the mass movements of Jewish ships began, and the British began to deport the Ma'apilim to offshore holding camps, Cyprus was back on the agenda.

25

ON THE PRISON ISLAND

Around ten the next morning the four deportation ships arrive at the port of Famagusta. It's a sunny day; the sky is clear and blue and there is a fresh breeze in the air. The passengers, broken and weary after their long night in the filthy cages, begin to disembark, marching in an orderly fashion on command. Dozens of military trucks are already waiting in the port, ready to transfer the Ma'apilim to the camps.

Here too the port looks like a British naval parade. British guards of various ranks. Troops in uniforms of many colors—all pomp and bombast, parading in front of the 1,500 wanderers. The transfer of passengers from the ships to the trucks happens so quickly it is as though the British are afraid the passengers will escape into town and disappear into the local population.

The trucks make their way along dirt roads surrounded on both sides by orchards: trees laden with oranges, bending under the weight of the ripe fruit. Here and there, Greek farmers toil with spades and hatchets. Seeing the trucks pass, they raise their hands in greeting, shouting to the Ma'apilim: "*Shalom!*"

The cries of "*Shalom*," the smiles, and warm greetings on this foreign island raise the spirits of the captive Jews.

The trucks come to a halt one by one in front of a heavy gate that looks like the entrance to a fortress. On either side of the gate stretches a fence of double rows of barbed wire, punctuated every fifty meters or so by a small guard tower. Between one tower and the next there are also stationed extra armed soldiers from the King's Regiment.

The arriving Ma'apilim make jokes, shrug their shoulders and wonder what the royal guard have done to deserve such a lowly assignment as guarding refugees.

The refugees are now streaming through the great gates, heading straight towards the military tents. The tents are long and white, each one housing eight to ten people. Here and there, between the tents there are cabins which serve as kitchens, with kerosene stoves due to the shortage of wood. With oil—the shmaltz of Ibn Saud's country—they heat the kitchens of Cyprus. Clouds of black smoke billow from those stoves and come to rest on the white tents and the skin of the half naked refugees warming themselves in the sun.

The arrival of the new refugees brings some of the old inmates, who come to welcome them and find acquaintances and relatives.

After crossing countries, traversing borders, and traveling over land and sea, the wanderers now find themselves in one of the eight refugee camps on Cyprus. They regard their new asylum with indifference.

"We'll be able to rest our weary bones here for a while," someone says, upon exiting the trucks.

"A fine long rest, six months guaranteed!" a second says.

"You'll be lucky if you sit here for eight months!"

"I'm not going to wait that long. Cyprus was never part of my plan. Palestine is where I'm headed."

"What are you going to do? Bring the English to court?"

"We'll have an uprising!"

A stocky Galitzianer Mizrachist, a man generally unfazed and unimpressed by most things, strides up to the group and says in a measured tone:

"I don't mind sitting here for a whole year, as long as I know it's the last stop along the way. They won't send me back to the camps on mainland Europe. What have I got to lose? From here to Palestine is only a hop, skip and a jump away . . ."

The most excited were the young people, those who sang when the British warships chased them in the middle of the sea, those who sang when their own, battered ship was dragged into the Port of Haifa. Even now, as they are led into camp Caraolos they have not abandoned song.

The armed English guards on the other side of the barbed-wire fence do not comprehend the high-spirits of the internees. The Ma'apilim continue to sing until they are all led into their new lodgings in the tents of Caraolos camp.

Caraolos is the largest of the eight camps around Famagusta, and is home to over four thousand refugees. They live in groups, in communities or in families. The total number of refugees in all camps is around 16,000, including 2,400 children, 600 pregnant women, 150 infant babies. Caraolos is by far the most boisterous of the camps, with frequent unrest, breakouts, protests and demonstrations against British rule. The British don't know what to do with the rebels. They try to move around the troublemakers, transferring inmates from one camp to another, but the results are always the same: as soon as a new group of refugees crosses the threshold into Caraolos they are infected with the spirit of rebellion.

I set off for a walk through the tents to have a good look around. My conversations with the veteran inmates prove very informative.

The extent to which the Caraolos inmates are rebellious can be seen in the state of the camp. Almost all of the tents are tattered. Strips of canvas are torn off to mend clothes. The clothing on their backs, which has travelled all the way from the German camps, over land and sea, via the briefest of sojourns in Haifa and on to Cyprus, is either worn out or has disintegrated entirely. The inmates, demoralized from the long months of waiting, demoralized by the treatment of the British, express their frustration by demolishing the British facilities.

But there are deeper reasons the inmates are resentful of their British hosts. When the British destroyers were hunting the refugee ships on the open waters they would constantly try to entice them through the loudspeakers:

"Give yourselves up! We will take you to Cyprus, where you'll get decent food, good clothes and comfortable lodgings!"

They brought the refugees to Cyprus, but they did not give them clothes, or good food. The refugees complain about the food not just because it lacks sufficient calories, but also because it is of poor quality and past its sell by date. The English regime is stingy to the point of criminality. They deliver canned food to the camps marked "Best before 1943" and hand out such perished, possibly rancid, food to refugees in 1947 ...

Here in the context of British trickery and unfair food distribution the "Joint"[23] has been forced to step in. This large Jewish aid organization has risen to the challenge of its stated mission. The Joint endeavors to supplement that which the British deliberately withhold. The Joint provides an additional 30 grams of bread and 400 grams of potatoes for each refugee every day, which adds up to about 500 calories a day. In addition the sick, pregnant women, children and camp workers receive extra rations.

....

23 The American Jewish Joint Distribution Committee, known colloquially as the Joint.

In order to give an idea of how dishonest the British food distribution efforts are we must go into some facts and figures.

Men receive 2,260 calories a day, women get 2,100 calories. Young people between twelve and twenty receive 2,500 calories. Children, according to their ages, between 1,400 and 2,000 calories.

Such numbers are, according to medical guidelines, less than the minimum recommended amount. Even a person who does not do any physical activity, who sits twenty-four hours a day in a state of pure relaxation, burns between 2,100 and 2,2000 calories a day. But people who are active, who move around, march, and perform certain tasks—as is the case for those in the camps—need to burn 2,500 calories, depending on how strenuous their labor is. The newly arrived refugees, who have traveled the pathways of the world, who are sensitive to the weather and sensitive to what they eat immediately grasped the significance of the food situation in the camps. No sooner had they brushed off the dust from their travels, put down their bundles, settling into their new home—gathering in family or community based groups—than they congregate to complain.

It's not just political matters, but also humdrum, routine daily problems, minor irritations and worries that are voiced in the short, clipped conversations between the refugees.

One boy with blond hair, the veteran from Stalingrad who walks around with pockets bursting full of medals, looks at the tattered tents and says bitterly:

"What is this? A concentration camp? A military barracks?"

He does not expect anyone to respond, and so he goes on to answer his own question:

"It's not a concentration camp. It's not a military barracks and it's not a refugee camp!"

"And this is where they invited us, the imperialists?" a plumb, blonde girl says, not without malice.

A skinny lad makes himself known, a young Agodah member, with long, flowing side-locks. His words came out as hard as nuts:

"I'm satisfied! I'm happier than I was a year ago. I'm happier even than I was a month ago! Now at least I know: this is it! the last stage of exile."

The Galitzianer Mizrachist with his gentle gait and measured speech, who as soon as he arrived had made his position clear, began to expound a scholarly explanation:

"When the Jews wandered in the desert they began to yearn for Egypt. Some of them even imagined returning there. Pharaoh had means to tempt them too ... The fleshpots of Egypt, the fish ... as it is written '*We remember the fish, which we did eat in Egypt freely; the cucumbers, and the melons, and the leeks, and the onions, and the garlick*'[24] with what can Britain tempt us with in Cyprus?"

24 Numbers, 11:5.

"Britain doesn't tempt, it deceives!" say the plump blonde girl.

"That's the foundations their empire is built on!" calls another.

There is no fish, and there are no fleshpots. But soon the newly arrived Ma'apilim are tucking into their meagre meals of herring, old soup, and stale vegetables. A quiet armistice settles in between the warring factions and parties in the camp. The Aguda members chat calmly with the Ihud people; members of Mizrachi, with those from Hashomer Hatzair.

I, who for practical reasons was supposed to join one of the factions back on the ship only to hesitate so long that I remained an outsider, can now stroll around the camp as a neutral observer. I decide to find out who's in charge, and seek out those committee representatives who deal with the British authorities.

The committee representatives explain that as recently as two months ago the situation was better. The British treated them in a formal, but respectful manner, sometimes even with understanding. But ever since a bomb was detonated on board the deportation ship the Ocean Vigour at Famagusta relations have soured between the refugee committee and the British authorities.

The British have adopted the tactic of collective punishment in retaliation for the terror attacks or violence acts perpetrated by individuals. Recently when a group of refugees rioted against the poor conditions, the British reacted by destroying camp property. They used live ammunition against the refugees and there was even a fatality. More collective punishment followed. Visitors are now forbidden, and letters are no longer delivered. All contact with the outside world has been severed.

These repressive measures lead to great unrest in all eight camps. The inmates decided to turn to the International Red Cross with a memorandum, demanding a commission be set up to investigate the situation.

The memorandum was understated and modest, the text an exemplar of naivety, typical of the helplessness of dejection and humility.

The memorandum appealed to the people of the world, "who need you to know how the victims of war are being treated . . ."

26

THE STRUGGLES OF THE SIXTEEN THOUSAND

In a world full of hate and indifference towards the plight of the Jewish people, it would be an unforgivable oversight not to highlight the warm relations between the refugees and the Greek population on Cyprus. At every opportunity they are happy to demonstrate solidarity and their opposition to the British regime.

As an example of such solidarity we must recall how, on the 1st of May, the local Socialist Workers' Party sent a greeting of warm encouragement to the refugees in the camps, underlining their sympathies for the Jewish people and for the Ma'apilim. The message also expressed the hope that the goals of the Ma'apilim and the aspirations of the Jewish people in relation to their homeland would be realized. With this public declaration the Cypriot Socialists demonstrated their open contempt for British rule.

Even declarations of sympathy and demonstrations of solidarity cannot lift the spirits of the camps. Morale among the long-term inmates is low. The early enthusiasm felt upon first reaching the island is long since gone. Some of the refugees have so little hope that they believe these military tents will be their permanent homes. Others believe that if immigration quotas are not increased they are doomed to at least a year's captivity on the island. The authorized organizers of camp life do everything they can to alleviate the suffering of those who may have to spend a long time on the island. In order to introduce a certain degree of stability into their lives, normalize the situation, raise their spirits and overcome their inferiority complex it is necessary to organize a full medical inspection of all refugees in the camps. The number of clinics and medics needs to be increased, as well as doctors and nurses.

It's not just the medical conditions that need to be seen to, but the psychological ones too, which have been terribly neglected. No one had thought to set up libraries or reading rooms. There's nothing to read, and no textbooks to teach from. There are barely any bulletins or newspapers to get the latest news from Palestine. There are also no tools or materials for those who would prefer to use their time doing meaningful work.

The only ones demonstrating devotion and a willingness to put themselves out for the Ma'apilim are the emissaries from the Jewish-Palestinian Yishuv and the Joint. The inmates in Cyprus are viewed as a potential part of the Yishuv, and so the Yishuv takes an active interest in their fate. The coordination of efforts between the Yishuv and the Joint is exemplary, but more aid is needed.

On my second day in Cyprus I spend my morning on a long walk around the camps. Strolling from one tent to another, I suddenly spot a sign hanging over the entrance of one of the tents, announcing an "exhibition." I walk toward the sign. It is a Hashomer Hatzair tent. The canvas walls are hung with artworks, wrought in the metals abundantly found on the island. There are lithographs etched in stone, copper carvings, sculptures, statues, marble figures and delicate tapestries. There are also models of Greek buildings in Cyprus and miniature maquettes of Jewish homes in Palestine.

The industrious hands of the boys and girls of Hashomer Hatzair have made these objects, showing perseverance during their period of exile.

It's still only 8 a.m. It's a foggy morning and through the chilly breeze my ear catches the sound of furtive voices, singing in prayer. It is the morning prayers, intoned by members of the Aguda and Mizrachi factions alike. Tallitim cover their heads as their bodies sway, their voices absorbed in pious thoughts. So sounds the second morning prayer of the Cypriot exile: solemn God-fearing song rising as high as the gates of heaven.

To one side, far removed from the worshipers, a dark-skinned Jew with a matted beard mumbles a silent prayer. In front of him he has an overturned barrel, on top of which sits an open book. From afar he looks like an ascetic, a recluse on the run from people and the world, who likes to pray on his own . . . He remains there in his corner long after the morning prayers are over and the others have dispersed. My curiosity draws me to the recluse and his barrel. Is this a modern Diogenes?

One glance at his dark, bearded face and another glance at his book is enough to dispel the notion. He is one of those Prisoners of Zion who joyfully sing the odes to Zion of the inspired and exalted poet Yehuda Halevi. Those songs, like fiery psalm-quotations, sound terribly melancholy and cheerless.

> "Who will give me wings to fly away,
> bearing the tatters of my torn heart
> To your cleft hills? . . .
> I would delight to walk, barefoot and nude,
> On the desolate ruins
> Of what was once your palaces . . .
> To walk on the site of your hidden shrine,
> To walk where your tomes once rested,
> In the hiding places of your rooms . . ."

> "Who will give me eagle's wings on which to fly
> To mix my tears with your parched clay.
> Your stones and earth will taste like honey when I kiss them.
> My heart is in the east and I am in the west.
> How can I expect the food I eat to be so sweet?"

Yehuda Halevi, the poet from Toledo, did not just sing the fiery ode to Zion, but traveled there himself in

1140, in the bloody year of the crusades. He traveled a great distance with daring determination. He could no longer stay in the west. He abandoned his daughter, his grandchild, his students, and his yeshiva and set off for the ruins of Jerusalem whence he never returned.

Now, over 800 years later, an ascetic Jew sits on the island of Cyprus singing the songs of the poet from Toledo, waiting for the day when he can walk through the rebuilt gates of the city of Jerusalem.

A few paces from the singing ascete, a group has gathered to discuss the latest developments. It is just past breakfast time. Someone has heard that a small radio has been successfully smuggled into the camp. No one can confirm whether this news is true, but if it is then 16,000 refugees will now be able to keep up with world events on a daily basis. They will even be able to listen to the sensational, exaggerated news bulletins of the BBC.

The speakers are no fans of the London-based radio station which spreads calumny about the yishuv. Every tiny event there is blown up out of proportion. Every third rate happening is falsified. The aim is to sully the Yishev's reputation in the eyes of the "civilized" non-Jewish world. When a few weeks ago a London Jew was arrested for trying to smuggle clocks into Palestine the BBC droned on about the event day and night. Whereas when bombs are laid in Egypt on an almost daily basis, when there are explosions in embassies and palaces, symbols of British power in Egypt—then the sensitive London radio remains silent, despite the rest of the world's press coming out almost hourly with alarming headlines about British casualties.

Everyone—be they members of Ihud, Hashomer Hatzair, Mapai,[25] or Dror[26]—have something to say:

"The problem is the British still have the upper hand."

"They've been driven from Egypt!"

"They say not a single one is left!"

"Is that why they don't say anything even though they are being hit there?"

"Exactly."

"And are they quiet about Sudan too?"

"They have no intention of leaving Sudan."

"They'll leave alright, mark my words, they'll leave!"

"Sudan is a gateway to the Empire."

"So there'll be one gateway less . . ."

"Gateways, windows, roofs, it's all got to go. The Empire will have to make do with just the walls."

Just beyond the rancor and bitter humor of this little circle of speakers, and newly arrived Ma'apilim are wandering past, walking through the tents, impressed by the size of the camp. They derive pleasure from seeing the growing number of refugees, and they are beginning to have ideas.

25 The Workers Party of the Land of Israel, center-left party whose leader at the time was Ben Gurion.

26 A Jewish labor Zionist young movement distinct from Hashomer Hatzair.

A pot-bellied man begins counting the tents with the bearing of one taking inventory, before eventually exclaiming:

"Let's set up a Jewish Yishuv here!"

"What, you want us to spread out and expand? As if we didn't have enough to worry about with accusations that we are rootless cosmopolitans." another man interrupts, "A new colonizer! From one exile right back into another one!"

"Cosmopolitans! Exile! Here he comes with his *zagranitsne*[27] words!" the pot-bellied man says, not allowing his fun to be spoiled, "none of that will bother us if we colonize Cyprus with a hundred thousand Jews."

"And just what do you want with a hundred thousand Jews in Cyprus?"

"I need a reserve!" he booms, "You know what a reserve is? A reserve for the Yishuv! Seeing as how we'll be surrounded by Arab countries, it will be good to remember that we have a spare Jewish Yishuv just in case!"

"He's right, you know!" another adds. "We could do with having another shelter . . . if things get crowded it would be nice to have a place to stretch out our legs . . ."

....

27 Foreign.

"A new territorialist!"[28] someone snorts derisively.

The group of new refugees moves from tent to tent, spreading their credo, unloading their suggestions and making the acquaintance of the long-term inmates. And by the time the evening meals are served, they already feel like locals.

In the evening the camp comes to life. The calmer, industrious inmates attend night courses to learn Hebrew, Jewish history and drawing. The wilder, more volatile inmates go to meetings where they discuss economic issues. By the light of kerosene lamps at the entrances of their tents, idlers play chess and dominos. From various corners the faint tones of violins and accordions can be heard.

Whether it was just how the imaginations of the embittered refugees worked, or whether it was the invention of malicious tongues, but rumors begin to circulate that amid the tattered tents, among the downtrodden survivors, a group of black market dealers have managed to smuggle their way in. Money is exchanged, American cigarettes are bought and sold, jewelry is stolen. In the distance, behind the tents, young people gather washed up casks and planks. They light fires. Crackling flames spit at the heavens. Huge rings of people gather around the fires

....

28 Territorialism was a movement in opposition to Zionism seeking an alternative location for the new Jewish homeland, suggested locations included Uganda, Argentina, Alaska, Australia to name but a few.

and the din of the Hora—the dance that speaks from all one's bones—spreads in every direction.

Late at night the light begins to waver: the fires have gone out. Another twenty-four hours have passed on the island of the dispossessed.

The central internment camp on Cyprus.

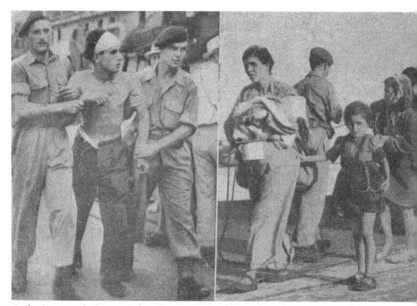

Left: A wounded man taken by British soldiers to a deportation ship.
Right: Mother with small children being led to deportation ship.

Jewish ship containing 1,577 Jewish refugees in Haifa port.

Britsh guards seaching refugees.

The Tradewinds, later renamed Hatikva.

"Illegal" Jews parting the waves.

British soldiers board the Hatikva.

Deportation of the Ma'apilim.

27

REFUGEES LEAVE CYPRUS

In certain corners of the vast Camp Caraolos, things are afoot from the crack of dawn. Feverish preparations are being made in the entrances of many tents: possessions are being packed away, rucksacks and suitcases are being crammed full. It is the day when almost 1,200 refugees are due to leave the island and return to Palestine. It is the final leg of their journey. A day which is marked as the "Flight out of Cyprus."

The problem is that the British camp-administration is in charge of enforcing the quota. Their bookkeeping is too detailed. They exhibit too much stinginess and deliberation in doling out their certificates, like a sly miser handing out pennies. They subtract from the quota every immigrant who manages to reach the shores of the Jewish land who had the good fortune to avoid the British watchmen.

According to the unjust balance sheet of the illegitimate White Paper 1,500 Ma'apilim should be allowed to return to Palestine. That is Cyprus's quota for the last two months. But the British administration—by means of its paid informers—discovered that 375 Ma'apilim managed to make it to Palestine from the ship, Shoshana. And so 375 certificates are sub-tracted from the total, meaning only 1,125 Ma'apilim can go. On top of this, the administration has the gall to declare that this number may be further reduced if more unauthorized refugees arrive in Palestine in the meantime.

The immigrants bound for Palestine are almost all Ma'apilim from the ship Latrun. They laugh at the British immigration law. Theirs is a level of faith and determination that transcends all laws. The statistics of the growing birthrate in the camps is spread with joy—in contrast to the tragically low number of surviv-ing Jewish children from Europe it is welcome news. There are 130 newborn babies in the maternity clin-ics. The Dhekelia camp, where there are two thousand Jewish children between the ages of three and eighteen is now the place with the highest concentration of Jewish children on earth. This children's camp will soon receive twenty-five additional teachers from Palestine in addition to the 150 teachers and instructors who be-long to the ranks of the Ma'apilim themselves. Medical aid is administered by four Palestinian-Jewish doctors, aided by twenty-five Ma'apilim doctors as well as seven dentists and fifty-two nurses.

The military hospital in the capital Nicosia has added a new wing with 200 extra beds for the refu-gees. There are currently 120 refugee patients there, being treated by twenty-seven nurses. British military doctors are also doing their part. But the most basic and elemental demands of the healthy refugees are criminally neglected by the British authorities. A salient example of the British authoritarian rule of the camps is the fact that, due to security reasons—oh those British and their commitment to security!—no workshops are permitted in the camps. Radios are also forbidden for fear that the inmates will listen to "illegal" programs.

I do my best to collect the chronicles of the island. I am the statistician tasked with recording the transgressions of the British regime. I jot down the details of all punishments and repressions. At around midday, when I have collected enough grievances and injustices, I go to the inmate who helps me hide my papers and documents. It is supposed to be a sort of checkup, to reassure myself that my American passport, my press pass, and my identification papers are safe and sound and likewise the man who is keeping them secure. I arrive at his tent and he comes to meet me, in a state of agitation. His brow is furrowed. His eyes, uneasy. He says:

"I think they are looking for you."

"Who's looking?"

"Our Friends . . ."

He justifies his suspicions in a few words. He tells me that early this morning an airplane brought over the Palestinian newspapers. There was an article about me, the reporter from the *Morgn Zhurnal* who went with the Ma'apilim from the Hatikva to Cyprus. The British immigration bureau are attentive readers of the Hebrew press. If they are reluctant to have uprooted refugees in Palestine and Cyprus, they certainly have no time for American tourists or newspapermen, especially when some American journalists succeed in debunking the British propaganda. The man who guards my documents is afraid that the British will sniff me out, as they will almost certainly start searching the camps. The news is bad enough to puncture my excitement. The plan was to stay on the island for several days. The Ma'apilim whom I have accompanied over seas, along shores, and past many ports have now been quartered on Cyprus. It is their temporary resting place. The island is their desert to cross; the tents are their sukkahs. My Ma'apilim voyage is over; my illegal mission is accomplished. But before going home I had intended to investigate the island, to scrutinize every inch of it from top to bottom. But the British are looking for me!

While I am worrying about what to do next, about how to buy time, I notice a group of visitors arriving hastily through the double entrance gates of camp Caraolos. The speed of their movements and their curiosity tells me they are tourists. Men in gray summer clothes and with large straw hats. They begin to sniff around the tents, mingling with the inmates, and asking the British guards if they can take photographs.

In a spur of the moment impulse it occurs to me that I should mix with the tourists. My freedom will now last only as long as it takes for the British to find my documents. With my clothes—which have always

made me stand out as a not quite convincing refugee—
I will be able to blend in with the tourists.

I approach the tourist guide. He is from Sudan,
and understands the language of bribery. The excursion hails from Egypt. I don't have a Cypriot travel visa,
but for a few pounds the Sudanese guide is willing to
integrate me into the group and pay off a couple of
English guards.

By the time the visit to the camp has ended, all
the formalities between me and the Sudanese guide
have been taken care of. We board a fantastically-
colored tourist bus which sets off toward town, toward
Famagusta.

The passage through Famagusta is short, but
in no other town have I ever seen so many mosques
and churches as in that Greek town. The majority of
the prayer houses are ancient and dilapidated. But
the best preserved of all is a huge Mosque. Its dome,
its walls, its whole massive structure bears a strong
resemblance to the Mosque of Omar in Jerusalem. The
streets of the old town are ancient. The buildings, a
mixture of Greek terraces, Greek columns and Roman
façades and arcades.

After lunch we head, avoiding the new town, to
the port where the walls are twenty feet thick.

The center of the town is dominated by the monu-
mental Othello tower, where Desdemona met her
tragic end. The guide spends a lot of time talking about
Shakespeare's drama, which has remained a firm fix-
ture in the world theater repertoire. The male tourists

take photographs. The women of the group want to hear more details about the Moor's love and jealousy.

From Famagusta we head to Salamis, the erstwhile Constantia, which boasts an impressive Roman-era agora. The town lies twenty miles to the north of Famagusta, and there is not much to see. Nicosia, fifty-five miles away, is considerably more lively and amusing.

Nicosia is the capital. It is full of noise and bustle, but it is a noise and bustle different to that of a western city. The noise lulls you. The bustle contains a synthesis of western speed and eastern sleepiness. Here too there is a giant minaret, surrounded by half-curved walls, watched over by eleven bastions which bear the name of old Venetian noble families. There are cathedrals whose walls are adorned with striking, colorful frescoes depicting the tomb of St. Barnabas of Cyprus. There are tombs of various crusaders hidden away in an Armenian church, as well as the great Arab Ahmet Mosque. The museum contains giant statues of bronze and gold, pottery and ornaments molded from various metals. Also there are the bronze statues of the Syrian-Roman emperor Septimus Severus who drowned the Judean uprising in blood. Next stop is the resort town of Platres, which is situated 3,700 feet above sea-level and is a popular destination for Egyptian tourists who cannot tolerate their native climate. The surrounding landscape is strangely reminiscent of the Swiss alps— the higher one climbs, the more warm clothing one needs to have.

The Troodos Mountains rise 5,500 feet above sea-level at their highest peak, the legendary Mount Olympus. In summer the government headquarters and garrison move there. The mountains are covered in forests; vineyards stretch from the peaks down to the valleys. High Season is June to October. From November to May the Troodos Mountains are capped in snow. The area is famed as the sanatorium of the Near East.

The climate is ideal for rehabilitation from tuberculosis and chronic malaria, as well as for those who suffer from chronic bronchitis and anemia. The spa is however unsuitable for those with heart conditions and kidney-disease.

The highest village in Cyprus is Prodromos, 4,600 feet above sea-level. It is ideal for all kinds of patients bar those with heart problems. The population is only 460. The village boasts an abundance of grapes, cherries, apples, pears and plums.

A spa renowned for its curative waters is Kalopanayiotis, frequented by those who suffer from paralysis, rheumatism and gallstones.

The village of Kyrenia is a charming little port sixteen miles from Nicosia. Four miles to the east lies Bellapais Abbey. It is a marvel of gothic architecture in the Near East, built in 1234. On a mountain peak 2,300 feet above Kyrenia stands the fortress of Hilarion. To enter one must first borrow the keys from either the commissioner of Kyrenia, or the police commander in Nicosia. The population of Kyrenia numbers 19,000 inhabitants. There are wonderful swimming pools and sports stadiums there.

It is night by the time we arrive in the port of Larnaca. It is an old Phoenician city, bustling and lively. Near the salt lake is the tomb of Umme Haram, the aunt of the Prophet Muhammad. The city of Larnaca was captured and ruled by Arabs in 632 AD.

In the new town there is a large church. On Cyprus, churches and places of worship are often destroyed in times of invasion or conflict between the various ethnic groups. Even as late as 1921 the great statue of Zeno the Stoic, a native of Larnaca, was destroyed.

The population of Larnaca is 10,000.

The Sudanese tourist guide does not want to miss pointing out a single important sight as the bus drives us through the mountains and valleys of Cyprus. It is now pitch dark. Half an hour after reaching our hotel, he takes us straight to Paphos to visit the birthplace of Aphrodite, the Greek goddess of love. The city is named Paphos after the son of Pygmalion.

Greek legend recounts that Pygmalion, a sculptor, carved out of clay a stunningly beautiful woman. Beholding the beauty of his work he prayed to Venus to breathe life into the statue. Venus granted his request and the statue was transformed into a living breathing woman. Pygmalion married her and she bore him a son, Paphos.

The entrance gates of the city of Paphos are adorned with historical dates.

Sergius Paulus, the Roman governor, was converted to Christianity here by the baptists Saint Paul and Saint Barnabas. Christian legend would have us believe that Elymas, who rebelled against the two Christians, was rendered blind. We see the pillar on which Saint Paul was tied by the locals.

The whole place smells of idol worship and Christian incense. No sigh of Jewish life for miles around. I almost begin to yearn for the camps of Famagusta, for the battered tents where campfires burn and people dance the hora. I miss the rebels of Zion, even though—as I'm well aware—the British are looking for me.

I spend the night in Paphos with the Egyptian tourists.

28

A CAPTIVE ON THE ISLAND OF THE DISPOSSESSED

The British are waiting for me.

The inevitable comes a lot sooner than I expected. The British who are so unruffled about implementing international responsibilities, so negligent when it comes to policing the Arabs of Transjordan—those same British are remarkably fast at tracking down one Jewish newspaperman, an illegal immigrant.

That same morning when I part ways with the tourists in Paphos and return to Famagusta, the keeper of my documents is waiting for me. He explains to me, in the curt tones of one handing out a verdict:

"Your documents are in the hands of the British."

"They searched you?"

"They searched four camps, all day long, from top to bottom. I had your documents moved around from one camp to another, from one hand to another, but by nightfall they'd been found."

"So I should be ready at any moment?"

"You can count on the British!" my accomplice smiles. "They even know about your little day-trip with those Egyptian tourists. They've got more spies than soldiers . . . so I guess we should soon say our goodbyes?"

"Why?"

"They're going to deport you . . ."

I know as well as he does that my time is up, that I'll be deported. Nevertheless the thought of what's coming gives me a little thrill, as well as anxiety.

A circle of people gathers around me. Some try to reassure me that the British can't do anything to me, a journalist. Others show no inclination to comfort me. On the contrary, they try to warn me that since the recent bombings in Acre prison, when over 200 prisoners, both Jews and Arabs, escaped, the British have been cracking down harder on everyone, no matter what their "crime" was.

A long term inmate, a young man with a long Tolstoy beard, says with a dismissive wave of his hand:

"You won't enjoy any privileges . . . they'll send you straight back."

"Since when are you an expert on immigration law?" my collaborator asks him.

"I don't need to be an expert," the Tolstoyan begins to explain, pointing toward me, "For me he's a genuine Jew, but according to the immigration laws he has committed what the British call an 'offense,' on top of which he doesn't have a Palestinian travel visa. The British will deport him."

"I notice they're not in any hurry to deport the Arabs coming in over the bridge from Transjordan . . ."

"You mean the Arab Ma'apilim?" someone laughs.

"Yes."

"You can call them whatever you like, it won't make a difference." says the Tolstoyan coldly.

The group gathered around me splits into two camps. One camp says they will go easy on me, while the other camp insists the British will throw the book at me.

I listen to the warnings, and remarkably they do not frighten me. But as with any unavoidable occurrence I'm eager to get the encounter with the British over with, the sooner the better. Realizing that these are my last moments on the island several Palmach boys come to give me a few small gifts for the road: a bronze ornament made by some inmates, a few local coins, and a badge of their Cypriot division in the shape of a Star of David. The emblem, made of nickel, is engraved with the number 13, and *Kaprissin 1947*. Such badges are usually only given to Palmach members who have visited Cyprus.

I hide the bronze ornament in my suitcase, put the coins in my pocket and I hide the emblem so that the British don't find it.

As I'm waiting to be taken, searched and deported, at the other end of the camp a stage is being built. Industrious carpenters are putting down boards, hammering in nails, and erecting walls.

Why are they building a stage? They are celebrating the tenth anniversary of the founding of the village of Masada in the Jordan valley. The Ma'apilim may be trapped in Cyprus, but they do not forget the jubilee of a Jewish village. Every outpost is important to the Yishuv and Cyprus too is an outpost. The important dates must not be forgotten. The principal participants in the celebration are members of Gordonia.[29]

Girls and boys, drenched in sweat lend a helping hand. They take pains to make sure the stage will be ready by evening. Amid the bustle and commotion they hastily recount the history of the young village Masada.

Ten years ago daring young Gordonians arrived at a desolate patch of land purchased by the Jewish National Fund. It was a decisive moment, the year 1937, in the midst of the Arab terror attacks, when forests and farmlands were burned and razed and the fruits of so much Jewish toil went up in smoke and the yishuv practiced restraint.

Then, at the height of the riots, the Jewish coloniz-ers engaged in a construction "*blitzkrieg*" of walls and towers—gates and spires. In the dead of night caravans and wagon-trains set off across the land. Heavy trucks loaded with prefabricated walls, with roofs, with sen-try towers. Tractors followed with farm machinery and water pipes. Work commenced with the coming of the morning star and by breakfast time that same morn-ing a new outpost had been built.

At midday Bedouins from neighboring villages come to greet the new residents.

....

29 A zionist youth movement.

Thus were outposts built in the Jordan Valley, in the Hefer Valley, and in Beit She'an. And thus, too, was Masada established.

Not all settlers endured the first harsh experiences in Masada. One went to Naharayim. Another fled to Sodom. But Masada remained. Masada grew. Masada set down roots.

In honor of Masada, which now counts 350 souls and boasts 800 hectares of grain-fields and 190 hectares of woodlands . . .

In honor of Masada, which has 105 cows, 2,200 chickens, 16 oxen, an inventory of machinery, tractors, a combine-harvester . . .

In honor of Masada, which each year produces 300,000 eggs, 200,000 liters of milk, 220 tons of bananas, 60 tons of grapes, 60 tons of vegetables, 30 tons of fish . . .

In honor of Masada, the fertile outpost; In honor of Masada, the watchful Jewish eye in the Jordan Valley— Cyprus will tonight put on a celebration!

I cannot keep my eyes off the nimble young people working so hard to build the stage, and so I wait there in front of my tent. Half an hour later a small military car approaches and a British soldier exits. He asks me my name and tells me I should gather my belongings because his orders are to escort me back to headquarters.

As I'm coming out with my suitcase Ma'apilim watch me from their tents with silent looks, as one watches a passenger setting off on a long journey.

The car drives through the camp gates, and follows the perimeter of the barbed-wire fence. As I pass I see how close to the fence the sailors from my Ma'apilim ship are. I see my captain standing there, the heroic crew, the brave commander, the helmsman of our ship—they are all now nameless, scattered anonymously among the other inmates of the camp.

The British headquarters is a white building surrounded by palm trees. The entrance is flanked by Greek columns in front of which stand stern British guards.

Inside, in a large administrative office, a major, a sergeant, and a private are waiting for me. All three are armed, but the private in particular carries an entire arsenal about his person. The long desk, illuminated by a green desk lamp, is covered in piles of paper, reports, and cards of fingerprints. There is also no shortage of photographs depicting suspicious individuals, and filled out forms. This is the typical mountain of files one finds nowadays in British administrative offices—the swollen headache of the British colonial apparatus.

I notice my passport and press pass lying on the table. I also notice an open book by Rudyard Kipling.

The major, a bent figure with an angular face not unlike King George V's, is pacing back and forth behind the desk. He is smoking a brown pipe. He invites me to take a seat and speaks to me politely in a tone as though he is continuing a conversation we had been having before:

"Your passport is American. You are a journalist by trade."

"Correct."

"And with these advantages you boarded a refugee ship?"

"Yes."

"Why? Out of curiosity?"

"More than just curiosity ... excitement."

"Excitement about what? About telling your readership an extraordinary story? Ordinary stories are ten a penny ... "

"Well put."

"You realize that by boarding such a refugee ship you are indirectly aiding illegal immigration?"

"I realize that."

"And that you encourage illegal immigration?"

"Yes."

"And that that's not the job of a journalist."

The major pauses for a moment. I speak up:

"You call the immigration illegal?"

"As long as refugee ships are outside the bounds of the law, they are illegal!" the major answers sharply.

"That is mere semantics, major."

"That is the law!"

"Do you recall, major, the year 1940?"

"That was only seven years ago, and I have an excellent memory ... "

"You remember how the British fought with their backs to the wall?"

"I remember."

"You remember Dunkirk?"

"As an Englishman I will never forget it."

"These refugee ships—they are the Jewish Dunkirk." I say.

"Come now!" the major protests, "that's hardly realistic."

"What's happening now in the ports of Europe is a brutal reality," I say, "and realistically speaking, the caravans of refugee ships are ten times more tragic than Dunkirk."

"These are emotions," the major interrupts me, "we are talking about the law."

"What do you call law?" I shoot out with a question.

"The law is a set of established systems for preserving order," the major answers succinctly, "Why such a question? Are you an anarchist?"

"No."

"And you as an American, do you respect the law?"

"As long as a law defends the rights of man. American laws are on the side of justice."

"British laws have thus far not violated the rights of any individual."

"Yes, but the British naval laws force the refugee ships to sail under false names and borrowed flags."

"As I've said before, the refugee ships are breaking the law ..."

"You understand, major, that we are not just running refugee ships, we are saving the survivors of a nation ..."

The conscience of a British major, who keeps a copy of Rudyard Kipling on his desk, might perhaps accept such a concept. But it is difficult for a British major who holds a position as investigator on Cyprus to exchange his military language for ponderings about just laws and unjust laws.

He is silent. Silence is often a comfortable escape when fleeing from a plagued conscience. After several minutes he says calmly:

"If you don't mind I will ask you a few questions."

"With pleasure."

"Who sent you to travel on the illegal ship."

"I was sent by my newspaper."

"Do you also belong to an underground organization?"

"No."

"Are you a member of the Haganah? You must realize that we are not an enemy of the Jewish Haganah ... I mean *Haganah* in the sense of "defense," the literal meaning of the word ... we have tolerated many of their activities. During the war we commended their courage ..."

I look at the major. He does not seem to be waiting for an answer because he immediately asks a second question:

"Your assignment, was it a quick mission?"

"Yes."

"And have you seen enough?"

"Enough to tell everyone on five continents what is happening to the people who lost millions of innocent lives in the war . . . I've seen the unluckiest, the most downtrodden and oppressed people on earth."

The major is ready to bring the conversation to an end. He scrutinizes my passport, makes a mark with a red pen and says:

"You are an American citizen. But your voyage and entry were illegal. An hour from now a ship will set sail for Haifa. You will be taken to the immigration inspector in Haifa. You can discuss your political convictions with the authorities there."

An hour passes, two hours, three hours, and they still do not take me to the ship. Officially I'm under arrest by His Majesty's government, but to the credit of that British major during that first hour I am not treated like a prisoner. They offer me cigarettes, bring me coffee with sandwiches and later they lead me into a small library.

Whether it is because the island of Cyprus has been spared the complex of a "National Homeland" and the British administration is spared the need to brutalize the local Greek population, or whether it is because the major has no backbone and has decided to hand me over to the Haifa functionaries, either way the reason for my delayed deportation is only made clear to me later when I have the chance to experience the hospitality of a British jail.

In the small library of the British headquarters I take down a book called *The Travels of Marco Polo*, a book about the voyages of a 13th century Venetian adventurer, who wandered distant exotic lands. I leaf through the book and find a page where it is written that when Marco Polo, traveling illegally through all the roads of the world—from Genoa through the deserts of Persia—arrives in Peking the gruesome overlord there, Kublai Khan, receives him with great hospitality. He appoints him as his trusted emissary, honors him with distinctions, and even keeps him for three years as governor of the city of Yangzhou.

In moments of distress, in moments of waiting and uncertainty, the imagination takes over. Tension grows wings. Reading that random page of Marco Polo I ask myself what distinctions the British administration in Haifa would honor me with once they have discovered that I have traversed so many lands, crossed so many seas by illegal means on illegal ships and with illegal Jews?

A guard arrives to accompany me to the ship.

29

THE FIRST NIGHT IN HAIFA PORT PRISON

After three days on Cyprus I'm sent back to Haifa under high security. It is late at night. The port is quiet, only here and there a lighthouse flashes briefly, and scattered spotlights send signals. As soon as I set foot on the pier I am handed over to the immigration authorities.

The British inspector, who guards the shores of Palestine against every step taken by a Jewish foot, leads me into the police headquarters with such ferocity as though I were a terrorist fresh from blowing up a police station or derailing a train full of British soldiers.

He is a tall man with three silver stars on his epaulettes. His full, red face with his watery eyes seethes when he sits down at his desk. He shoots hateful glances in my direction and he sighs, whether from troubles, or anger.

"This is how they delude themselves in this country..."

An adjunct appears by his side, a stiff, obedient sergeant who stands ready to agree with every word his superior utters. The angry inspector prepares for the interrogation as though preparing for a lecture. He glances at his adjunct, then glances at me. He skims through the pages in my passport and asks:

"You're an American citizen?"

"Yes."

"And you think that gives you the right to come here on an illegal boat?"

"The right to come aboard that ship was granted to me by my Jewish identity and my profession as journalist."

The inspector is far from polite. Little devils burn in his green eyes. He looks at my press pass and once again leafs through my passport:

"You don't have a visa either, do you?"

"No."

"Which means that not only did you come here on an illegal ship, but you also entered the country illegally."

"Is that what it means?"

I know that my back-answering is not going to win me any favors. But once I've taken such a tone I have to commit to it. Whether it's because I feel protected by my American passport and press credentials, or whether I'm convinced that this British satrap can't do me any harm, my boldness is awakened. The recalcitrant words seem to come to my tongue unbidden.

The inspector had no time for my arrogance:

"I'd like to point out that your attitude will do you no favors. This is not the United States . . . here British regulations apply.

"I know."

"And you must follow them!" he adds.

"Even foreign citizens?" I ask.

"In this country and under the circumstances, yes!"

He subjects me to a piercing stare and says:

"If you wanted to come to Palestine, why did you go to Cyprus?"

"Curiosity . . ."

"Without Cyprus your enterprise would not have been complete?"

"I accompanied the refugees all the way to the shores of this country; I wanted to come with them to the island where they are being banished."

"Are you a member of an illegal organization?"

I decide it is time to explain my mission to this dull Englishman and I say:

"I am exclusively a newspaper man, sir. My employer authorized me to travel on one of the refugee ships to accompany the unfortunate refugees on their journey. I accepted the mission."

"And you intend to write about the voyage?"

"Yes."

"There are certain factors that even newspaper men cannot ignore . . . the press consider themselves as privileged people. They forget that there are things which even they must respect. That is respect for and loyalty to the rule of law."

"Which laws exactly, the ones which prevent Jews from entering this country?"

The inspector once again glares at me with an angry flash of his green eyes and responds sternly:

"You don't have the authority to change British laws."

Throughout the whole time this stereotypical British bureaucrat, this de facto boss of Haifa port, is getting himself worked up about me, his adjunct stands opposite him with servile obedience, willing to do anything to ease his boss's nerves. The inspector gives me an order:

"Empty your pockets! Put everything you have on the table!"

As I begin to empty my pockets the inspector's impatience grows. He hastily taps and prods my coat, my jacket, my hat. The search is so thorough he asks me to remove my shoes and socks. The desk is soon covered in a pile of my personal belongings. I am relieved of my documents, my wallet and address book, my notebook, pens and watch. My finished notes are hidden on a garter around my waist. The experienced inspector relieves me of this too. His eyes light up as he tosses the bundle of sheets, covered in my dense handwriting, onto the desk. He looks at the Yiddish handwriting with the face of a hen trying to understand human affairs and says:

"You must understand Hebrew well?"

"Yes, sir!"

Having finished with my pockets he opens my suitcase, where a world of work awaits him. The cynic in him takes over and he rummages in things that have no place in formal searches. He shakes out every piece of my clothing one by one. He turns each of my ties over in his hands, peers into the innards of my watch. He disassembles both of my fountain pens searching for explosive material. He opens the packets of American cigarettes. He even removes the silver wrapper from each piece of chewing gum casting them down onto the table one by one. Looking at the aftermath of the search leaves a bitter taste in my mouth. I point to the chewing gum strewn across his desk.

"Mind if I take a piece?"

"Take one of the unopened ones!" he grumbles severely.

I chew loudly. The juicy paste refreshes my gums. He asks with feigned surprise:

"Is there dope in this chewing gum?"

Instead of answering I cast him a scornful look. I don't see an obedient British agent carrying out his official duties. I see a colonial schemer who embodies corruption in all its forms—sadism included. His expressions become stiffer, more merciless. The jacket of his uniform becomes a suit of armor; his revolver, a halberd. His British pith hat becomes a Roman helmet. This is what the ancient rulers must have looked like in the occupied province of Judea.

The inspector has not finished with me yet. He picks up my bundle of keys and begins to inspect them one by one.

"What's this key for?"

"For my suitcase."

"And this one?"

"My apartment in New York."

"And this?"

"My mail box."

"And these other five keys?"

"The drawers of my desk."

The inspector grumbles:

"It cannot be hard for you to understand our thoroughness . . . after the explosion in Acre prison no search methods are too harsh."

All the indignities suffered now are attributed to the Acre prison bombing. It has become an excuse for a new wave of chicanery and repression against the whole Yishuv. It has become a daily occurrence for arrests to be made in the hundreds based on nothing more than unconfirmed suspicions.

I look at the port inspector. He goes out of focus. The distance between me and him increases until I see marching before me lines of Ma'apilim, rows of captured Jews, trudging toward the deportation ships. The wooden pier is packed with armed military guards directing the migrants. The pain of the world is etched on their faces. The sorrow of all the victims looks out through their eyes. They march obediently, the persecuted and uprooted . . .

The suffering of all wandering people since the six days of creation accompanied those beaten Ma'apilim when they boarded the prison ships to Cyprus.

Ten minutes later my inspector takes my passport and press pass and all my documentation. He confiscates my notes along with a hundred blank airmail envelopes under the suspicion that they contain messages written in invisible ink . . . he confiscates all my papers, two English magazines, two of my own books: my Palestinian short stories, and a book in English about the Nazi terrors. He tells me he will send it all to be examined.

I point out to him that my books were printed years ago. One book, *On the Scaffolds*, in 1936 and the other, *Between 100 Gates*, in 1942, both of which are fiction. They have nothing to do with the current British adventures in Palestine. The inspector answers:

"Personally, I am not interested in the contents of these books. They will be sent to the examiner in Jerusalem . . ."

The inspector is clearly finished with me as he whispers to his taciturn adjunct:

"He was looking for adventures and he found them; I'll show him a good time . . ."

He turns to me:

"Your punishment will be deportation, and until the day of your departure you will be our prisoner. You will be liable to pay the travel costs and other expenses yourself. How would you like to return to America? By plane or by ship?"

"Before I decide," I say, "I will get in contact with the American consulate and with the Jewish Agency. I would also like to send a telegram to my newspaper in New York to tell them where I am."

"Do you think that intimidates me?" the inspector smiles cynically.

"I've been sent by the New York paper the *Morgn Zhurnal* and they need to know what the situation is."

"They must also be worried about you," the inspector teases.

"I would like permission to send a telegram immediately," I say, standing my ground.

"I won't grant you any such permission. You are in our custody and will be treated according to our regulations.

"Even as a suspect I have my rights, and as a foreign citizen I have privileges."

The inspector has no desire to hear my demands, saying:

"We will inform the American consulate that you are here."

"I would like to be in contact with them myself!"

"What gives you the right?"

"The fact that I'm an American citizen. You've looked at my passport and no doubt you've read the part where it states that in the event of problems in a foreign country every American must contact the consulate immediately. This right is set down in the American code of citizens' rights."

The inspector is in an awkward position. I can see his hesitation growing. Not to give in would be against his hardline commitment to the letter of the law; to give in, a sign of weakness. He attempts to soften his tone:

"It's the middle of the night, there's nothing to be done until morning. The American consul will be automatically informed about you."

"I want to telephone the consulate, I insist!"

He leads me into the front office where a British sergeant and maybe a dozen Arab policemen are. On the walls hang heavy-gauge rifles. The sergeant counts my confiscated travelers' checks, and my cash in French and Italian currencies. He notes down a number in his books. He puts the money in a safe and asks me to sign.

With a raised voice I repeat my demands to speak to relevant authorities. My entreaties fall on deaf ears. I find myself between thick walls and iron gates. The inspector leaves me in the hands of his adjunct and, as he takes his leave, says:

"Take him to his cell. You don't need to search him again—all he has is a pen."

As the iron door of the dark cell closes behind me I am suddenly paralyzed. It is not the fear of the cell walls that gets to me, but the feeling of offense and humiliation that overpowers me.

Someone once told me that a journalist's medals do not hang from his uniform, but are the marks of indignity born on his back. At this moment I feel those marks being laid down like hammer strikes. I am not alone. Two other prisoners lie on the ground. Their beds are nothing but dirty sheets on a hard stone floor. Grates cover the windows through which the cold moonlight shines in.

In the dim gloom I can make out the faces of the other prisoners. Lying next to one wall is a half-black Arab with his sheet wrapped around his head, and by the other wall—a white man who has made a makeshift pillow from a piece of wood. Between the two men lies a sheet destined for a third inmate. The message is clear: this is where I will spend my first night in Palestine after an absence of ten years. This is my guest house and these are my roommates.

I am hungry and thirsty. My naïveté, or my ignorance of prison life, causes me to dwell on my every urge and desire: to drink, to eat something, to go to the bathroom.

I bang on the door and call out to the supervisor, but my call goes unanswered like a cry into the desert. I repeat my requests only to hear my echo bouncing along the long, empty corridor.

30

TWO TYPICAL PRISONERS

I continue to bang on the iron door and call out to the guards. By now it is long gone midnight and, although I can hear the measured footsteps of the guards on the other end of the corridor, I receive no response.

My banging and shouting in English seem to have roused one of my cellmates from his sleep. He gently raises his head the better to hear what I am shouting and then comments, phlegmatically, in English:

"It's no use shouting. They won't come back until morning."

In surprise I step back from the door and turn around to face my neighbor. In the darkness I can make out a young man with a head of blond hair. His angular countenance is of a pale white complexion. He does not have a typically Jewish face. I ask him:

"Are you a foreigner?"

"I'm an American, from San Francisco. They brought me in here this morning."

Upon first meeting another inmate in jail, it's best not to ask about why they've been arrested. Either you wait to get better acquainted, or the other prisoner volunteers the information themselves. My neighbor it seems is a follower of this prison etiquette. He says nothing. I rebel against discretion and remark bitterly:

"I've just come off a refugee ship without a visa and they locked me in here."

"You come from America?" my neighbor asks sitting up.

"I'm from New York."

"What moved you to come here on a refugee ship when it would have been easier if you just got a visa?" my neighbor asks, becoming curious.

"I'm a journalist and it was for a story I'm working on, following the plight of the refugees."

I see the San Franciscan is intelligent enough to understand the significance of my journey because he starts to speak with great insight about the refugees whom he has encountered himself on his travels through various countries. One question leads to another and soon his tight lips begin to loosen. It turns out he is a professional mariner. He works on tugboats around the Mediterranean. What his position is he does not say, but he is currently a crew member of a Greek vessel. How does he come to be here in Haifa port jail when his ship is sailing legally under a Greek flag? Is he a pirate? A smuggler? A people trafficker?

Here is what he has to confess:

"So many times I've sailed past the ports of the Holy Land and felt an urge to go to Jerusalem and visit the holy sites . . . I'm a Catholic. The urge always remained and my ship always sailed past. But this time I took advantage of a moment when the captain wasn't there. The ship was anchored a hundred meters from the shore. I jumped into the water and swam ashore..."

"And the British picked you up like an illegal immigrant?"

"No, I came ashore on a beach far from a port. I managed to make it to Jerusalem and saw all the holy Christian sites . . . I was already on my way back but the captain was looking for me . . . I was denounced by informers. And the British locked me up..."

"What sort of punishment do you expect to receive?"

"Just a fine. The Arab policeman who's taking me in to court tomorrow told me they can ask up to two hundred pounds..."

"And you don't want to call a lawyer to defend you? Have you tried to contact the American consulate?"

"I'm willing to pay the fine. I don't want to draw things out longer than I need to . . . If the trial is fast I could be out of here by tomorrow..."

His story is hard to believe. There's something he's not telling me. An American abroad, in a tight spot, awaiting sentencing in a foreign land. He knows what his punishment will be and doesn't try to seek protection. Something just doesn't add up, an impression further confirmed by his off-hand remark:

"The British don't like us Americans. They suspect we're smuggling in weapons."

Perhaps these words contain a veiled confession. Arms-smuggler or not, his words do nothing to alleviate my feeling of bitterness. I dwell on my own predicament. Here I am between prison walls without contact with the outside world. And the worst part is no one knows I'm here. As far as anyone knows I'm still in Cyprus.

The rest of the conversation centers on my troubles. The San Franciscan declares that he intends to do something to help me once he's released. The suggestion comes from him spontaneously:

"Give me some names, and I'll tell people what's happening to you."

The plan is to smuggle out a letter. I have a pen, but where to find some paper? We find a piece of greasy cardboard from some food packaging lying on the floor. I pick it up. Who should I write to first? I decide to write to the Hebrew Journalists' Union. The ink will not hold on the greasy card, so I decide to write in English so that my accomplice can copy the message onto white paper.

As we are working out the details of our conspiracy we hear the Arab with the sheet over his head snoring and talking in his sleep, with such intensity it sounds as though he's haggling at the Haifa camel market.

By the moonlight coming in through the grated windows I write my letter to the Hebrew Journalists' Union requesting they inform the Jewish Agency and the American consulate about my arrest as I suspect the British will attempt to keep my presence here a secret.

My cellmate stuffs the note straight into his shoe and promises to take care of everything. Reassured by his promise I lie down on my hard prison bed.

I cannot sleep for long. When I wake up, morning is still far off. Both cellmates are snoring soundly. I begin to pace up and down across the cell. Plans and schemes float through my mind not one of which is feasible. My mouth is dry; my stomach, empty. What hours of sleep I managed to catch were full of restless dreams.

The Arab is the first to open his eyes. He sits up hastily and gazes at me in surprise with his deep dark eyes. He is a youth of about twenty. His face is dark and muscular with a thin mustache on his lips. His upper torso is covered in thick hair. By my conduct and colorful tie he recognizes that I am not a "native" and asks me in halting English:

"Not a Palestinian, *Hawadja*?[30]"

"No."

"*Inglizi*?"

"An American."

"I knew it!" the young man switches to his mother tongue and his face lights up with complicity "*Inglizi* are not good ... they lock everyone up! Even Americans! Why? My name is Ahmed Abdul Aziz. I need to serve time, I can't help you ... I'm done for. *Hawadja*! I pickpocketed a tourist at a hotel ... I swear by the Prophet! Not entirely my fault. I'm as poor as the night! I stole

....

30 Honorific used when addressing Jews and Christians.

eighty pounds from him . . . I've been locked up for three days now. Today I see the judge, *Hawadja*. How much time can I get? A few years?"

After his confession I offer Ahmed Abdul Aziz my last stick of chewing gum.

Ahmed chews quickly. With his fingers he pulls the gum out in long sticky threads. In that moment it occurs to me that I should be content with my situation, happy that my pockets have already been emptied so my new friend won't be tempted to slip his fingers into them.

I try to recall the few Arabic words I used to know back in the old days and explain to him that in America stealing is also punishable with prison. Ahmed swallows this news and grows enthusiastic.

"I'll go to America too one day, *Hawadja*. By Allah! I'll go! In my village there was a young *fellah*,[31] as poor as a beggar in front of the Mosque! He didn't have the money for a camel, a donkey, a wife. So off he goes to America . . . ten years later he returns to our village for a visit . . . and how did he look, *Hawadja*?" in his enthusiasm Ahmed extends his arms, "As fat as this, with yellow shoes and a gold watch . . . he'd become as rich as a caliph!"

The Arab's excitement wakes up our other cellmate, the American. He gets up, puts on his shoes and prepares to be picked up by the policeman to be taken to court.

....

31 Agricultural laborer.

An hour later Ahmed is led out of the cell. The American, two hours later. Before leaving he manages to use my pen to write the address of the Hebrew Journalists' Union on his arm, just in case the guards find the letter he's smuggling in his shoe.

I am left alone. Through the long empty corridor I hear the muffled footsteps of the prison guards. Through the grating in the iron door, I can make out the open door of an office down the hall, and inside I can see an Englishman in uniform sitting at a desk. I call out to him politely through the door. At first he sits there, unresponsive, as stiff as a mummy. The second time I call he slowly hauls himself to his feet and approaches the door. I explain that I'm a foreigner, that I've been held here fourteen hours already, without food, without having any contact with a prison employee. Perhaps he can do something for me?

He answers in a sedate manner that this is a provisional arrest station of Haifa port. The real prison is a few blocks down the road. There's no food to be had here no matter how long I wait. But seeing as how I'm a foreigner I can buy food with my own money, he'd have to discuss that with the orderly. He says he'll be back in a couple of hours.

I don't so much need more information about the "provisional arrest station" so much as a human ear ready to listen to a human voice and be willing to answer with a human tongue. It must be late in the day by now as there is more activity in the corridor. I call out through the grating toward every uniformed passerby. Eventually I succeed in catching the attention of a young sergeant and unload my grievances on him. That sergeant with a Jewish face, with sad, gentle eyes listens to me attentively. He promises firstly to find me some food. A few minutes later and he is back with the receipt for my money which is in the safe, and asks me formally:

"With which money would you like to pay for your food? You have some French Francs, some Italian Lira, some Irish Pounds and American Dollars . . . You understand? We first have to exchange the money from the safe, and we can't open it until the corporal returns . . . he usually comes in late."

The sergeant does not step away immediately. He drops the formal tone and looks around nervously to see if anyone is listening and suddenly begins whispering in Hebrew:

"Don't worry . . . The Jewish Agency knows you're here. Your arrival has been announced over the radio and in the press. The police, however, did not say where you were . . . the best thing would be for the Jewish Agency to arrange food for you. And don't worry about what they're going to do with you; the end result will be deportation."

These are the first kind words I've heard in fourteen hours in this stone cell. I sit down patiently to wait it out.

An hour later a civilian Englishman knocks on the door

"Take your things. You need to go to a hearing."

I pick up my coat and hat and stand by the door. The Englishman leads me into an office where a sergeant greets me with a smile. It's the first smile I've seen on the face of a British functionary. The sergeant has dark hair, a muscular face and kindly eyes. He is dressed in civilian clothes with the style and polish of a Levantine. He invites me to take a seat, while he perches on the edge of the desk. He begins:

"Well then, are you still interested in writing about your experiences?"

"The more I see, the stronger my desire to write." I respond.

"Understandable. It will be an exciting story I'm sure," he chuckles affably.

There is exaggeration in his words. No malicious fire burns in his eyes. A policeman arrives and begins filling out a questionnaire. Date of birth, profession, purpose of your visit. Afterward they bring me into a second room where they want to take my fingerprints.

The sergeant says, softly and apologetically:

"I'm afraid we're going to have to take your fingerprints. It's just a formality. We do it with all journalists. In the event that anything happens to you we will be able to identify you."

I see an opportunity to win a concession and say:

"Sergeant, I'm hungry. I haven't eaten in almost twenty-four hours. I'm not going to do anything else until I get something to eat."

"Someone is already on the way with some food as we speak. In the meantime, why don't we just get the formalities out of the way. It would be a shame to waste any more time."

Taking my fingerprints is a whole process. One finger isn't enough, but they want a print of all ten fingers from both hands on special paper. The whole thing is carried out in such a meticulous pedantic fashion that I'm almost prepared to take off my shoes and let them take my toe prints while they're at it. I respond to the whole scene with sarcasm and disdain.

Ten minutes later they bring in my breakfast. A bottle of Tnuva milk and two cheese sandwiches. I throw myself on the food like a starved wolf.

With the last morsels still clinging to my teeth they lead me to an automobile which is supposed to take me to the Haifa remand prison. On the short ride I manage to see the main street, the Kings Way, from Haifa port, teeming with life and bustle, with Jewish life and bustle.

The multistory buildings, the latest in architectural achievement, are like palaces bathed in the harsh light of the Palestinian sun. The signs on the buildings, with all their colorful writing, scream down in a thousand different voices, declaring that beyond the walls of the British prison, in contempt of the British usurpers, a Jewish country is cooking and brewing.

31

THE WRITING ON THE WALL

The Haifa remand prison where I am taken is located opposite the bright new Kings' Way street, by the entrance to the Arab Quarter which forms an Arabic island in the 80% Jewish city of Haifa.

The old Ottoman building is surrounded by Arab coffee-houses and playgrounds. Around the doorway is a low sandstone wall topped with a spiral weave of barbed-wire. The barbed wire is, symbolically speaking, the wall of thorns through which the British must pass in order to maintain their brutal police regime.

There are entire squadrons of the British air division dressed in their red berets—whom the locals call the "Red Devils"—specialized in adorning every government building and police station in these crowns of thorns.

The seat of every British ruler—large or small—is hidden behind an arc of barbed wire.

We walk through two high gates until we reach the interior courtyard which leads to the cells. Even on the walls of the courtyard there are metal cages packed full of Arab arrestees, most of whom are here under suspicion of theft, murder, smuggling, hashish dealing and various crimes of a violent nature.

A prison guard leads me up a winding staircase to one of the higher floors. On the half-open door of my cell I see the number 20.

My entrance is greeted by four smiling Jewish faces. The Jewish policeman closes the door behind me and mumbles quickly:

"This is a Jewish cell, you'll be more comfortable with these boys . . ."

Indeed I do feel more comfortable as soon as I cross the threshold into my new cell. There are no suspicious glances; no doubt my cellmates already know who I am. Nevertheless, there are four pairs of eyes looking at me, eager for more details.

"Are you the correspondent who came on the Hatikva?"

"Yes."

"They won't keep you here long. We Palestinian Jews are being held as 'natives' . . . but the British respect the Americans."

That's the narrative one hears all over the world, and one I believed before falling into the hands of the British myself. Maybe it's because I'm Jewish, or maybe it's the resentment the British feel because the Americans are helping the Ma'apilim . . . Either way, so far the British have enjoyed taking out their anger on a journalist who accompanied illegal immigrants. I am the first Jewish journalist they have succeeded in capturing. Before me there were just a few non-Jewish journalists, informing the world about the Jewish refugee situation in a perfunctory manner.

A journalist is a stumbling block for the British propaganda effort.

I take off my jacket, my tie, my shirt and look around my new stone accommodation, getting my bearings.

The four walls are covered in graffiti: writing, drawings and caricatures. It's clear that among the prisoners who passed through here at some point were people with artistic abilities, or at least with a tendency to draw, because some of the caricatures and cartoons are fitting depictions of the corrupt word of British prison life. Many slogans express rage against the British authorities. But there are also others of a more satirical bent, sarcastically extolling the virtues of His Majesty's government.

I note one piece of writing that seems to serve as an instruction for newcomers:

"To those who come after us! You can get anything here for money. All the guards take bribes. Don't let them overcharge you!"

Among the usually slogans and popular song lyrics my attention is drawn to a note written above the barred window, with the following patriotic call:

"I love you, even in chains, Fatherland.
Zion, you will greet your captives!"

Signed: Leone Hasson

Next to this a note in a flamboyant hand, with a hint of self-aggrandizing pride:

"In this cell I served three months for my fatherland. Long live the Jewish people!"
Signed: The Assistant-Commander of the Jewish People

On the western wall, in gothic calligraphy, a citation from one of the *Herrenvolk*, a German with a swollen ego who did not hesitate to address the Haifa prison walls with his full military rank:

"Hans Dietrich, Panzer division, Panzer °5, Afrika korps."

Next to a caricature of a fat Arab policeman opening a cell door is the English caption:

"Dr. H. Cohen spent two weeks in this charming vermin nest."

And a little further, next to a sketch of a British soldier jumping from an exploding train, I'm greeted by a familiar slogan, one which can be found on every New York subway station: *Kilroy was Here!*

Good old Americans, wanting to bring a little familiar private joke to the unfriendly walls of a Haifa prison.

One of my cellmates, Gavriel, wants to help me decipher the graffiti, some of which is cryptic and laconic, like a secret code. Gavriel has been here for over a month and knew some of those who wrote them. He knows that some of them are now in Latrun, the British concentration camp, where one may grow old and gray without knowing the date or time of day . . .

In Latrun, local boys are held without evidence, without being charged, held on the grounds of pure suspicion alone. There are as yet no laws that allow people to be detained for two years without judge or jury. The British take such drastic measures in order to have a free hand in rounding up the Sons of Israel and throwing them in prison. It is fully in accord with the authoritarian tendencies of British rule to turn this devilish practice into law.

Gavriel is pale and thin. A month's worth of British hospitality has left its mark on his young face, and on his body. The twenty-eight year old Gavriel has the body of an adolescent boy: his eyes are hollowed holes; his cheeks, sunken. His shoulders are as bent as those of an old man. Gavriel is forthcoming enough to tell me exactly who he is. A fighter with Irgun. He does not shy away from his offense, for which he is sure to serve a full prison sentence. He forged checks to raise money for his organization. It was his role. Revolutionaries are fond of the motto that the end justifies the means.

Rebels in other nations have also robbed banks to fund their revolutions. Stolen money is, according to Gavriel, the grease in the wheels of every revolution. After his swift confession Gavriel becomes more discreet. He does not wish to discuss the ideological differences between the different Jewish fighters in the Yishuv. He notes however that in comparison to the tigers of the Stern Gang the Irgun are lambs . . . the Stern Gang wants to annihilate the British; their animosity will not cease until the end of time. They will never forgive or forget the British who murdered their leader Stern in such a cowardly and treacherous manner. The extremist Gavriel considered the terror acts of the Irgun as strategic moves. No bomb is set off and no bullet fired unless it furthers the national cause. "Only thus will the Fatherland be conquered!" Gavriel says, repeating the slogan of the Irgun, like a pious Jew quoting scripture.

I look at Gavriel, the Irgun soldier. He has been led astray. His beliefs are my doubts. The destruction, the terror attacks shake things up, but they also harm the Yishuv. I refrain from arguing ideological differences in a Haifa jail. Gavriel is misguided, but he is a Son of Israel. He suffers physical pain, but he possesses spiritual strengths. He is the product of British provocation, a victim of their power.

The second of my new cellmates is Daniel, a member of Palmach, the elite fighting force of the Haganah. He has served on several Ma'apilim ships as a Haganah escort. He was in Cyprus, suspected of being involved in the explosion on board the deportation ship the Ocean Vigour. There is no evidence, but the British claim they have some. He smuggled his way into Cyprus with three other Palmachniks. Two men took part in the bombing that destroyed a deportation ship. But Daniel and the others did not arrive in Cyprus until two days after the explosion. Based on nothing more than the conjecture that a man like him would be capable of being a saboteur Daniel was punished with two months in a Cypriot prison. Later he was sentenced to deportation back to Palestine. British functionaries were waiting for him in Haifa port and he has been jailed here—indefinitely—ever since.

Daniel is full of life. This is his sixth day in Haifa prison after serving two months in Cyprus, but there is no sign that this has brought him down. His thick mane of hair like a thoroughbred horse, his large body like an athlete, the fire in his eyes, and the conviction that freedom for the People of Israel will come.

The two months of prison in Cyprus have not broken Daniel, but have given him experience. He knows how to break the monotony of prison life by establishing a routine. In the mornings he sings; in the afternoons, he learns ballroom dancing and discusses how Aliyah Bet can be used to bring about a swift Jewish demographic advantage. To kill time he tells stories of his experiences with the Arab Bedouins around Nablus. He used to be a land surveyor in that region. The Bedouins have respect for people who come to their land, burdened with maps and charts. They see the map-bearers as holy people. During World War I it was using the power of a map that British Uber-Adventurer Colonel Lawrence managed to recruit legions of armed Bedouins to fight on his side against the Ottoman armies.

The next player in this dark prison arena is my third cellmate, the Stern Gang member Zebulun. His words contain the entire condensed program of the self-styled Fighters for the Freedom of Israel, the so-called Stern Gang. Zebulun has no time for sentimental language. He formulates the aspirations of his fanatical companions in concrete terms.

Palestine is not just a ring, but a hub in the chain of the British Empire. That's why the British can't afford to leave Palestine. It is in the Empire's interest to keep Palestine in the dark, to keep it backward. And the result—the more the Jews achieve here, the stronger British opposition to a Jewish state becomes.

Britain must leave the Jewish Homeland. There can be no common understanding with the occupiers who have time and again shown their intention to undermine the work being done by the Yishuv.

The Jewish people are fighting the British alone, but they could find allies among the other peoples fighting for their freedom. The allusion is to the Indians, the Burmese and others under the yoke of the Empire. The war has multiple fronts. One could argue that any gains made by the Jews against the imperialists here, also help the liberation struggles in other lands across the empire. The Palestinian divisions can indirectly embolden the Indians or even the Sudanese. The Stern Gang's orientation also positions itself in relation to Russia. The end goal—Brits out! Out with the enemies of Jewish self-determination as a people.

The fourth occupant of the cell, Baruch a former Jewish brigadier, does not fail to introduce himself to me. He carried a British rifle on many fronts. He guarded the borders of the Netherlands and Belgium. He drove back the Nazis at El Alamein and Tobruk. The Germans never managed to capture him. But after the Allied victory—a victory he played a part in winning— he became a captive of the British. Why? Because he has a suspicious face. And what did they suspect his face of doing? Of taking part in a rail explosion. Was there any evidence? The British don't have time to look for evidence against the "natives," against Palestinian citizens.

The ex-brigadier is not an excitable person by nature. He is saddened to have to sit in jail after having been awarded three medals and distinctions from His Majesty's government. There is no cup of coffee to be had. No cigarette to be found. So he tries to keep his spirits up with wit and anecdotes. He tells the story of how when a unit of the Jewish brigade served in Holland, the local Jews were surprised to see a few dozen Yemenite Jews among their number. They asked:

"Who are they? You have black soldiers too?"

"These are our colonial troops" came the answer from the Jewish sergeant.

Entirely out of harmony with the atmosphere cre-
ated by these Jewish political prisoners, was a fifth and
final occupant of the cell. A non-political, ordinary
criminal. A chubby Sephardic man who refuses to pay
support to his wife who won't grant him a divorce.
For defaulting on his fine he is paying his debt with a
month in prison. This Sephardic "anti-feminist" wants
to tell me his ordinary life-story, but just then the iron
doors of the cell open and the Arab guard comes to
take us out to stretch our legs for an hour in the yard,
where we will also eat lunch.

32

CELL NUMBER 20

The prison yard, where we are brought out for an hour to have lunch and get some fresh air, is a typical Arabic courtyard with stone walls and bordered gateways, and white domes on the roofs like a mosque. It is twelve o' clock. The sun blazes down, baking the rough stone floor.

The cook—an Arab convict who's served ten years of a fifty year sentence and for his good behavior has been put in charge of the prison kitchen—is standing in the doorway of the kitchen, which looks like a cave, handing out metal bowls with black olives, *zaytun* in Arabic. Each bowl is filled a third of the way up with olives and is supposed to be shared by four inmates. To fill the bowls the cook adds a piece of dark flat bread, which the locals call a *pita* and is as bitter as maror. This is lunch from a kitchen ruled by the British, but operated by the Arabs. A long-term prisoner, half Greek, half Arab from Alexandria, whispers to me as we walk around the yard:

"The olives are vanishing, *hawadja* ... a month ago the bowls were full, and shared by only two people.

Now it's a third for four people ... a pack of thieves! The British sergeant, the cook, the guards, all of them ..."

So I never found out how many missed calories each prisoner was owed by the British. But I did discover how many olives were stolen each day, under the nose of and with the tacit approval of the British sergeant.

As my first meal in ages, the whole thing leaves me feeling nauseous, and the pita gives me stomach cramps. I decide to keep my complaints to myself for now and wait for dinner and familiarize myself with the diet as a whole.

I take off my shirt, leaving my torso uncovered, and take in some of the sun's rays. I think of my sunbathing as a down-payment for the vitamins I'm going to be deprived of from the food ...

Striding across the courtyard I look up toward the highest story where the women's wing of the prison is located. They too are out on their balcony taking their midday exercise. The female convicts, mostly fellahs from the villages in grubby clothing, their faces mostly covered, shuffle around quietly and modestly. They are barefoot; some of them are women of the streets. But these female prisoners receive special supervision.

There are three women in gray police uniforms busying themselves all day. These members of the Arab prison underworld are very active in their complaints against how things are being run. They tell me that they would not tolerate the flea infested blankets and began to hit their heads against the walls. After that, they were given mattresses. After their second protest, they were given white blankets, and after the third, pillows. One of the women is heavily pregnant, and there is an Arab midwife who looks after her day and night.

I notice that not just the Arab women but also the men—some of them violent offenders—get food sent to them from their relatives: white bread, onions, tomatoes, cucumbers and falafel. For the Jewish prisoners, it is forbidden to bring food in from outside. The prison authorities are shameless enough to justify this by referring to the Acre prison bombing. Since the Irgun blew up the fortress-prison in Acre, where 160 Arab and 40 Jewish prisoners escaped, while eleven Jews—and not a single Englishman—paid with their lives, the British have decided to punish all Jewish prisoners in Palestine by withholding food. Until then the Jewish Agency and the Jewish National Council used to send food for the Prisoners of Zion. Now the ban is in full force . . . even the Arab policemen, so fond of bribes, are afraid to smuggle anything into the Jewish cells.

I observe the Arab prisoners who dominate the yard. In Haifa, a Jewish city, in a British prison, forty-five cells packed with Arabs, and only one Jewish cell. The Arabs march in rows, as though in a procession. Here comes Halil who runs the commissary, a fat man with a bulging belly, serving a seven year sentence for dealing Hashish. There is Younis, an Egyptian from Port Said, a liar, a sycophant, who screams that all Palestinian Arabs stink and that American Jews should take over the country. In front of the door to the prison workshop sits a Syrian from Beirut with tangled hair and a black goatee. He fought for Britain, sat for four years as a prisoner of war in a German camp and now here he is, obediently washing and pressing British uniforms in a Haifa jail.

Among the prisoners sits Abu Hasan, a money lender who stabbed one of his clients for not paying on time.

The thin Yusuf Dervish, eating his olives and pita, is in for raping an Arab girl. He's terrified that the victim's brother is going to castrate him when he gets out.

Watching over everyone is the corporal, who can help or denounce, can take bribes or betray . . .

Most of the arrestees have no idea how long they will have to stay here. No one gives them any indication when their cases will be heard in court and the investigations drag on without end. Each one dreams of the moment when the lazy prison guards will slowly surround the iron door and yell out: "Clear out!" The phrase "Clear out" is like a magic spell for every prisoner. It means freedom. For the sinner who repents it means he will be able to turn over a new leaf. For the criminal with ambitions it means he'll be able to spread his wings . . .

Yard time is over. The pitas have all been swallowed, the olives gnawed, and we are led back to our cells.

On our return, we meet a new guest, a Jewish arrestee. He's come to the cell as if it were an excursion, with his own blanket and pillow. He's no stranger to the place: this is the fourth time the British have brought him here. He does not see eye to eye with the standard-issue flea-bitten blankets and so he brings his own bedding with him. His name is David Bouzgalo. He works for the Mirzachi in Carmel. He is a character-istic example of a young man in Palestine who has had his freedom permanently stolen. Two months he spends under house arrest, followed by one month in prison. And a year only contains four such trimesters. This time when the British came to his house with a blank arrest warrant—only his name needed to be added—he called out to his mother:

"Mother, bring me a blanket and a pillow. They're calling me to the British hotel . . ."

David Bouzgalo's crime is that his brother Isaac, a member of Irgun, is accused of throwing a pamphlet bomb: a kind of bomb containing pamphlets. Agitating against British rule. The bomb, which is fired upward into the air, is not designed to harm anyone, but to scatter hundreds of propaganda leaflets. Isaac came across the pamphlet bomb by accident, and when he picked it up to see what it was it detonated and he ended up losing seven fingers from both hands—the fingers had to be amputated. Isaac is now in a hospital bed in Acre prison and the British are trying to build a case against him for handling explosives, a conviction that carries the death penalty.

David Bouzgalo, is Isaac's brother, flesh and blood. Why have they arrested him four times already? So that he can give the British information about Irgun's activity, and strengthen the case against his brother who could find himself being led to the gallows.

But David Bouzgalo is not discouraged. He is not just a prisoner. He is also a courier who brings in news from the outside. With enthusiasm he recounts the events of the previous twenty-four hours. Since yesterday, a band of murderous Arabs has been decimated by the Haganah.

For some time now Arab gangs have been attempting to terrorize isolated outposts in the Yishuv. The attacks are carried out under the pretext of robbery, but the truth is that the Mufti had begun to organize gangs with the aim of destabilizing the country. The gangs attracted all sorts of unsavory elements, even former Nazi officers.

The Haganah, the mighty defensive arm of the Yishuv, which knows that it's best to chop off the snake's head at the beginning, has launched a campaign of annihilation against these bands before they become a threat to the Yishuv. The attack took place in an Arab coffee-house in a village near Nablus where the bands were hiding out. Solomon Miller, the brave commander of the Haganah battalion fell during the attack, but the entire criminal gang was destroyed.

At four in the afternoon the cell doors open once again. It is time for the last meal of the day. At the same time the arrestees have to pick up their lousy blankets for their beds.

The Syrian tailor stands in front of his workshop handing out the blankets, like a sergeant handing out rucksacks to new recruits. The cook hands out communal bowls of pea-soup, which the half-starved arrestees grab impatiently. This is the most nutritious meal of the day. The soup with accompanying black pita will have to keep us going until morning.

While the prisoners sip their soup the prison sergeant enters the yard. He is the boss here in the prison. He is strong and tall with wide shoulders, hot-tempered and short-fused. His pristine uniform indicates that his appearance is not something he takes lightly. His clothes are ironed. His shoes shine. The stiff visor of his hat is pushed to one side, like a Nikolayevsky soldier. The arrestees know him; they know he is a monster who administers with an iron fist. To my unpleasant surprise I discover that he is an Irishman. What kind of Irishman serves as an enforcer in a British jail?

The sergeant carries out his inspection of the yard with such theatricality you could swear he expected applause. He regards the teeming yard full of arrestees as a guard in a zoological garden regards the animals.

I approach him and inform him that I'm a foreign citizen, and that I don't sleep on lousy blankets or eat bitter pitas and that I demand food from outside even if I have to pay for it myself.

The sergeant looks me over with his wolfish eyes for a moment and snaps:

"You can complain as much as you like, sir. For me you're just an arrestee like any other . . ."

"Arrestee or not, I'm a foreign citizen. I'm awaiting deportation, and as long as I'm here, I'll stand up for my rights."

"If the president of the United States were to walk in here, even he couldn't help you!" the sergeant says."Here you are subservient to British prison laws."

"I don't need the president; calling the consulate should be enough! They'll convince you to change your tune," I say.

The sergeant is silent for a moment. He does not like to speak impulsively. He is not used to being spoken back to; his stern demeanor is somewhat deflated. He begins to explain:

"Since the bombing in Acre, sir, I'm under strict orders not to allow any exterior food for Jewish prisoners."

Such a bloodhound, I think, I hope he gets what's coming to him! How dare he punish me for being Jewish? In the prison registry I'm marked as an American citizen and I should be treated as such. How can I even be sure the consul knows I'm here? The newspapers say that, according to a police report, I'm still in Cyprus.

I call out:

"What has the explosion in Acre got to do with me? You want to punish me just for being Jewish? Are you practicing racial descrimination here?"

The sergeant becomes agitated:

"Be careful how you speak, mister! I'm no Gestapo officer and racial discrimination is not my job. I'm only following orders."

"Even those kind of orders?"

"I myself am no Englishman," the sergeant continues, "I'm an Irishman. But when I go out into those streets I'm in just as much danger of being shot as any Englishman!"

"Let's not get bogged down in political discussions," I implore, "You are a functionary here. And as a functionary you are committing an injustice! I demand to be put in immediate contact with the American consulate."

"The American consul is already informed about your—"

"I'm having serious doubts about that. And even if it is true, it is not much. I want to telephone the consul and invite him to come here."

"You can't do that from inside the prison. Your freedom is curtailed. Besides, you should have to pay for the consequences of your actions. We didn't ask you to come here on an illegal ship."

Arguing with this Irish brute—who twenty-five years after Irish independence still has a heart to serve the British—is not worth my time. I return to my cell.

The mood up in the cell among my five roommates is not one of defeatism. One member of the Palmach, one of the Stern Gang, two of the Irgun and a former brigadier—one could almost forget we were sitting in prison. They chew on the leftover black pita and discuss the wondrous growth of the Negev. Prison comes and prison goes but in the meantime we need to plan how to increase Aliyah Bet, to bring in more and more Jewish refugees. They gush with enthusiasm about how fast the settlements around Haifa are growing.

From the Arab coffee-house next door to the prison, we hear hoarse voices. It is a radio program from Jerusalem, an Arabic voice intoning the news with drawling monotony. Gradually the repetitive tones of the radio lull, one by one, the prisoners of cell number 20 to sleep.

33

THE BRUTAL TREATMENT OF THE PRISONER

I awake from my second night in prison with a start. My cellmates are all sitting up bursting lice between their fingertips. There is no shame in the enterprise, nor do they find anything funny about it. It is simply part of the daily routine of Haifa prison, like washing oneself or tying one's shoelaces.

From outside, we hear the clatter of metal plates and voices in Arabic. It is the cook and his helpers preparing breakfast for the inmates. Soon half-filled cups of tea are being handed in through the bars. The cook's helpers distribute the sour pitas which the inmates throw themselves on as though after a long fast.

A hand throws a newspaper through the bars. Is it the hand of the Jewish policeman? Or an Arab? It does not matter. The paper is the first signal from outside, a sign that someone out there is keeping an eye on cell number 20.

I pick up the newspaper; a copy of the *Palestine Post*, an English-language Jewish newspaper, which is read by all the British in the land, friend and foe alike.

The front page is still talking about the Refugees from the Hatikva being deported to Cyprus even though the landing was several days ago by now. One headline stands out: a column about my arrest.

The article says that I, a correspondent for the *Morgn Zhurnal*, was traveling with the Hatikva and was brought to Cyprus where I was captured and sent back to Haifa, where I am currently being held. The column also indicated that I have not been in contact with the Jewish Agency or the American Consul and that I am demanding intervention. The American Consul, having been asked to respond, released the following statement:

"It is unusual that an American should find himself in such a situation . . . " and "The consul has taken immediate action to intervene."

The results of their intervention have so far not been noticeable, but the knowledge that my complaint has at least reached somebody's ears buoys me up.

My spirits improved, I sip the half-cup of tea on an empty stomach, and it hits me like a shot of strong liquor.

My cellmate David Bouzgalo tells me that the British have never before shown such impudence to a foreign citizen. When the Ottomans were in charge, foreigners were treated with the privileges of a prince. In the Sultan's days, insulting a Russian Jew could cost an Arab guard a flogging. For threatening a French Jew, one Arab was sent to Acre. David's own father was a political prisoner in Ottoman times. He was jailed for two days. But every night the Turks allowed the prisoner's father to enter the prison and stay with him, in case he was afraid to spend the night alone . . .

An hour later, as we're going out to the yard to wash, I hear a commotion coming from one of the lower cells; someone is kicking against the iron door. The banging is followed by shouting in Arabic. All the Arabs are already down in the yard except for this one. Some of the others come up and gather around the cell door. They are laughing;

"A crazy *Yahud*!"

I approach the locked cell. Behind the iron grating of the door, I see a Jewish arrestee, an old Sephardic-Ottoman Jew from Jerusalem. He has been transferred to Haifa and he does not know why. Neither does he know why he is in prison in the first place, but he cannot praise the Jerusalem prison enough. "A paradise!" he keeps repeating, touching his lips with two fingers, "A real paradise!"

The Ottoman Jew does not want to share a cell with Arabs. He wants to join the Jewish cell. He wants to pray, and to eat Jewish food as is his right. But the British sergeant and the Arab guards are deaf to his pleas. The dark skinned Ottoman is enraged. His hard cheekbones tremble. His lips bubble. His whole body is in revolt. He screams:

"Two peoples happily sharing one land, along come the *Inglizi*, those swine, and cause turmoil . . . Upon my life! *Inglizi*—to hell with them!"

His cries and the scene he is causing make him seem to be unhinged, but he is not crazy. It is only a moment of confusion, a passionate outburst. He appeals to the Jews in the prison to help him, he wants to be among Jews. Suddenly his mood lightens, and he shouts out:

"Why did they arrest me? Because of a fight? I didn't beat up any Englishman! But I'll tell you the truth! To help build this land I'm willing to do anything, even if it means killing a few Englishmen. They've earned it, the scoundrels!"

All the while he continues to kick the iron door with his foot. By now he's practically hurling himself against the walls, and his cries turn to warnings:

"When I get out of here, upon my word, I'm going to join the Stern Gang! I'll throw bombs . . . I'll derail trains . . . I'll blow bridges to smithereens . . . no Englishman will escape my clutches alive . . ."

The sergeant comes striding toward us in a state of concern. The Ottoman's screams have put him in a difficult situation. They have a rule that whenever an inmate makes violent threats the British officers are not to allowed show fear. The sergeant attempts to threaten the inmate with solitary confinement down in the old dungeons, but in reality he does not know what to do. The Arabs standing around are laughing into their fists, enjoying his powerlessness. Eventually, the sergeant orders the cell open and, mumbling curses, drags the rebellious Ottoman to the Jewish cell.

An hour later the sergeant has a second insurrection to deal with. This time it is an Arab who has caused some offense to the cook. The sergeant has him taken to a large, dark cell. His sadistic power over the "orientals" now finds its full, brutal expression. He shoves the Arab up against the wide window and chains his hands and feet to the iron railings. When the prisoner trembles—in the same pose as Jesus on the cross—and begins clanging his chains, the sergeant shouts from the other side of the yard:

"That's what you get, you son of a bitch!"

The Arab is in pain. He flails his arms and legs like an animal in a cage. He screams that he will smash his head against the walls, that his friends on the outside will blow the prison to pieces. Nothing helps him. The sergeant watches the Arab—writhing and twisting—as though he is watching a performance at a circus.

Several British soldiers in red berets—the Red Devils—arrive in the yard carrying beams, shears, and rolls of barbed wire. They are on their way to repair the "wall of thorns" around the main entrance of the prison. The sergeant calls to the Red Devils, inviting them to watch the chained Arab in his torment. With a red face, inflamed with sadistic pleasure, he says:

"Watch how an Irishman deals with insurrections . . ."

No sooner do the Red Devils leave than the sergeant frees the Arab from his chains, and assigns him the chore of helping to wash the toilets, thereby giving him a little more liberty. This is the sergeant's habitual trick. Whenever someone rebels against his authority he first comes down on them hard, and then gives them a "commission," a place in the ranks of prison order. In this way both sides come out as winners. The arrestee can put down the flag of rebellion and the sergeant has one less troublemaker to worry about. Indeed the arrestee will go on to serve the sergeant with subservient loyalty. The sergeant looks around for further signs of insubordination. I decide I will no longer touch the prison food. Twice a day I send their paltry bowls—whether half-full of olives or sticky soup—back to the kitchen. I have only one aim: to receive food from the outside. For now my hunger grows and torments me. The prison guards, who generally regard a foreign arrestee as a creature from another world, regret my behavior. One of them, the chief bribe-taker himself, visits my cell at night with a bowl of groats, begging me to eat. When I push the food away he squints in dismay, succinctly expressing his philosophy concerning the general world order with the words:

"Eat, *Hawadja*, eat! *Khulo dunya zift!*[32]

But his world does not stink. Twenty minutes later he takes my money: two British Pounds for chocolate and five packets of cigarettes per Jewish prisoner. He comes back with only one packet of cigarettes with the excuse that the rest were taken from him as he re-entered the prison. Poor crooked screw, and a lousy liar; he lied with the same squint and tone as when he declared that the world stank.

The cell door opens and the guard calls me out. Down in the yard a policeman is waiting for me with

32 The whole world stinks!

an enormous camera. He is here to take my picture. I sit down on a chair next to another arrestee who is also here to get his picture taken. As the photographer fiddles with the settings on his camera and prepares the slides, I sneak a glance at my neighbor. It is an elderly Arab as hairy as a wizard. His diminutive body is wrapped in a robe, striped like a tallit. On his head he wears a yellow turban. He sits stiff and unmoving like a clay statue. His eyes dart toward me, then toward the photographer; waiting is clearly a torment for him.

The policeman is taking too long preparing the camera. Sitting there in front of him is uncomfortable and boring. In my impatience I feel like doing something. But as the policeman is inserting the slide he whispers to me in Hebrew:

"I can do something for you outside . . ."

I look at him in surprise, and answer impulsively:

"Can you take out a letter?"

"No letters. No notes. They search our pockets. Everything has to be passed on orally. You speak—I'll listen."

"Do you know who to go to?"

"You can trust me."

I decide to trust him. In a few words I tell him about my situation. He continues to fuss over his camera while I speak. When eventually he snaps my picture I feel elated to have encountered an unexpected courier.

Before I even make it back to my cell I am summoned a second time, this time to the prison administrative office. Two plain clothes policemen are waiting to take me to the inquiry.

An automobile is waiting for us outside the main entrance. Both escorts are armed with two revolvers each—one in the right trouser pocket, the other in the left. They take such precautions that during the short walk from the gate to the car their gazes dart frantically in every direction.

Leaving behind the prison walls, I'm hit by the blinding light of the street. The sunlight on my skin is invigorating. The automobile tears through the bustling Haifa streets with seeming haste. We hurtle past pristine white buildings. The city is spread out over a large mountain. From the top, a glorious panorama unfolds, the hills undulate like camel humps, alternately decked with greenery or exposed purple rock.

The colorful houses are bathed in sunlight. The automobile races on, avoiding the Arab quarter with its limestone buildings and *nargile* smokers sitting on wicker chairs in the middle of the street. The car circles around a narrow alleyway packed with women in rags selling fruit and vegetables.

The car comes to a halt in front of a new white government building where signs of a recent detonation are visible. The driver exits first and opens the doors for my police escorts whose hands were poised ready to draw their revolvers if necessary.

In front of the government building are several familiar looking military cars parked in rows. I am in a good mood and my escorts seem like friendly enough sorts so I point to the small green vehicles and say:

"American Jeeps!"

"And what good do they do us?" One of the escorts says: "Even before we get them here, they are already destroyed by terrorist bombs . . ."

We enter the dark building and head up the stairway that leads to the administrative office of the English investigator.

34

THE HEARING

In the British investigator's office everything is ready for the hearing. Three stiff, cold bureaucrats are waiting for me. One is a man with thin red hair and cherub-blue eyes. The other is a large muscular man with the build of a boxer. The third, a bespectacled man with the appearance of a hard-working student. The last sits in front of a typewriter, fingers at the ready.

Perhaps it is just a coincidence, but as I step over the threshold, the muscular investigator is playing with his revolver. His fidgeting with a loaded weapon does not even stop when he begins to question me—now moving the revolver from one pocket to the other, now checking to see if it is loaded. His fingers edge along by the trigger. His gestures seem entirely innocent, but he does not forget to subject me to his long, lingering gaze.

The red-head paces impatiently back and forth, then he lights his pipe and positions himself opposite me:

"What can you tell us about the illegal ship?"

"Nothing."

The inspector does not consider the answer as definitive. He takes a deep puff on his pipe and continues:

"According to the information I have you flew from New York to Paris with the express intention of joining the ship. A ship would have been too slow, so you flew . . ."

"That's correct."

"Could you tell us, what was the reason for such haste?"

"What modes of transport I take on my trip," I say, "is my own private affair. My newspaper is covering the travel expenses."

The red-head sits down in his chair. He shifts his weight nervously from one side of the chair to the other, makes a movement as though he is about to stand up again and says sharply:

"Your passport indicates you arrived in Paris on the 20th of April. Who did you meet there?"

"You expect me to give you all the names of the people I come into contact with on my travels?"

"As a professional newspaper correspondent you have enough experience to know what I mean . . . who did you meet in relation to the illegal ship? Someone brought you to the ship, did they not?

"Oh, that's what you mean? I met a man."

"What was his name?" the inspector grows tense.

I'm not obliged to name any names, but to indulge my love of playfulness and to keep my inspectors on their toes I say:

"Abraham."

"His surname?"

"I don't know. The people who run illegal ships don't identify themselves to journalists . . ."

The inspector exchanges eye-contact with the secretary whose fingers have paused over the typewriter. The inspector mumbles something to him and then turns back to me:

"And where did you meet this Abraham?"

"In a café."

"In which café?"

"Somewhere on a boulevard."

"And I suppose you don't remember the address?" the inspector smiles bitterly.

"I don't remember."

"And who put you in contact with this Abraham?"

"No one. I recognized him via a prearranged signal." He wore a white flower in his lapel."

"Who told you what the signal was? And where? In New York?"

"Yes. A man, whose name I don't know and whose address I don't know either."

My red-haired inquisitor claps his hands together in frustration and turns to the secretary:

"Write this down! Mister Samuel Isban, the American traveling correspondent, met with nameless people who don't have addresses . . ."

Still angry, he turns back to me:

"Let's get back to this mysterious Abraham for a moment. What did he tell you? Where did he send you?"

"He sent me to a second man."

"His name?"

"Isaac!"

"Issac! Like in the Bible," the inspector lets out a diabolical laugh. "First Abraham, then Isaac . . . and where did you meet this Isaac?"

"Somewhere in a European port town."

"And what did Isaac do with you? Did he lead you aboard an illegal ship?"

"Yes."

"Which port was this?"

"Somewhere on the coast. I don't know the area as I was driven there in a closed automobile at night. For security reasons they did not want me to know where I was being taken."

"That is false! The Hebrew newspapers reported that, according to the passengers onboard, the ship set sail from Genoa. So how could it be that you don't know the name of the port?"

"I don't know what the passengers have been telling the newspapers. I boarded the ship at night from a stretch of isolated coastline."

"When you boarded the ship were all 1,500 passengers already on board?"

"Yes."

Our dialogue is not a simple game of cat and mouse. I know that I won't ask him for any concessions, and don't try to gain his sympathy. I know that they already have a warrant to hold me for several days. There is nothing they can do to force any more information out of me. After all: the British don't stoop to Gestapo methods against foreign citizens. So why not get my own back for being locked up, for not being allowed to set foot on Palestinian soil, for the sleepless nights and the lousy sheets?

The red-haired inspector shares a bitter look with his secretary who has barely even been able to fill a half page worth of information. He is pained; he sucks on his pipe in silence.

To give the red-head time to catch his breath the second inquisitor, the boxer, takes over. He asks me:

"Which cabin was yours on the ship?"

"A cabin?" I laugh, "I was lucky to get a space on a plank with the other passengers. I did not ask for or receive any privileges."

"Did you see the captain?"

"I never met him. The captain of a refugee ship is anonymous. None of the passengers know who he is."

"And who were the crew-members? Do you remember them?"

"I don't know. It was hard to tell the difference between the passengers and the crew. There were no uniforms. Everyone wore the same tattered clothes."

"Astonishing! You mean to tell me that the crew did not have their own cabins?"

"A tiny cargo ship packed with 1,500 passengers doesn't exactly have room to spare for private cabins."

"And did you see the captain's cabin?"

"Seeing as how I didn't know who the captain was, I wasn't exactly interested in finding out where his cabin was."

Here, the red-haired inspector takes over again. He is visibly agitated, running his fingers nervously through the thin strips of red hair combed over his head. He knows I'm lying, but is powerless to squeeze any information out of me. The British have not yet passed a law forcing foreign arrestees to become informers. In his helplessness the inspector attempts to provoke me, to insult me. Perhaps that will move me? He speaks, observing both me and his secretary at the same time:

"What kind of story will you write for your readers if you don't even remember any details from your voyage? A fine correspondent you are! If that's the standard of journalism today I could do better myself."

"If you have aspirations in that direction it's a real shame you're wasting your time with such a thankless job as interrogating uncooperative arrestees."

He does not respond. He taps his pencil against his lips and scrutinizes me. The staring contest does not last long; I break the silence. I look toward the secretary, whose fingers have long ago stopped typing, and say:

"Gentlemen, let's make one thing clear. If you are expecting to get information out of me you've got the wrong guy. You understand that, don't you? Even if I had a wealth of information I wouldn't share it with you. I have responsibilities as a journalist, and as a

Jew. My employer sent me here to follow the travails of the most unfortunate people on earth. I've seen how the hated and hunted are trying to escape from a continent that has for them been transformed into a graveyard ... does one really need to be a Jew in order to feel their pain? And does one need to be British to play around with dry, formal protocols about their hardships?"

"We share your sympathies with the suffering refugees, Mr. Isban," the inspector says, "But we look at these problems not from a Jewish perspective, but a human one ..."

"1, 500 passengers heard those very words blasted at them from a megaphone on a British warship in the middle of the sea ... the same phrase 'we sympathize with your suffering' ... but with a nasty caveat 'you are not permitted to enter Palestine illegally' ... 'anyone who violates the law will be punished' ..."

"Illegal immigrants *do* violate the law!" the inspector replies obstinately. "Has that never occurred to you?"

"If Jewish immigrants and those who help them reach their homeland are breaking your wicked laws then they are doing a great historic deed. They drag one small ship after another out of the European hellscape toward the Promised Land. If, in your rigid pedantry, you call that a criminal act then there will be a lot more criminal acts to come."

"You've begun to answer honestly! the red-head inspector smiles. "And you know perfectly well that up to now approximately thirty ships have come carrying 20,000 immigrants."

"For the record, sir, I believe your calculations are not correct. The statistics is one thing I am privy to and not all the ships have been captured by the British blockade . . . there are happy exceptions and lucky escapes. I believe there have been at least forty ships with over 60,000 Jews on board. . ."

The inspectors face registers this surprise with a grimace. His demeanor becomes less confrontational, gentler. But the rest of the exchange does not lead to any better results. Exhausted and spent, he takes down the details of my date of birth, place of residence, age, nationality, etc. He re-reads me the dry report and tells me to sign.

He offers me a cigarette with the assurance that I may smoke it in the office before having to return to my cell. I pass.

The secretary looks at me in surprise, and then smiles:

"What a life! At the end of the day it must be interesting for a journalist to spend time in jail . . ."

35

THEFT AND CORRUPTION IN THE PRISON

The same evening I return from my hearing, the prison receives an unexpected visitor. The government medical officer responsible for overseeing the prison arrives for his weekly inspection. I am glad to see an outside face between the prison walls. I stubbornly seek out contact with anyone I can from the outside, knowing that each one is an indirect messenger, a link to the outside world.

The doctor, a short gray-haired man with the bearing of a typical Turkish bureaucrat, turns out to be in fact a Sephardic Jew.

The Irish sergeant is accompanying the doctor around the prison, and as they pass our cell he attempts to distract the doctor into overlooking cell number 20. I call out through the grating, pouring out my grievances as loud as I can.

When the door is eventually opened three people stand at the threshold: the doctor, the sergeant, and an Arab guard. The sergeant, agitated, comes running up to me and asks:

"You want to register your complaints again?"

"Yes. But this time to the doctor," I answer.

"Are you a foreigner?" the doctor asks, "feel free to speak any language you wish: English, German, French, Hebrew," the doctor says with a smile.

"I'd like to make a complaint, doctor, I'm an American citizen and I'm waiting to be deported. But my treatment here is unacceptable. I haven't eaten in two days. They don't let me bring in food from the outside, and I haven't spoken with my consulate."

The doctor steals a glance at the sergeant, seeking either confirmation or denial. The sergeant begins his old refrain:

"Since the bombing in Acre outside food is forbidden for Jewish prisoners."

"But the gentleman is a foreigner," the doctor protests gently, "He's within his rights to ask for food from outside . . . he also has a right to see his consul."

"But doctor, who will send in the food? The Jewish Agency? That is strictly forbidden. I cannot allow any contact between the Agency and the Jewish prisoners. And as far as the consul is concerned, we've already had two American prisoners in here who caused the consul nothing but headaches . . . he's not the one who asked them to travel on illegal ships."

"That's not our business, sergeant," the doctor answers. "The gentleman would like to see his consul; you have to put them in contact. The consul can take care of the food problem. Arrestees should not be allowed to go hungry."

Encouraged by the doctor's words I add: "If I don't receive outside food I'm going to formally declare a hunger strike!"

The sergeant, enraged by both the doctor's intervention and my threat, begins to bellow:

"If you go on hunger strike you will get sick, and if you get sick, I will send you to the hospital. What's more, if you don't stop your protest, I will have you transferred to Acre this very day! You're the first American who's caused me so much trouble . . . the two Americans who were here before you both served a month. I've also had a French journalist here for thirty-eight days. None of them ever complained . . . I have a warrant to keep you here for seven days. But if your bad behavior continues we may just have to issue a second warrant for a further seven days, after that another fifteen days . . ."

"Are you authorized to issue these supplementary warrants?" I enquire. "Or are you just a supervisor here? Aren't you just following orders, as you said to me yesterday?"

"You'll find out what I'm authorized to do!" comes the sergeant's furious reply.

The doctor, somewhat impatient that the conversation has descended into a heated, personal exchange, turns to the other cellmates:

"What about your blankets? Are there any lice?"

"Whole armies of them!" Gavriel answers.

"They breed so fast we're practically swimming in them," another says.

The sergeant cannot tolerate the insubordination and loses his temper:

"I have over 190 Arabs in this prison and not one of them has complained about lice! You Jews are the only ones asking the earth of us!"

"But we're the ones with the lice!" the arrestees answer obstinately.

"And what do you want me to do about the lice? Sit down and pick them off your bodies?"

This cynical utterance is not enough for him, the sergeant—who had a tendency to admit to criticism only to deny it a moment later—screams:

"You're all liars! You don't have any lice! Go on then, show the doctor, show the doctor where you have lice!"

One arrestee steps forward. No sooner does he lift the hem of his shirt than an enormous louse crawls out. The arrestee looks at the sergeant, the sergeant looks at the doctor and the latter says:

"Tomorrow you will carry out a thorough disinfection. Don't spare the DDT. And if that's not enough, get them some new blankets."

Before the doctor sets off to inspect the women's ward on the top floor, I manage to whisper to him reminding him not to forget his promise about sending food, and informing the consul. Just at that moment the prisoners are being let out into the yard for their third meal of the day. The meal consists this time of a black pita with a quarter bowl of a brown, sticky substance called "deeb". This small dribble of sweet liquid is intended to nourish four arrestees for the next fourteen hours.

The sergeant now finds himself in a tight spot: he tries everything in his power to delay the meal until after the doctor—that thorn in the sergeant's side—has left. He winks at the cook, at the guards. They do what they can, but are unable to keep the hungry prisoners away from the bowls.

The long term inmates are well aware that it's gone four o'clock, and everyone, be they counterfeiters, hashish-dealers, or murderers, expects to have their portion on time.

One of the Arab guards succeeds in pushing the arrestees who already have bowls to the back of the yard, and the doctor is by now near the front steps, ready to leave. After my confrontation with the sergeant I'm in no mind to let him get away with his trickery. I snatch a bowl of the treacly substance, slip through the crowd and call out to the doctor. The doctor turns around, and I approach him with a question:

"Do you think, doctor, that this bowl contains enough food for four people?"

The doctor seems to be embarrassed. Questions like this are usually reserved for the offices of the Ministry for Health, or in laboratories where one weighs and measures the portions but not bellowed out loud in prison yards. But the doctor takes the bowl in his hands as though estimating its weight and says:

"How much does it weigh? I'd say about 400 grams..."

With that he hurries off to find some scales. The sergeant, who has seen the whole thing, follows him. The Arab guard follows them both. All three are gone for some time, and when they return the doctor's verdict is:

"150 grams less than it should be!"

Whoever it was that has been stealing food that should have been feeding the two hundred inmates of Haifa prison is not discovered immediately. But the fact that 150 grams of food from each bowl is stolen each day, and that this has probably been going on for months if not years, has been confirmed. And confirmed by chance. The hand that steals is rewarded; the four hungry mouths that should eat from each bowl are swindled. The discovery of the theft sends the sergeant into a fury. The Arab guard walks behind him, his brow drenched in sweat. The doctor scolds both of them with hasty, agitated words. Afterward, he approaches me and says:

"There was only 250 grams in each bowl. The government pays for 400 grams. Tomorrow the portions will be as they should be . . ."

During all this commotion the Arab inmates eat and watch as though the whole thing were a show put on for their entertainment. Once the doctor has left they come to congratulate me. The pot-bellied hashish-dealer, dressed in a pair of red pajamas and with a yellow hat on his head, shakes my hand with a warm smile.

"Inti kuwais, hawadja! khuli palastin-arab zift!"[33]

Another inmate, a Transjordanian arms-dealer, slaps the fingers from one hand against the palm of his other hand and says:

"Where were our heads? We are asses not to have seen what was happening! We had to wait for an American to tell us that our blankets were full of lice and our food was being stolen from us . . ."

A third man, the Syrian tailor, makes a racket:

"Such cowards, such sheep! Even before the doctor entered the cells the sergeant gave us a signal behind his back, warning us not to complain, and we, frightened little lambs, obeyed!"

There is soon talk of organizing a prison strike. What kind of strike? A full-blown hunger strike—that is to say: they will not touch the tea in the morning until all the louse-infected blankets are burned in the yard. There is only ten minutes of yard time left, but the organizers work fast, passing on instructions from ear to ear. The Jewish cell number 20 is also to take part in the strike—the prison's new motto: all for one and one for all!

I watch the rebelling Arabs and I smile. I'm no stranger to these people and I know their revolution is all hot air. In the morning, the revolutionaries will drink their tea just like every other morning. And if anyone asks them who tried to organize the strike, they will point to the Jews . . .

....

33 "You're something else! All the Palestinian-Arabs are useless!"

I keep my distance. The next morning my skepticism is proven to be correct. From up above we hear the clatter of metal cups. We hear the slurping of the Sons of Ishmael. No sign of a revolt. Not a word about insurrection.

36

JEWISH POLITICAL PRISONERS STARVED

The failure of the Arab prison strike transpired just as I had predicted. But then something happens which leaves me in a state of shock for several days.

Just after morning tea the face of the sergeant appears between the grating of the cell door. He throws in a packet of cigarettes, two Hebrew newspapers and addresses me in a mild tone of voice totally at odds with his Irish temperament. He gives me four pieces of news at the same time:

"I've called the American consul . . . at 8 o' clock a lawyer from the Jewish Agency will come to see you . . . your breakfast is being brought in from a restaurant . . . If you want, later you can come down to my office and have a shave . . ."

So many concessions at once from such a despotic functionary is a little too much for me to take. But he keeps his word. At 8 o' clock a basket of food arrives from a nearby restaurant. Milk, eggs, white bread, butter, cheese and jam. The prison police take every piece of food and crush it looking for hidden messages or explosive materials. The food was clearly meant for one person—for the American. In our cell there are six people. My cellmates stare at the basket with mouths watering, and so I divide up the food equally between us.

Officially the food was ordered by the lawyer of the Jewish Agency, with express written instructions that only I eat it. But the sergeant turns a blind eye as we retire to the pantry behind the kitchen to share a secret feast.

After breakfast comes the morning walk and we residents of cell number 20 are in such good spirits that as we walk and talk—hotly debating various problems of Yishuv politics—we almost forget that we are in a prison yard and could almost imagine we are strolling down Allenby Street in Tel Aviv or Ben Yehuda Street in Jerusalem. The Palmach member talks about the terrible hardships endured by new settlers in the far flung outposts. They are fighting on two fronts. Aside from their daily toil in the fields as farmers, they must also protect their outposts against British terror and provocation. He mentions the heroic battle of Al-Bireh where two unmatched powers—the British military and the Yishuv—vied against each other, and the weaker side—those with justice on their side—came out as the winners.

Al-Bireh symbolizes Jewish determination to endure.

David Bouzaglo finds himself as almost the sole moderate among the zealots. He speaks calmly, and always tries to convince his opponent with charming phrases. He tries to win his debates using logic and common sense. His clever arguments are often accompanied by comparisons. He says:

"In essence, we in the Irgun are against terror for the sake of terror. But there are times in the history of every nation when gruesome acts are unavoidable. We pick up arms against the occupiers because they seek to destroy the Yishuv. Our foe is brutal and so we must respond with brutality . . . Did America not decide to use the atom bomb against Japan when the moment came? And what were the results of the atom bomb? The end of the war and sparing of a million American lives!"

"But is this a convincing argument? Does Palestine find itself in a position to tolerate terrorism against the occupier?"

Amid the heated debates in the prison yard individual voices come to the fore—the young Sephardic husband who prefers to do time rather than pay his wife's alimony; the explanations of Gavriel, that forging checks to finance terror is also a form of courage and devotion.

The discussion continues until we are called back to our cells.

A few hours later, I am called to the administrative office. Waiting for me there is the lawyer representing the Jewish Agency. A warm smile, a firm handshake. He offers me a full packet of cigarettes. I do not need to tell him of my difficulties getting in contact after three days of captivity; he was well informed about the details. He tells me the Jewish Agency's first priority is to get me out on bail so that I can move around freely in the days leading up to my deportation. Their first attempt has failed. The American consul, too, is working in the same direction. If things work out I should be able to visit Tel-Aviv and see my family, my city, my streets which, once upon a time, I helped to pave; my gardens, which I helped to plant.

"In the meantime," the lawyer says, "We're doing what we can to guarantee that you get daily meals from outside. The food should nourish not just your body, but also your soul—give you that little boost that you need to survive the British prison."

I am not permitted to send any letters or telegrams, but I come to an arrangement with the lawyer and I dictate what I would like him to telegram to the *Morgn Zhurnal*, to my family in New York, and to my relatives in Tel-Aviv. Over the next twenty minutes I pour out my heart. I demand to have my materials returned to me: my documents, photographs, my personal affairs. The lawyer leaves with the promise that he will visit me twice a day.

When I arrive back to my cell, the Jewish policeman who first brought me here is waiting for me—the sole Jewish guard in the whole prison. He speaks with a triumphant smile:

"Well, who do you think got the word out for you? I ran out and found the first Jewish activist I could find and said to him 'You've already eaten breakfast, but there's an American Jew in prison right now, a writer, and he has a right to eat breakfast too, right?' The activist rushed off to tell his people . . . and here's the result! Now you're under the care of the Jewish Agency. And I didn't do any of that for a bribe like the Arab guards . . . I did it out of a sense of duty, I did it as a Jew!"

Outside the disinfection crew is arriving: two uniformed Arabs armed with nozzles and cans of DDT powder. They arrive with such an uproar as though they mean to smoke out the whole building. In fact it is only the inmates themselves who will be disinfected. One by one the cell doors are opened and each prisoner's naked body is covered head to toe in powder—eyes, hair, even nostrils. One Arab points the nozzle at the inmate like a machine gun and the second turns the unfortunate naked prisoner like a carousel, around and around . . .

During this refined spectacle the Irish sergeant watches, melting for joy. His green eyes are filled with laughter. His large nostrils and thick lips flare like a winded animal. It is not a desire to vanquish the lice that drives him, but the satisfaction of a sadist to see his wards so degraded and humiliated.

I am spared the DDT disinfection, but he takes revenge on the other five Jewish inmates. He points to each one in turn and commands:

"Give that one a double helping; I saw lice on his body. Let him have it!"

"And don't spare that one either! He ratted me out to the doctor!"

The unhinged Irish sergeant seems to have reached the height of his madness, as that evening he concocts a new plan. He decides to take an interest in the physical shape of the inmates. Sport and exercise have been neglected in the prison far too long for his liking: that evening he orders all the Arab inmates outside on the terrace to do some jogging, to clear out their lungs, and no doubt build a little muscle tone.

The prison terrace takes the form of a gallery around the cells. The Arabs do as they are told and run, though they could have declined. At first they run like bent camels. Soon the race is transformed into a circus performance. A full fifteen minutes the sadist stands there with a whip in his hand, urging the Arabs on, whipping them, driving them to the point of collapse, panting all the while:

"Faster! Faster, Lazy orientals!"

When he is finished with the Arabs, he comes to the Jewish cell to ask if we would like to do fifteen minutes of exercise. When his offer is rejected he stands there for a moment in disbelief before saying:

"What's that going to look like? The Arabs are willing to do a spot of exercise, but the Jews refuse?"

Food arrives for me twice a day now, with six people sharing a portion meant for one. We share what we get and eat frugally. My request to have food for six sent in does not help: the prison guards will not let in food for any more than one.

The lawyer visits daily. His progress is modest. The British seem to have decided that I'll stay in jail until the day of my deportation. There is still a risk that they will issue a second seven-day warrant once the first one expires. For five days I wrangle with the idea of inviting my family to visit me here in prison. It would be humiliating for my mother to see me here. I have not seen her in ten years. The idea of having to leave again without seeing her first is painful. My brothers know that I've been captured, but, because of the articles in the press, they thought I was in Cyprus. The indecision plagues me. I ask the lawyer to telegraph my youngest brother asking him to pay me a visit. On the sixth day, as I sit in my cell waiting for the visit, I allow my imagination to run wild, and I daydream about the consul coming to see me all the way from Jerusalem. He is polite, formal. His appearance is intended to inspire me in my hour of need: "Don't forget that you are an American. The Stars and Stripes will always have your back!"

My daydream continues, my imagination adding more details: the emissary from Washington wants to know why anyone, even a journalist, would get it into my head to traverse such a thorny path when all legal avenues were open to me. My imagined explanation did not help, my enthusiastic declaration that the Ma'apilim sea-crossings were a one of a kind opportunity in our days. My fantasy consul listens with the attentiveness of one hearing romantic travel adventures. He is astounded what ends a journalist's curiosity can lead to. But the result is the same. He repeats the words his real-life counterpart released to the press: "It is unusual that an American should find himself in such a situation . . ." Americans are respected wherever they go, and can always avoid problems if they follow the legal pathways as they are marked on the official maps.

My imagined consul fades into the backdrop of the prison walls, leaving me alone with my own thoughts once again.

I have not followed the legal pathways. Our seamen drew their own maps while our ship sailed under a false name and under a borrowed flag.

That evening my mother visits me, accompanied by other family members.

It would smack of a desire for overly dramatized sentimentality, If I were to describe the private, intimate meeting with my mother, my brother and sister. I will skip over this scene. When the Arab policeman leads me into the darkened visiting room and I see my kind, aging mother and she rushes toward me with outstretched arms, crying:

"My boy, why is this happening to you?"

The sergeant, who is there in the room watching, and who understands both Yiddish and Hebrew, could certainly not answer her question.

I find an answer for her:

"I'm here, mother, because I helped bring 1,500 Jews here to Palestine . . ."

"May God bless you for that, my child!" my mother sobs.

In that moment I am sure that the quiet plea of my pious mother reaches the very gates of heaven.

37

FROM JAIL TO THE AIRPORT

After eleven days sitting in jail, the time has finally come for my deportation. My arrest warrant expired five days ago but in the meantime Shavuot came along, followed by Sunday. The combination of Jewish holiday and Christian day of rest leads to delays in processing my paperwork and I have no choice but to spend an extra three days in jail.

On the morning of the eleventh day the lawyer comes from the Jewish Agency accompanied by a British civil servant with the rank of sergeant, who has the face of an Armenian but who speaks with a Scottish accent. They both assure me that if we hurry to arrange a ticket I can be out of here and on a plane to Cairo this very day. The civil servant explains in an affable manner:

"The port inspector wants to keep you in jail for another two weeks. If he wants he can issue a second warrant. I would advise you to hurry out of here, fly to Egypt and avoid any more hardship . . ."

I decide to follow his advice.

In the haste, hurry and bustle of rushing from one barbed-wire-fronted port office to another I make the most of my few instances of freedom. I catch a glimpse of Haifa, flooded in sun and blue light.

Inside, between the four walls of the prison: Arabia of old lives on. The guards, both British and Arab—gruesome satraps. The inmates—hideous counte-nances, masks from Baghdad, shades of Sheherazade's tall-tales. Whereas outside—the burgeoning Kingdom of the Jews is growing. Here is Haifa's main thorough-fare, Kings' Way, entirely Jewish. The shops, the banks, the cafés and restaurants. Across the hill stretches the neighborhood of Hadar HaCarmel—a colorful pan-orama. One could take Herzl's book, *Altneuland*, and almost use it as a guidebook. A half century ago that visionary, that creator of political Zionism, sketched the squares and lighthouses of this colorful Mount Carmel. If imagination can build plans, then a vision is reality itself. What an unparalleled imagination! Haifa, the gateway to the valley has grown into a mili-tary arsenal, into a coastal-fortress of the British army, which is sitting atop a volcano, on barbed-wire, afraid of Jewish explosives.

The civil servant, after collecting all of seventy signatures for my deportation—booked me a seat on a flight to Cairo. Why Cairo and not straight to France? The clerk in the travel agency explained that there are no direct flights to Paris, that the best thing for it is to get out of trouble as soon as possible in case the British find some excuse to keep me another half a month in prison, or to delay the return of my personal effects any further.

The time of the flight remains to be determined. My lawyer stays with the travel agent while they wait for information from Lod airport, while the Scottish sergeant and I go to drink coffee in a resplendent Haifa café.

After the first sip, the generous sergeant, who is the polar opposite of every British officer I've encountered up to now, smiles and says:

"Next time you come here on an illegal ship you need to be more polite to the port inspector . . ."

"More polite?"

"For your own good."

"How do you mean?"

"The port inspector never forgave you for speaking back to him or for hiding your notes from him."

"I was tired of saying 'yes, sir' to their insults."

"He's a tough man and the most powerful authority in Haifa port."

"That doesn't give him the right to seize my papers, materials, private documents or carry out his search while shouting insults against American journalists."

"Is that what he did?" the sergeant asks with a grimace—it is clearly not easy for him to serve under such a boss.

"Is that why he still hasn't given back my documents and papers, even now just before my departure?"

"It's hard for me to say. We'll try our best to get them back, as soon as we have confirmation of the flight-time."

The sergeant leans toward me. A smile, which comes even to stiff British bureaucrats during moments of intimacy, spreads over his face.

"Your story must be interesting . . . up to now American journalists have only come here with legal ships and visas. But you do the opposite—a passenger on an illegal ship and without visas to boot . . . "

"I was prepared for trouble," I say, "but not quite as much as this."

"In a way it's good for you. It will make your story better, more entertaining. We've given you a look behind the scenes of our prisons . . ."

"I'm very grateful for the opportunity to spend time in your prisons. But I won't be so quick to forgive the treatment I received."

"Did you find the prison regulations too strict?"

"They are brutal. As a journalist I will indulge in a little critique. What kind of show are you running here in this country? British rulers using Ottoman laws?"

The sergeant is embarrassed. He shifts his weight on his seat, lights a cigarette and says:

"I have nothing to do with any of that. That's up to higher authorities. I perform my bureaucratic functions . . . and, to tell you the truth, I don't like my job. A nasty business! The truth is many British functionaries are unhappy with the situation . . . I have many Jewish friends, but because of the tense situation we find ourselves on opposing sides."

The sergeant is telling the truth. There was no exaggeration in his declaration. The classic refrain:

"I don't like this nasty business" . . . is something I've heard many times from various functionaries, both in the prison and in the bureau of immigration in Haifa. But they are all obedient functionaries. They carry out their nasty business diligently and efficiently.

The sergeant, it seems, cannot abide that one would pity his station, that one should observe his weakness. The British man in him awakens, he regains his equilibrium and says:

"Things would be worse if it wasn't for us. If the world is in a hurry to solve the Palestine problem, let them take a shot at it . . . If it were up to me, I'd pull out all British troops in two weeks' time . . . the problem would solve itself pretty quickly after that."

These words contain a sly innuendo, a threat. He means to imply that what follows would be a bloodbath. A civil-war between Jews and Arabs. He also knows that British intrigue in the colonies can engineer bloodbaths between one part of a population against another. Though he also knows that the situation in Palestine is now a little different. Since the Jews have ramped up their aggressive tactics on all fronts, no Arab would dare brandish a stone against a Jew.

The sergeant wants to keep our conversation light and convivial, and so he adds:

"Don't forget to send us press clippings of your story. I want to hear what you have to say about us. I've read some reports from another American correspondent and I didn't like it one bit. Too many exaggerated descriptions. You newspapermen can have very active imaginations sometimes . . ."

The sergeant stands up. Coffee hour is over. The Lawyer returns, joined now by someone from the immigration bureau. In a confidential tone the sergeant says to me:

"Don't say anything to the port inspector about the money you have with you. According to the new rules they can confiscate any extra money you have above the exact amount necessary for the travel expenses."

From the travel agency next door we hear that the reservation has been confirmed. My plane is scheduled to leave Lod at two o' clock. It's now twenty to twelve. The trip to the airport will take two hours on top of the time needed for the deportation formalities and to pick up my documents and personal affairs from the port inspector. We head to the main office of the immigration bureau.

The port inspector casts me an insolent look. He recognizes me. He answers my lawyer cynically that all my documents and personal items are being examined in Jerusalem. He has no way of knowing if the examination is finished or if it will take another two weeks. The matter is out of his hands. My lawyer glances at the sergeant, who glances at me, and I realize that the port inspector is up to his dirty tricks. He wants to delay my deportation by another week. He would enjoy nothing more than the satisfaction of having me sit in jail for an indeterminate amount of time. Back outside, my lawyer and the sergeant come to the agreement that

I should not delay my departure. We'll have to hurry. The plane leaves at two. Meanwhile the lawyer will intervene on my behalf in Jerusalem. He will retrieve my documents in the next few days and will send them to the American consulate in Paris.

It's midday. The taxi driver who is waiting for us is instructed by the sergeant to break the speed limit and to drive at eighty miles an hour.

"This gentleman must not miss his flight!" the sergeant orders.

"What if I'm stopped by a patrol?" the taxi driver asks.

"The policeman who will accompany the passenger will take care of that." comes the response.

The policeman, an Arab with a black rifle and a revolver, climbs into the taxi next to me. The sergeant bids me a warm farewell. Before shaking my hand he gives me a copy of the Jerusalem English-language Newspaper, the Palestine Post and smiles:

"Read about Eddie Cantor ... I like him ... the best American actor of all ..."

As the taxi tears away, I open the newspaper. In the center page there is a picture of Eddie Cantor and next to it the words: "they warned men not to take a critical stance toward the British handling of Palestine, because they could boycott my films. Well, it doesn't bother me none whether they see my pictures or not. I don't want to make one nation laugh, while my own nation is weeping ..."

I settle back into my seat. The armed Arab sits there like a wall. I think about the Scottish sergeant who has to distance himself from his Jewish friends, who likes Eddie Cantor and whose job is to deport "illegal" Jews . . .

The taxi is driving at full pelt, the driver bent forward, hands on the wheel, eyes on his watch. He puts his foot down and the road flies past beneath us.

This Palestinian driver—a seasoned courier who can whiz over roads and make the miles vanish in times of danger, in times of unrest—is showing me what he's made of. The wheel in his hand is transformed into a magic circle, a sorcerer's plaything. The vehicle races into the distance.

38

OVER THE "DARK CONTINENT" BACK TO EUROPE

The automobile winds through twisting roads, at a dizzying speed, like a demon. The Arab policeman by my side is silent. The revolver weighs heavily in his hand. The rifle weighs heavily on his shoulder. He keeps shifting his weapons from one side to the other. The driver is doing eighty miles an hour, pushing the engine to within an inch of its life. I call out:

"Careful, driver! We don't want any accidents to happen."

"Let them happen! I'm not afraid of any accidents," the Arab policeman says with a resigned sweep of his hand. "I don't care if I live or die—I'm so tired of these torments with the British ..."

I regard the policeman a little askance. Is he joking? Is this a provocation, or a political discussion? The Arab's face appears weary, apathetic. His dark eyes appear dull. His mustache is unraveling, unwaxed. Every wince and grimace on his face speaks of resignation and indolence. It is not a joke. The Arab is deadly serious! I offer him a cigarette and a piece of chocolate and the hold on his tongue slowly begins to loosen.

"We don't need the British here! Jews and Arabs can live here together *sawa sawa*, without any problems." as he says this he brings his two forefingers together until they touch. "The English are nothing more than exploiters... *in al din a buk khulo inglizi!* (the devil take every one of them!)

"They exploit you in the police service too?" I ask.

"A band of despots!" he says half in English half in Arabic. My shift is eight hours. The pay is twenty-five pounds a month, less than six pounds a week. But instead of eight hours I usually work ten or eleven hours..."

"Do they pay you overtime?"

"Not a penny! And every British soldier gets to shout at me or have me punished by a sergeant... Look, you're the passenger. You need to catch your plane at 2:00. According to my schedule I should have finished my shift at 2:30, but I won't get back to Haifa before half past four... the driver is pushing this engine for all it's worth to get you to your plane on time. He's right too: get as far away as you can from this place! Get away from the British police!"

The policeman moves his rifle from one shoulder to the other. He wipes away his sweat. I share the chocolate with him that my sister brought me in prison. The Arab says:

"I know your predicament. You're an American. They'll deport you. I also know what conditions are like in Haifa jail where they kept you. When the Turks were in charge they'd treat an American like a caliph!

But the British are not ashamed to arrest Americans and then go to your president to borrow money! Have they even paid their debts for the first war yet?"

The world-weary, embittered, resigned Arab policeman from the British port prison has no shortage of insults for the British king, the queen, the princess, or the prime minister. Not a single minister in the entire British cabinet is spared his invective. I do not say anything, and the policeman soon dozes off.

The driver picks up even more speed. We are approaching Netanya—the new, white city on the shores of the Mediterranean. Blinding sunlight pours over the buildings. Netanya is in the process of growing, expanding. Netanya will be the Palestinian riviera. Our vehicle cuts through the inner streets. The city lies there, scattered like an unfinished artwork. But the traces of the sculptor's hammer and chisel are unmistakable in every line on the ground.

The entrance to Netanya is full of life. It's already high summer here. Buses growl, chauffeur's bustle. Our vehicle flies through the streets. We pass the hotel Eran, surrounded by gardens. There is the "Klub Hayedidim" (the Friends' Club), the coffee house Gan-Vered (Rose Garden), which was built by Jewish veterans. We drive past Wauchope Square. From the terrace of Gan Hamelech, on the water's edge, we hear music. We hear the sounds of the future Jewish riviera. We see the post office from the front, rows of gleaming buildings from behind, and soon our vehicle has already left the city behind. From Netanya the automobile travels along the fishing village Mikhmoret, just to the north of Vitkin Village. The fishing village is as radiant as a young bride. They are preparing to celebrate the birthday of a new fishing boat: the "Shark."

"How did these boys get it into their heads to build a fishing village?" I ask.

The driver explains that the idea came about because of a strange coincidence. The fishermen here were guards during the war, manning the machine-gun posts set up to protect the shores around Haifa. One day they spotted something in the water that looked like an enemy ship. They sent out warning signals. The vessel stayed where it was. When they approached it, it turned out that it was a Jewish fishing boat. The encounter led to a friendship. The guards were impressed with the deeds of the Jewish fishermen. After the war they retired from the navy and went to Italy to learn the fishing trade. Afterward they returned to Palestine and the result was the fishing village of Milkmoret.

The car drives past Hadera. We are not far from Ra'anana. The landscape before us is divided between patches of arable land, and stretches of sandy desert filled with spiky cacti. This is the patch of earth ruled over by the phlegmatic sons of Ishmael. The soil remains untouched by Jewish pickaxes. But the flat asphalt roads transport truckloads of Jewish workers, on the way to the city with provisions from the colonies and kibbutzim. There are packed Jewish buses, British patrol jeeps with machine guns, even here and there a caravan of camels.

On the one hand the driver is pushing the vehicle to the very brink, while on the other hand also worrying about getting a puncture, the roads being prone to Jewish sabotage attempts against the British occupiers.

At ten past two we arrive in Lod and enter the airport.[34] The plane is due to leave at half past. In the twenty minutes till my flight I once again have to sign British deportation documents. I am also obliged—after eleven days in jail—to pay a fine of two pounds for entering the country "illegally." The heavily-armed Arab policeman accompanies me as far as the steps of the airplane. In contrast to the regulations back at the prison he warmly shakes my hand as we part ways.

I depart from Lod at exactly 2:30. Fifteen minutes later our plane is flying low over Tel Aviv. According to British rules I'm classed as an "illegal" Jew, even during my deportation, and so I am not allowed to set foot on the streets of my Tel Aviv, my city where I spent my youth, in the city where I helped pave the streets, and build the first buildings. After ten years of absence I am destined to only see Tel Aviv from the air this time. I look down from up high and see the main squares of the Jewish metropolis. There is the city hall, there is the colorful Dizengoff square.

We fly past the Greek columns of the new Habima Theater. The green Rothschild Boulevard winds in a

---

34 Translator's note: the geographic details of this journey seem confused. I have given the details as they stand in Isban's account.

zigzag, shaded by eucalyptus and palm trees. The city is laid out in a grid of squares and triangles, tightly packed with buildings and gardens. Is this the same Tel Aviv that in 1908 was little more than a pile of sand where Meir Dizengoff the merchant laid the first foundations of the little neighborhood of Ahuzet Bayit—a residence for himself and a few other bourgeois families from Jaffa?

The buildings grow smaller, shrinking. Our plane, which has only seven passengers not counting the pilot and co-pilot, is flying now along the Mediterranean coast. I am the only Jew among the seven passengers. The others are three Egyptians in red fezes, a Frenchman and two Englishmen.

One of the Englishmen, a tall, broad man in a canvas suit and an Indian pith hat, is conversing with the Frenchman. The theme of their conversation is the Jewish land. Flying over Tel Aviv brought the Jewish problem to mind. He repeats the old refrain that the Jews are ungrateful to the British for all they've done. The composed Englishman is transformed by the heat of the plane into a passionate debater. He is fired up with imperialistic fervor and diplomatic emotions. No verbal acrobatics are being spared to win over the naive Frenchman that the British Empire was the first to protect the Jews of this world, and that all of Europe's Jews would be dead if Britain had not come to the rescue. The fiery defender of English imperialism, sweating on a hot plane flying between the continents of Africa and Asia, does not consider that Britain was an indirect partner in the annihilation of European Jewry. It does not occur to him that in the very height of the war, when hundreds of thousands of young Jews were fighting on the battlefields, and there was still a chance to snatch them away from the bestial fangs of the Gestapo and take them to the Jewish Land, the shores of Palestine were being blockaded by the British, and the gates locked.

I look down once again at Tel Aviv as it fades into the distance, as the land and coasts disappear and the plane flies out over the hazy sea.

The flight across the coastline of Africa reveals poor landscapes. Stretches of desert, strips of marshland and small islands.

I sink down deeper into my padded seat. The hum of the propellers grows louder. The wings lift the steel whale higher and higher. I look down through the window. Behind me lies Cyprus. Behind me lies the British jail. The "illegal" Jewish fleet continues to sail over the seven seas. While I, a free, legal man make my way from the dark continent of Africa back to Europe.

New York, 1947

Glossary

GLOSSARY

Aguda: The ultra-orthodox political party Agudat Yisrael.

Aliyah Bet: Aliyah Bet was the code name given to illegal immigration by Jewish refugees, and later Holocaust survivors, to Mandatory Palestine between 1934–48, in violation of the restrictions laid out in the British White Paper of 1939. The term Aliyah Aleph was used to refer to legal immigration.

Amalek: A nation described in the Bible as an enemy of the Israelites.

Betar (fortress): The Betar fortress was the last standing Jewish fortress in the Bar Kokhba revolt of the 2nd century CE, destroyed by the Roman army of Emperor Hadrian in the year 135.

Betar Movement: Right wing Revisionist Zionist youth movement, founded by Vladimir Jabotinsky.

Biluim: A movement of agricultral settlers in 19th century Palestine.

Bund: The General Jewish Labor Bund in Poland (Yiddish: *Algemeyner yidisher arbeter bund in poyln*) was a Jewish socialist party in Poland which promoted the political, cultural and social autonomy of Jewish workers, sought to combat antisemitism and was generally opposed to both Zionism and Communism.

Dror: A Jewish labor Zionist young movement distinct from Hashomer Hatzair.

Fellah: Agricultural laborer.

Galizianer: A Jew from Galicia, a historical region spanning Central and Eastern Europe which included those parts of Poland ruled by the Austo-Hungarian Empire.

Gematria: An alphanumeric code of assigning a numerical value to a name, word or phrase based on its Hebrew letters

Gordonia: A zionist youth movement.

Habonim: A Jewish Socialist-Zionist cultural youth movement predominant in Anglophone countries.

Hora: A circle dance originating in the Balkans. Part of the Klezmer dance repertoire it had a major influence on Israeli folk dance.

Haganah: Haganah (lit. The Defence) was the main paramilitary organization of the Jewish population in Mandatory Palestine between 1920 and 1948.

Hashomer Hatzair: Socialist Zionist youth movement.

Ihud: Zionist party founded in Lublin, Poland, in 1944 with the aim of uniting various Zionist factions.

Irgun: The Irgun ("The National Military Organization in the Land of Israel") was a Zionist paramilitary organization, that operating in Mandate Palestine between 1931 and 1948, that broke away from the Haganah.

Kaddish: "The Mourner's Kaddish", said as part of the mourning rituals in Judaism in all prayer services, as well as at funerals and memorials.

Landsman (pl. landslayt): Compatriot; people from the same town or region.

Lechu neranena: A liturgical song.

Ma'apilim: Name given to those Jewish Immigrants involved in Aliyah Bet (see: Aliyah Bet) also known in Hebrew as Ha'apala (lit. ascension).

Maariv: Evening prayer service.

Mapai: The Workers Party of the Land of Israel, center-left party whose leader at the time was Ben Gurion.

Maquis: Rural guerrilla bands of Resistance fighters in Nazi occupied France.

Maror: refers to the bitter herbs eaten at the Passover Seder.

Masada: An ancient fortification on the edge of the Judean desert. According to Josephus, the siege of Masada by Roman troops from 73 to 74 CE, at the end of the First Jewish–Roman War, ended in the mass suicide of the 960 Sicarii rebels who were hiding there.

minyan: A quorum of ten adult Jewish men, required for various religious obligations. Here the term refers to a gathering for prayers.

Mitzvah: Good deed or commandment. While Gentiles are expected to follow the Ten Commandments, the Torah contains 613 commandments which an observant Jew must endeavor to follow.

Mizrachi: Members of Mizrachi, a religious Zionist movement.

Nikolayevsky soldier: Nikolayevsky soldiers: Jews drafted into Russian military service from 1827 to 1856.

Palmach: The Palmach was the elite fighting force of the Haganah.

Shel rosh: Tefillin worn on the forehead.

The Stern Gang: AKA the Lehi ("Fighters for the Freedom of Israel"), was a Zionist paramilitary organization with the avowed aim of evicting the British authorities from Palestine by resort to force, allowing unrestricted immigration of

Jews and the formation of a Jewish state, a "new totalitarian Hebrew republic." The group self-identified as a terrorist organization and made no bones about the nature of their tactics.

Tallit (pl. tallitim): Prayer shawl.

Tefillin: Tefillin, often called phylacteries, are small leather boxes containing tiny scrolls of parchment, worn during morning prayer, on the forehead and arm, secured by leather straps.

Terratorialism: Territorialism was a movement in opposition to Zionism seeking an alternative location for the new Jewish homeland, suggested locations included Uganda, Argentina, Alaska, Australia to name but a few.

Umschagsplatz: (German: collection point or reloading point) a term used during The Holocaust to denote the holding areas adjacent to railway stations in occupied Poland where Jews from ghettos were assembled for deportation to Nazi death camps.

Yishuv: The community of Jewish residents in Ottomon Syria and later Palestine prior to the establishment of the state of Israel.

Yodfat: The Siege of Yodfat was a 47-day siege by Roman forces of the Jewish town of Yodfat which took place in 67 CE, during the First Jewish-Roman war.